GETTYSBURG

GETTYSBURG

HUGH BICHENO

CASSELL&CO

Cassell & Co
Wellington House, 125 Strand
London WC2R 0BB

A catalogue record for this book is available
from the British Library

ISBN 0-304-35698-0

Designed by Goldust Design
Printed and bound in Spain

CONTENTS

Chronology   8

Foreword by Richard Holmes   9

Introduction   15

1 **THE ARMIES MOVE TO GETTYSBURG**   33

2 **BUFORD'S AND DOUBLEDAY'S BATTLE (DAY 1)**   43

3 **HOWARD'S BATTLE**   55

4 **SLOCUM'S FRONT**   67

5 **MEADE'S AND LEE'S PLANS (DAY 2)**   75

6 **PLUM RUN VALLEY**   85

7 **STONY HILL**   97

8 **WHEATFIELD**   107

9 **PEACH ORCHARD**   117

10 **CEMETERY RIDGE**   127

11 **CEMETERY HILL**   137

12 **CULP'S HILL**   147

13 **THE RIGHT WING (DAY 3)**   155

14 **THE ARTILLERY**   165

15 **PICKETT'S CHARGE**   177

16 **CONCLUSION**   189

APPENDICES   201

Appendix A – Meade's Pipe Creek Circular   202

Appendix B – Order of Battle – Army of the Potomac   204

Appendix C – Order of Battle – Army of Northern Virginia   215

Appendix D – Dramatis Personae   224

Bibliography   229

Index   231

To Ned

CHRONOLOGY

1861

4 March Abraham Lincoln inaugurated President.

12–13 April Bombardment and surrender of Fort Sumter, South Carolina.

21 July Confederate victory at First Manassas (Bull Run), northern Virginia.

1 November McClellan appointed general-in-chief of the Union armies.

1862

February Grant captures Forts Henry and Donelson in upper Tennessee.

17 March Start of McClellan's campaign in the Jamestown Peninsula, Virginia.

6–7 April Grant's victory at Shiloh, lower Tennessee.

May–June Jackson defeats three Union armies in the Shenandoah Valley, Virginia.

26 June–2 July Lee defeats McClellan in the Seven Days' Battles.

29–30 August Lee defeats Pope at Second Manassas.

4 September Start of Lee's first invasion of the North.

17 September Drawn battle between Lee and McClellan at Antietam, Maryland.

22 September Emancipation proclamation.

7 November McClellan replaced by Burnside.

13 December Lee defeats Burnside at Fredericksburg, Virginia.

1863

25 January Burnside replaced by Hooker.

30 April–4 May Lee defeats Hooker at Chancellorsville, Virginia. Jackson mortally wounded.

May Grant's campaign in Mississippi, siege of Vicksburg begins.

3 June Start of Lee's second invasion of the North.

9 June Union cavalry fights Confederates to a draw at Brandy Station.

28 June Hooker replaced by Meade.

1–3 July Meade defeats Lee at Gettysburg, Pennsylvania.

4 July Fall of Vicksburg.

14 July Lee completes retreat to Virginia.

19–20 September Defeat of Union army at Chicamauga, border of Tennessee and Georgia.

24–25 October Defeat of Confederate army by Grant at Chattanooga, as above.

1864

9 March Grant appointed general-in-chief.

May Union armies under Sherman and Meade/Grant invade Georgia and Virginia.

5–6 May Drawn battle of the Wilderness, Virginia.

8–21 May Drawn battles at Spotsylvania, Virginia.

1–3 June Union defeat at Cold Harbor, Virginia.

15–18 June Failure to take Petersburg by storm, beginning of nine-month siege.

17 July Johnston replaced by Hood.

2 September Sherman captures Atlanta.

8 November Lincoln re-elected President.

November–December Sherman's destructive march from Atlanta to Savannah, Georgia.

November–December Hood's counter-invasion of Tennessee, crushed at Nashville.

1865

February–March Sherman's destructive march through South Carolina.

30 March Start of Grant's final offensive in Virginia.

3 April Fall of Richmond.

9 April Lee surrenders to Grant at Appomattox.

14 April Lincoln mortally wounded by assassin John Wilkes Booth.

FOREWORD

Gettysburg is one of the most written-about battles of history, and, as Hugh Bicheno observes in his introduction, it carries weighty symbolical baggage. It lies at the very epicentre of 'Lost Cause' mythology, with the heroic failure of Pickett's Charge catching the smoky glint of the Confederacy's dying fall. Yet it appeared as one of history's great climactic clashes only in retrospect: at the time the Union capture of Vicksburg was more alarming to Confederates. And, as we shall see, Gettysburg did not break General Robert E. Lee's Army of Northern Virginia. A redoubtable opponent to the very end, scarcely less formidable in defeat than in victory, it was never, for all Lincoln's rhetoric, at the mercy of Major General George Meade's Army of the Potomac immediately after Gettysburg. And not least amongst that irascible officer's virtues was the ability to recognize that.

Yet if Gettysburg was not the beginning of the end for the Confederacy, it was without doubt the end of the beginning for the Union. To understand why, we must look at what had happened in the war thus far. Brian Holden Reid is right to hail it as 'the most important event in the history of the USA', and to observe that it resulted from a fundamental disagreement about the place of slavery in the Union. 'Without slavery,' he stresses, 'there would have been no war.' The election of Abraham Lincoln in the 1860 presidential election was speedily followed by the secession of seven slave states in the Deep South and the establishment of a Confederacy under the presidency of Jefferson Davis. In mid April 1861 war broke out when the Confederates bombarded the Union garrison of Fort Sumter in Charleston harbour, and four states of the Upper South, unwilling to assist in the coercion of their sisters, joined the Confederacy.

In terms of material resources it should have been no contest. The Confederacy had less than one-third of the population of the entire USA, and just under half its population were slaves. It had only 9,000 of the 31,000 miles of railway track in the USA, and the Union states of Massachusetts and Pennsylvania on their own out-produced the entire Confederacy. Its economy was heavily dependent on cotton, and the Union's crushing naval superiority, applied through the slow but certain constriction of blockade, announced the week Fort Sumter fell, would at one and the same time destroy the cotton trade by cutting off exports and render it difficult (though never wholly impossible) for the South to import the arms its own undeveloped industry was unable to produce.

Yet if there was ever a demonstration that war does not follow a linear path driven steadily onwards by big battalions, the Civil War is it. The Union's elderly general-in-chief, Winfield Scott, favoured a methodical campaign – dubbed by the press the Anaconda Plan – aimed at the slow strangulation of the South. But political pressures demanded quick action to end the 'rebellion', and in a misguided attempt to take the Confederate capital, newly established at Richmond, Virginia, the Union army was soundly trounced at Bull Run in June 1861. In the following spring the war seemed to turn in Union favour, with a victory at Pea Ridge, Arkansas, in March, opening western Tennessee to attack, and the capture of New Orleans in April. U. S. Grant, fast establishing himself as the rising star amongst Union generals, took Forts Henry and Donelson, leading to the fall of Nashville. The Confederates counter-attacked, but were fought to a bloody standstill at Shiloh, and Union troops went on to occupy Memphis.

Little came of this early promise, and by mid 1862 the war had adopted the pattern it was to retain for three long years. There were three major theatres of operations, linked by railway. In the west, where the Union strove to complete its conquest of the Mississippi basin, and was to capture Vicksburg, splitting the Confederacy, in July 1863; in the centre, around the key railway junction of Chattanooga; and in the east, between the Potomac and Rappahannock rivers in northern Virginia. There was little doubt as to which was the most significant. Both the proximity of Washington and Richmond, the rival capitals, and the close attention of European powers put events in northern Virginia under a spotlight which rarely shone so brightly elsewhere. A successful Confederate invasion of the North might have encouraged Britain and France to join the war. Britain's economy was damaged by the cessation of cotton imports, and France was engaged, in Mexico, in precisely that adventure which the Monroe Doctrine ('the American continents...are henceforth not to be considered as subjects for future colonization by any European power') had forbidden. But neither wished to join the losing side, and so, to gain that external support which might have enabled it to win, the Confederacy had to demonstrate that it could win without it. Thus the eastern theatre saw the main contending armies march and counter-march in an area which, although a mere fragment of the theatre of war as a whole, became the conflict's vital ground.

In April 1862 the Union commander George B. McClellan launched an enterprising amphibious thrust towards Richmond, only to be roughly handled by Lee, appointed to lead the Army of Northern Virginia when its commander was badly wounded. Lee went on to win a second battle at Bull Run and advanced into Maryland, only for a fortuitously captured order to enable McClellan to attack him on 17 September at Antietam before his concentration was complete. A combination of Union mistakes and Confederate resolve produced a drawn battle – and the bloodiest single day in American history – but Lee had to fall back. And in early October, in the central theatre, the Confederate commander Braxton Bragg mishandled an attack into Tennessee. Both Confederate offensives, which might just have persuaded Britain and France to intervene, had failed.

McClellan was replaced in November: the fact that he was to stand against Lincoln in the 1864 presidential election emphasizes just how political generals could be. The following month his successor, Ambrose E. Burnside, attacked Lee in a strong position at Fredericksburg and was roundly beaten. He was replaced by 'Fighting Joe' Hooker, who, pressed by Lincoln to 'give us victories' marched west of the Fredericksburg position and prepared a ponderous master-stroke, only to be taken in the flank at Chancellorsville by 'Stonewall' Jackson, Lee's ablest lieutenant. He was drubbed in a battle marred, for the Confederacy, by Jackson's fatal wounding. Hooker was remarkably frank in dismissing two reasonable explanations for his collapse. He was neither drunk nor concussed by the impact of a nearby shell: 'I just lost confidence in Joe Hooker.' So too did Abraham Lincoln, and replaced him by George Meade, prompted to do so, at least in part, by the fact that Meade had been born in Spain of American parents and was thus unable to run for president.

This, then, was the background to Gettysburg. Despite enjoying both a comfortable numerical superiority and being equipped by the burgeoning industry of the busy North, the Union army in this crucial theatre had been comprehensively beaten. It was beaten at Antietam even when its enemy's plans were known to it; beaten at Fredericksburg with an imbalance of casualties more than two to one against it; and beaten again at Chancellorsville though with odds two to one in its favour. Small wonder that with the news of this last defeat Lincoln's face turned grey. 'My God,' he muttered, almost dazed, 'what will the country say?' In fact there was no new outcry against the war, although the anti-war Democrats known as Copperheads (from their lapel pins fashioned from an Indian's head cut from a coin) were as active as ever. And the Union army's spirit was not broken. Indeed, in the opinion of one of their number, the men of the Army of the Potomac showed 'nothing of that spirit of insubordination and despondency ... which had prevailed in the middle of the winter.' But the facts remained that the North was not winning; that even Lincoln could not guarantee to hold the ring politically; and that a significant Confederate victory on Northern soil might provoke foreign intervention.

Meade, then commanding one of Hooker's corps, was astonished to be woken in the early hours of 28 June to be told that he was in command of the army. He had already told his wife that he did not expect to be appointed because 'I have no friends, political or others, who press or advance my claims', without realizing that, in the prevailing circumstances, his hand was actually strengthened by the absence of scheming supporters. He told her that even his critics must recognize that he was both brave and competent, but added: 'The only thing they can say, and I am willing to admit the justice of the argument, is that it remains to be seen whether I have the capacity to handle successfully a large army.' That capacity was to be tested to the full in just two days' time. And if George Gordon Meade did not have the real opportunity of winning the war for the Union in July 1863, he had every chance of losing it.

I commend Hugh Bicheno's admirable study of the battle for three particular reasons. Firstly, because it seeks to explain it as a Union victory, for which Meade and his hitherto-baffled army deserve credit, rather than a Confederate defeat in the Lost Cause tradition. Secondly, because he has spent much time on the battlefield itself. It was, I think, my former Sandhurst colleague Paddy Griffith who coined the neologism 'microterrain', and it is an inescapable fact that too much military history has been written without proper consideration of the impact of the ground upon the events that unrolled across it. And finally, because this book recognizes that what happens on the battlefield often has little to do with industrial capacity or demography, though both, in their way, may bear upon it. It is an affair of the human spirit, played out in an environment characterized by chance and uncertainty. If you believe in the inevitable supremacy of sheer numbers, read his account of the charge of Barksdale's Mississippians, or of the defence of Little Round Top by the 20th Maine. It was the latter's commander, Joshua Chamberlain, as college professor turned infantry officer so characteristic of the armies that fought at Gettysburg, who caught the emotions that still haunt these Pennsylvania fields: 'In great deeds something abides. On great fields something stays. Forms change and pass; bodies disappear; but spirits linger, to consecrate the ground for the vision-place of souls.'

RICHARD HOLMES

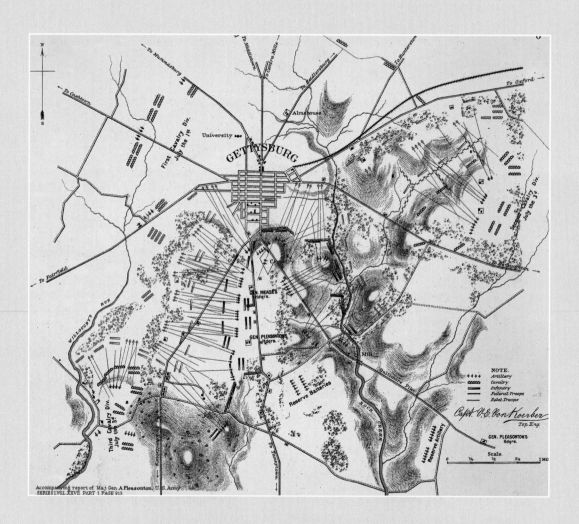

INTRODUCTION

The field of battle exists at three levels: there is the ground as it was fought over; then the preliminary grading by the participants, seeking to create a coherent context for their fragments of an intense reality; and lastly the interpretative tarmac that sometimes obliterates the underlying features. The higher the historical stakes the greater the probability that the event will be politicized beyond recognition and that special pleading, 'what ifs' and self-perpetuating controversies will assume a life of their own. No battle carries greater symbolical baggage than Gettysburg, regarded as the turning point of the Civil War, itself the most contentious event in the history of the States thereby reunited.

Waterloo occupies a similar place in British historical consciousness and there are parallels, particularly between Pickett's Charge and the equally ill-fated advance of Napoleon's Old Guard forty-eight years earlier. But at Gettysburg there was no Blücher to arrive in time to turn a repulse into a rout and, although the significance of French mistakes at Waterloo has certainly been emphasized, the historiography of Gettysburg has been unduly slanted towards discussion of Confederate errors and bad luck. When asked who was responsible for their defeat, Major General George Pickett drily answered, 'I've always thought the Yankees had something to do with it', but for over a century this common-sense guide was ignored, mainly because the result was so unpalatable to partisans of the South's romantic 'Lost Cause'. Their interpretation prospered partly because Major General George Meade,

> **Composite map of the battle: the only reasonably accurate part of the Union cavalry commander's report**

CONFEDERATE COMMAND TREE

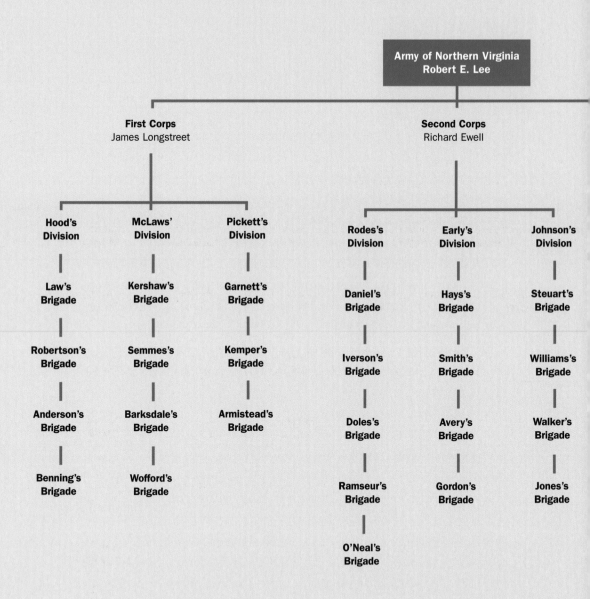

Army of Northern Virginia
Robert E. Lee

First Corps
James Longstreet

Second Corps
Richard Ewell

**Hood's
Division**

**McLaws'
Division**

**Pickett's
Division**

**Rodes's
Division**

**Early's
Division**

**Johnson's
Division**

**Law's
Brigade**

**Kershaw's
Brigade**

**Garnett's
Brigade**

**Daniel's
Brigade**

**Hays's
Brigade**

**Steuart's
Brigade**

**Robertson's
Brigade**

**Semmes's
Brigade**

**Kemper's
Brigade**

**Iverson's
Brigade**

**Smith's
Brigade**

**Williams's
Brigade**

**Anderson's
Brigade**

**Barksdale's
Brigade**

**Armistead's
Brigade**

**Doles's
Brigade**

**Avery's
Brigade**

**Walker's
Brigade**

**Benning's
Brigade**

**Wofford's
Brigade**

**Ramseur's
Brigade**

**Gordon's
Brigade**

**Jones's
Brigade**

**O'Neal's
Brigade**

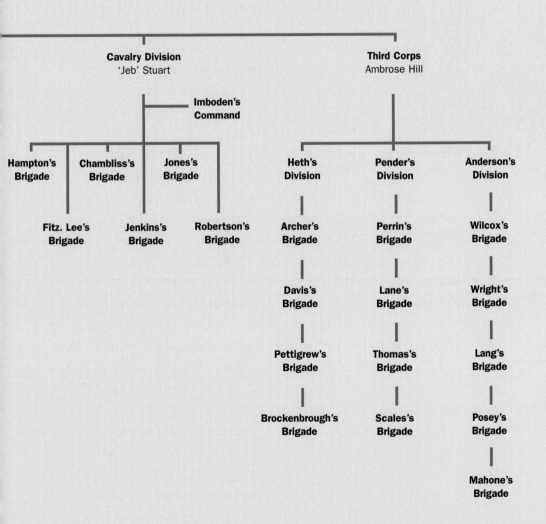

Cavalry Division
'Jeb' Stuart

Third Corps
Ambrose Hill

Imboden's
Command

Hampton's
Brigade

Chambliss's
Brigade

Jones's
Brigade

Heth's
Division

Pender's
Division

Anderson's
Division

Fitz. Lee's
Brigade

Jenkins's
Brigade

Robertson's
Brigade

Archer's
Brigade

Perrin's
Brigade

Wilcox's
Brigade

Davis's
Brigade

Lane's
Brigade

Wright's
Brigade

Pettigrew's
Brigade

Thomas's
Brigade

Lang's
Brigade

Brockenbrough's
Brigade

Scales's
Brigade

Posey's
Brigade

Mahone's
Brigade

Abraham Lincoln

the journeyman Union commander who checked General Robert E. Lee at Gettysburg, was studiedly uncharismatic and made no secret of his contempt for politicians and journalists, who were accordingly receptive to false accounts of the battle provided by officers identified with Meade's predecessor, Major General Joseph Hooker.

But as in anything to do with the Civil War the greater responsibility rests with President Abraham Lincoln, who in full Old Testament prophet mode blamed Meade for not finishing the enemy off after the battle. 'If I had gone up there, I would have whipped them myself', he wrote. 'Our army held the war in the hollow of their hand and would not close it. … We had them within our grasp, we had only to stretch forth our hands and they were ours. And nothing I could say or do could make the army move.' Today we would call that 'spin'. Lincoln defined the war as one against traitorous individuals with whom there could be no compromise and he well knew this made it a struggle to the death. But it was only human to yearn for a quick end to the bloodbath his election had precipitated, and to blame Meade for not achieving a quick result.

Lincoln also knew he was vulnerable to the charge that political deals had resulted in an army hollowed out by haphazard recruitment policies, themselves partly the product of wishful thinking. He knew himself to be the keystone of the Union effort and it was sensible to use an officer without powerful friends as a lightning rod. In the context of the crushing moral responsibility he undoubtedly felt for the hundreds of thousands of young men who died to make a reality of his vision of a greater United States, the scapegoating of one general weighed less than a feather in the balance. Unfortunately for Meade's reputation, Lincoln's assassination upon the hour of victory transformed him from the necessarily devious and compromised politician he was known to be into the marmoreal 'Honest Abe' he has been ever since, and the sentiment cited above became lapidary.

Lincoln's Othello also had an Iago in the flamboyant political Major General Daniel Sickles, who capitalized on the credibility bestowed by being maimed during the battle and rushed to Washington to promote his poisoned version of events. Desperate Dan never gave up, becoming instrumental in turning the battlefield into a National Park, getting himself awarded the Congressional Medal of Honor in 1897 and successfully portraying himself as the true architect of victory, all at the further expense of Meade. This issue need not detain us: Sickles wilfully disobeyed orders and deserved to be court-martialled, and since Meade would certainly have been blamed had the outcome been otherwise, he should be given the credit at least for not losing a battle fought on almost equal terms against a general who had made fools of all previous Union commanders, even when their armies grossly outnumbered his.

Brevity demands likewise cursory consideration of other controversies. Lee's army was weaker than it could have been because the individual states were anxious to retain control over their own resources, yet since that was what the Confederacy professed to be about it is difficult to see how it could have been otherwise. The same can be said of the Union policy whereby conscripts could buy their way out of their obligation and the profiteering that characterized procurement – war increases government revenues and patronage and that was what Lincoln wanted to do anyway. War came, as most do, because of the ambition and reckless vanity of politicians on both sides, and it was fought, as most are, to answer Humpty Dumpty's question: 'which is to be master – that's all'. If the weaker party throws the first punch, no matter how much he is provoked, it ill behoves him to complain if he is then pounded into submission. He may win a round or two, but assuming a more or less equal will to win the outcome cannot be in doubt. Confederate leaders were acutely aware of this, which was why the implacable Lincoln filled their horizon and rightly dominates the historiography of the Civil War.

Although the Gettysburg campaign witnessed the deepest penetration by a substantial Confederate force into Union territory, whether it was the military 'high water mark' of the rebellion is open to doubt. There is a stronger case to be made that the Confederate apogee in the eastern theatre came on 30 August 1862 at Second Manassas, where Lee won the last in the series of victories with which he and his great subordinate Major General Thomas 'Stonewall' Jackson turned back three separate Unionist invasions of Virginia. But eighteen days later, after following through with a lightning counter-invasion of the North, Lee took the outrageous risk of offering battle at Antietam (Sharpsburg) with his back to the Potomac river when outnumbered nearly two to one. Although his army was not destroyed he was compelled to retreat, and the hoped-for political benefits of taking the war to the enemy evaporated when, five days later, Lincoln issued a proclamation emancipating slaves in Confederate territory. Although it was overtly an act of economic warfare, it added a moral dimension to the struggle and thereafter any realistic Southern hopes for diplomatic recognition by the European powers dwindled.

George Meade

Lee's second invasion of the North, the Gettysburg campaign of 1863, did not immediately follow upon his brilliant victory at Chancellorsville on 30 April–6 May, dearly bought when 'friendly fire' mortally wounded the irreplaceable Jackson. It was instead conditioned by events in the no less vital western theatre, where Confederate fortunes had declined steadily since they lost control of the Upper Tennessee river and were obliged to evacuate Nashville in February 1862. In mid 1863 Federal forces were closing on the last stretch of the Mississippi river still controlled by the Confederacy, in fulfilment of a strategy of maritime and riverine blockade known as the 'Anaconda Plan', and Lee's raid was in part an attempt to relieve the pressure by striking at the reptile's head. But while the two eastern armies glowered at each other from their respective ridges on what might have been the fourth day of battle at Gettysburg, the fortress of Vicksburg and an army of nearly 30,000 men fell to Major General Ulysses Grant. Contemporary Confederate opinion was far more shaken by the fall of 'the Gibraltar of the Mississippi' than by the result at Gettysburg.

Jefferson Davis

Among other reasons to question whether the battle was the turning point in the war, the most salient is that Lee neither intended nor indeed was equipped to assault Washington or Baltimore, even though fear that he might do so dictated Union strategy. No less significant was that the full fruits of battlefield success are only harvested in the ensuing pursuit, something the cavalry of neither side accomplished throughout the war. Even if Meade had been driven from Cemetery Ridge, he would have fallen back on a previously identified, stronger position covering the cities and Lee would have lacked the men and the ammunition to mount another attack on him. Outright military victory was never a possibility for the Confederates and the strategy they adopted was defensive, its maximum aspiration being to sicken the North of the war in general and of Lincoln in particular.

At the operational level the formative experience for Lee and many other senior officers in both armies was General Winfield Scott's brilliantly conducted fighting advance from Vera Cruz to Mexico City in 1847, in which they learned that the side retaining the initiative suffered the least casualties. Gettysburg was no watershed at this level either, because even when forced onto the defensive Lee succeeded in obliging his opponents to conform to his dispositions, something he continued to do almost to the end, an extraordinary achievement given the growing disparity of resources between the two sides. On occasion – and Gettysburg was one – he erred in believing his army capable of more than it could accomplish, but the feeling was mutual and Grant, not a man given to overstatement, judged Lee's presence on the battlefield to be worth 20,000 men.

In studying the battle itself, unless there is convincing testimony to the contrary it is prudent to assume that after two years of war most field officers knew what could and could not be required of the men under their command. While hindsight may serve to elucidate why certain tactics did not prosper, contemporary accounts are generally misleading about the reasons why they were adopted in the first place. Even today, commanders in battle seldom have enough information to plan in a linear, logical sense and there is something inescapably intuitive about the mental process involved. It is a rare officer who will admit that a successful tactic was adopted on the basis of false assumptions, while contrived excuses for failure are all too common. The line between boldness and rashness, or between prudence and timidity, is often difficult to draw.

Robert E. Lee

In a slim volume such as this we cannot explore whether in tactical terms this was the last of the Napoleonic wars or a precursor of World War I and, anyway, the simple answer is that it was neither and can only be studied within its own terms of reference. Some considerations are eternal and these can be broadly divided into quantifiable factors such as firepower and concentration, and intangibles such as morale and shock. The basic unit of each army was a regiment, in theory of ten 100-man companies, although a glance at the Orders of Battle in the Appendices will reveal that at Gettysburg few regiments on either side were even half this strong. These were grouped in brigades, these in divisions and these in corps. Confederate infantry units at every level were larger, until they were double the size of their Union equivalents at corps level. This had little to do with different perceptions of combat efficiency and much to do with the politics of the two armies, which we shall examine in Chapter 5. The artillery was an exception to this general rule and Union batteries averaged six guns to the Confederates' four.

In attack the conundrum was how to achieve the necessary shock without presenting the enemy artillery with a concentrated target during the advance. Columns, at this point in the evolution of the range and lethality of weaponry, were used mainly to move troops within one's own lines. Although

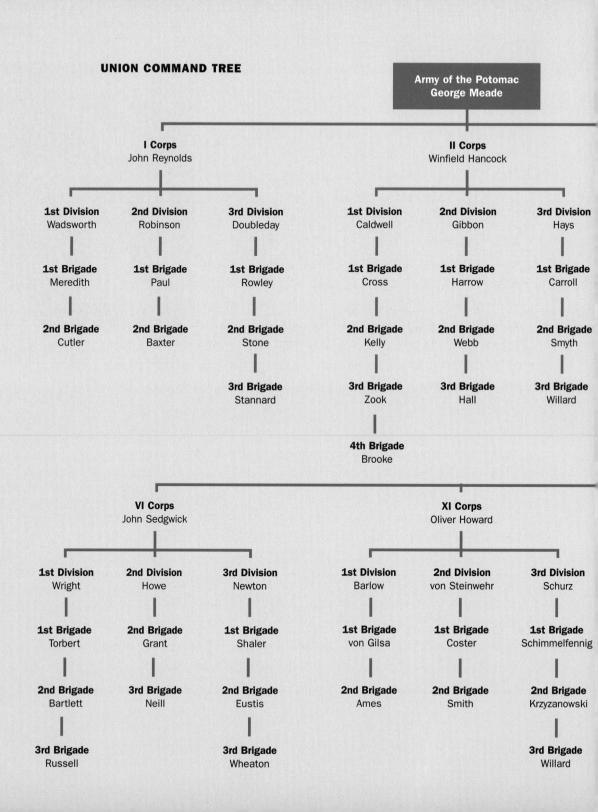

UNION COMMAND TREE

Army of the Potomac
George Meade

I Corps
John Reynolds

II Corps
Winfield Hancock

1st Division
Wadsworth

2nd Division
Robinson

3rd Division
Doubleday

1st Division
Caldwell

2nd Division
Gibbon

3rd Division
Hays

1st Brigade
Meredith

1st Brigade
Paul

1st Brigade
Rowley

1st Brigade
Cross

1st Brigade
Harrow

1st Brigade
Carroll

2nd Brigade
Cutler

2nd Brigade
Baxter

2nd Brigade
Stone

2nd Brigade
Kelly

2nd Brigade
Webb

2nd Brigade
Smyth

3rd Brigade
Stannard

3rd Brigade
Zook

3rd Brigade
Hall

3rd Brigade
Willard

4th Brigade
Brooke

VI Corps
John Sedgwick

XI Corps
Oliver Howard

1st Division
Wright

2nd Division
Howe

3rd Division
Newton

1st Division
Barlow

2nd Division
von Steinwehr

3rd Division
Schurz

1st Brigade
Torbert

2nd Brigade
Grant

1st Brigade
Shaler

1st Brigade
von Gilsa

1st Brigade
Coster

1st Brigade
Schimmelfennig

2nd Brigade
Bartlett

3rd Brigade
Neill

2nd Brigade
Eustis

2nd Brigade
Ames

2nd Brigade
Smith

2nd Brigade
Krzyzanowski

3rd Brigade
Russell

3rd Brigade
Wheaton

3rd Brigade
Willard

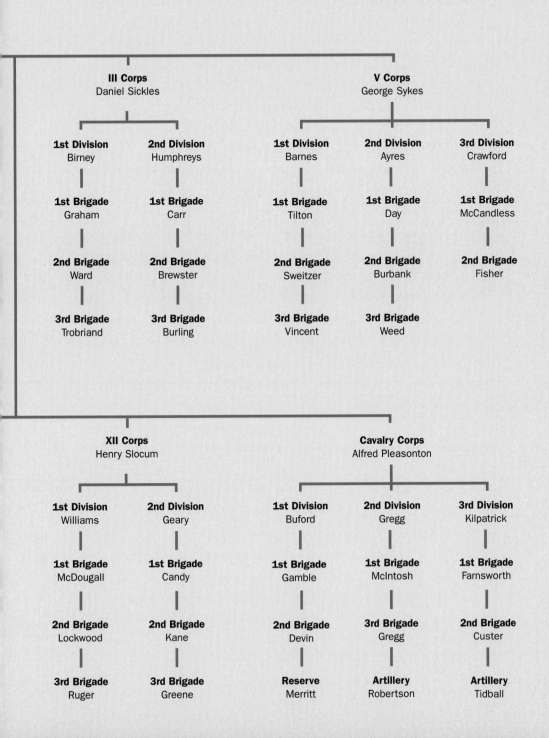

III Corps
Daniel Sickles

1st Division
Birney

2nd Division
Humphreys

1st Brigade
Graham

1st Brigade
Carr

2nd Brigade
Ward

2nd Brigade
Brewster

3rd Brigade
Trobriand

3rd Brigade
Burling

V Corps
George Sykes

1st Division
Barnes

2nd Division
Ayres

3rd Division
Crawford

1st Brigade
Tilton

1st Brigade
Day

1st Brigade
McCandless

2nd Brigade
Sweitzer

2nd Brigade
Burbank

2nd Brigade
Fisher

3rd Brigade
Vincent

3rd Brigade
Weed

XII Corps
Henry Slocum

1st Division
Williams

2nd Division
Geary

1st Brigade
McDougall

1st Brigade
Candy

2nd Brigade
Lockwood

2nd Brigade
Kane

3rd Brigade
Ruger

3rd Brigade
Greene

Cavalry Corps
Alfred Pleasonton

1st Division
Buford

2nd Division
Gregg

3rd Division
Kilpatrick

1st Brigade
Gamble

1st Brigade
McIntosh

1st Brigade
Farnsworth

2nd Brigade
Devin

3rd Brigade
Gregg

2nd Brigade
Custer

Reserve
Merritt

Artillery
Robertson

Artillery
Tidball

the term was often used to describe an attacking formation, this was a misnomer applied to the tendency of soldiers to bunch together during the last stage of a charge. The norm at the start was for the regiments of the leading brigade or brigades to advance in a double-ranked, five-company front, followed by a similarly constituted and deployed second line. Support troops might be formed in 'columns of regiments', that is with each regiment formed four or more deep as for a route march, only facing right and stacked one behind the other. This permitted maximum concentration to be maintained during a rapid advance to exploit a penetration achieved by the first waves, but only if the latter had suppressed the enemy artillery, or occasionally when terrain or reduced visibility provided cover. Even in Napoleon's day a column was never intended to engage an unbroken line of infantry and, if in nothing else, infantrymen were thoroughly drilled in deployment from column to line.

The brigade commanders usually decided how many regiments went into each wave, how dense each line was and how widely spaced the waves were. Although the manuals employed by both sides prescribed a line of 2 feet per man, this was a parade-ground optimum seldom achieved in battle and at Gettysburg only Brigadier General William Barksdale's Mississippi brigade charged literally shoulder to shoulder. Contact could be a protracted exchange of rifle fire at relatively close range when momentum failed or, when it did not, a charge in which the bayonet emphasized the attackers' determination to close. In protracted firefights it should not be thought that men stood and killed each other at close range – inexperienced troops might do so, but frontiersmen knew very well how to use cover and even in the open they loaded their rifles while lying on their backs and rolled over to shoot. Those not reared in Indian fighting territories learned quickly from their western comrades.

In attack or defence, company commanders were supposed to form on the right of their units to set the pace and maintain dressing (hence the order 'eyes right'), but in practice during the advance they, their lieutenants and senior NCOs acted as 'file closers', placing themselves behind their companies to push falterers back into line and to close up gaps made by casualties. The price of epaulettes was paid when the opposing sides came within flat trajectory small-arms range of each other (about 200 yards even over open ground), in particular on the attacking side, when officers normally had to lead by example and thus attracted preferential attention from enemy riflemen. Many maps and a number of battlefield markers give the impression that defending troops and guns formed along the crests of hills, but they did this only in exceptional circumstances. The norm was a first double-ranked line on the forward slope with a second on the reverse, although sometimes a favourable feature permitted a commander to shelter all his troops and guns from direct artillery fire while maintaining their own lines of sight.

Indirect fire, that is engaging the enemy beyond the line of sight, was in its infancy and seldom intentionally employed, the fuses of case shot packed with musket balls (shrapnel) and shells that broke up into fewer (six to eight) but deadlier fragments being notoriously undependable, especially on the Confederate side. The first pages of Appendices B and C present some technical notes on the ordnance employed, but the king of the Civil War battlefield was certainly the bronze smooth-bore 12-pounder Napoleon. A battery of these firing canister – thin-walled cans containing approximately thirty 1-inch-diameter iron balls packed in sawdust (sometimes called grape shot, although this was properly a load used by naval ordnance with a smaller number of larger balls) – could sweep its front far more effectively than even a large regiment of infantry and its shock value was infinitely greater. The longer accurate range of the rifled cannon made them more suitable for counter battery fire, but their lower throw-weight and blast (shock) made them less useful within the ranges at which Civil War battles were commonly fought.

The two sides were evenly equipped with small arms and artillery, thanks in part to the capture of large quantities of stores by the Confederates, but the communications, logistics and of course the industrial infrastructure of the Union war effort were so superior that only astounding mismanagement can

Individuality and self-reliance: Confederate infantrymen

explain why it did not prevail sooner, given that the inadequate Confederate quartermaster/commissary arrangements were further weakened by endemic corruption and incompetence. The effect of superior resources was most clearly seen in the cavalry: underlying the gradual erosion of Confederate superiority in this field was the fact that their cavalrymen had to provide their own mounts, so that a horse lost was also a trained trooper lost for as long as it took him to return home and obtain another. This meant that the born-to-the-saddle south-westerners could play no role in the eastern theatre, whereas the Union was able to make cavalrymen out of less promising material by keeping them in the field with government-supplied remounts.

Since the animals were a major investment for the individuals involved, the wonder is not that there were relatively few Confederate battlefield cavalry charges, but that there were any at all.

After a century dominated by Lost Cause historiography, Edwin Coddington's posthumously published *The Gettysburg Campaign: A Study in Command* set a new standard and more recently Harry Pfanz's two exhaustive treatments, rightly concentrating on the second day, are unlikely to be superseded. What these studies make clear is that, without disrespect to the genius of such as Jackson and Lee in knowing how to take full advantage of it, the power of the Confederate armies came from below, as movingly expressed by the detested Braxton Bragg, for much of the war commander of the Confederate army in the West, whose men would have been most surprised to know how he felt:

> We have had to trust to the individuality and self-reliance of the private soldier. Without the incentive which controls the officer, without the hope of reward and actuated only by a sense of duty and of patriotism, he has in this great contest justly judged that the cause was his own and gone into it with a determination to conquer or die.

There is a wonderful moment during the TV version of Gettysburg when Union Colonel Joshua Chamberlain asks some Confederate POWs what they are fighting for. 'Our rahts', they answer. 'Rats?' echoes Chamberlain uncertainly. 'Rahts [rights]', they repeat indignantly, nicely encapsulating the problem of two peoples divided by a common tongue, usually said of the Americans and the British. The latter will identify easily with those Rebs, because they have more recently seen the fruits of their patriotism and courage in adversity frittered away by a self-serving political class. They may also better appreciate the corrosive snobbery of an upper class that objectively preferred defeat to the social consequences of a mass mobilization, the only way the South could have compensated for a white population less than a quarter that of the Union.

As to the battle itself, we cannot presume to second-guess any commander's decisions on the basis of information not available to him at the time, and in the absence of evidence that he failed to respect the best practices of the time he deserves the benefit of the doubt. In Lee's phrase, the most that any officer can hope to do is 'bring the troops to the right place at the right time' to the best of his ability. Thereafter soldiers will gravitate away from the areas most exposed to enemy fire, to rally and continue to fight in the case of those better motivated, or to help the wounded to the rear or just sit out the rest of battle if they judge they have done enough.

Such revisionism as this account contains emerges from a belief that the only dependable witness is the terrain and from a deep appreciation that in these indifferently trained citizen armies, men from frontier states made markedly more effective soldiers. In what the great Prussian contemporary Field Marshal Moltke (the Elder) unkindly called a struggle between armed mobs, short-term enlistment coupled with high battle frequency meant that few units had the time and personnel continuity to achieve the machine-like battlefield discipline of, for example, the Vermonters who shattered Pickett's Charge with point-blank volleys. Also, while it is not possible to write about Gettysburg without some reference to what went wrong on the Confederate side, this account seeks to emphasize what the Unionists did right. Lastly, although history is hindsight, I have tried to respect the fact that both sides were acutely aware of their own errors and weaknesses, without the consolation of knowing that things were just as chaotic on the other side of the hill.

In order to give as complete a picture as possible in relatively few words, the text often requires the reader to refer back to the maps at the start of each chapter, and on occasion also to the tabular Orders of Battle in the Appendices. Larger units are identified by their commanders' names, not their administrative numeration, and for ease of reference appear in the Orders of Battle approximately in the order in which they are introduced in the text. Although regimental strengths and casualties provide a useful dimension they should be treated with caution: Union returns provide an accurate picture of the state of that army before and after the battle, but Confederate calculations are less trustworthy and differently arrived at. The 'missing' figures are particularly slippery, but if proper corrections are made for the situations in which they were placed, the casualty returns give a fair indication of each unit's performance.

The casualty figures for recently fought Chancellorsville have been included because the attrition of those literally prepared to kill or be killed is an important factor in battlefield momentum. There is a tendency to value 'blooded' troops more highly than the untried, but the latter, if well trained and led, may perform tasks that their more experienced comrades judge too difficult, while the former may have been diminished more than numbers indicate by the loss of natural as well as starred and chevroned leaders. The curve of combat usefulness that came with experience peaked relatively soon, as the randomness of death and injury on a smoke-shrouded battlefield eroded a soldier's faith that it could not happen to him. The smooth-bore musket ball was really only lethal to about 100 yards, but a rifle firing the Minié bullet, whose base expanded to fit the grooves in the barrel thereby gaining both velocity and stabilizing spin, could kill out to 1,000 yards, while at shorter ranges the greater-than-half-inch diameter, 1-ounce projectile literally smashed a man into the ground. Accurate fire was another matter, but it was not the ball or bullet with his name on it that a soldier feared, but the many addressed 'to whom it may concern'. If death or injury at extreme range was still uncommon, the distance over which they might travel had greatly increased.

The human element will always remain the most difficult to assess, yet strategy, logistics and battlefield tactics are ephemera by comparison with thirst, fatigue, terror, confusion and the counter-intuitive but undeniable fact that only a minority of soldiers fired their rifles with studied intent, even when their weapons were clean and before smoke enveloped them. Indeed many soon ceased firing altogether: after the battle 27,574 rifles were recovered, most of them loaded and almost half with multiple charges. Multiple loading is the signature of a stunned, frightened soldier going through the motions but not actually committing the aggressive act of pulling the trigger and we may safely assume that many similarly disabled rifles left the field on soldiers' shoulders. A large number of the discarded rifles had probably become unserviceable or so fouled that the recoil had become too brutal to bear, but many of these were probably exchanged for functional replacements that other soldiers had thrown away in their haste to be elsewhere. Battlefield evolutions are described in terms of divisions, brigades or regiments, but we must bear in mind that the success or failure of each of those manoeuvres was decided by countless individual choices among fight, flight and the many alternatives in between.

On 1 June 1863, Robert E. Lee's Army of Northern Virginia began to disengage from the positions overlooking the Rappahannock river at Fredericksburg it had defended with conspicuous success for the preceding six months and marched towards the Shenandoah Valley, the bread-basket of Virginia but also the covered way to the North. Major General 'Fighting Joe' Hooker, commanding the Union Army of the Potomac, wanted to bring Lee back by attacking at Fredericksburg, but his superiors in Washington demanded that he keep between them and the Confederate menace, so by 14 June the whole Union army was also marching north. But the Confederates did not debouch from any of the intermediate passes and kept going across the Potomac river, along the Cumberland Valley and into Pennsylvania. Four weeks into the campaign the leading elements of Lee's army were opposite Harrisburg and Colombia on the Susquehanna river, while

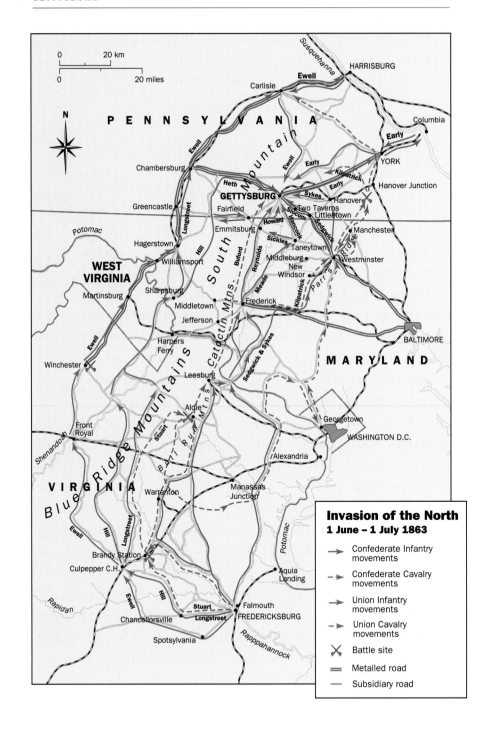

0   20 km

0   20 miles

N

P E N N S Y L V A N I A

Susquehanna

HARRISBURG

Ewell

Carlisle

Columbia

Ewell

Chambersburg

Ewell

Early

Early

YORK

Kilpatrick

Hanover Junction

Heth

Sykes

Early

Greencastle

GETTYSBURG

Fairfield

Slocum

Hanover

Two Taverns

Littlestown

Emmitsburg

Howard

Hancock

Sedgwick

Manchester

Potomac

Sickles

Taneytown

Longstreet

Hagerstown

Hill

Buford

Middleburg

New

Windsor

Westminster

WEST
VIRGINIA

Williamsport

Reynolds

Meade

Parr's Ridge

Martinsburg

Sharpsburg

Frederick

Kilpatrick

Middletown

M A R Y L A N D

Jefferson

Catoctin Mtns.

South Mountain

Harpers
Ferry

Sedgwick & Sykes

BALTIMORE

Ewell

Winchester

Leesburg

Shenandoah

Aldie

Bull Run Mtns.

Stuart

Georgetown

WASHINGTON D.C.

Front
Royal

Alexandria

V I R G I N I A

Warrenton

Manassas
Junction

Blue Ridge Mountains

Ewell

Hill

Longstreet

Potomac

Brandy Station

Aquia
Landing

Culpepper C.H.

Rapidan

Ewell

Hill

Stuart

Longstreet

Falmouth

FREDERICKSBURG

Chancellorsville

Spotsylvania

Rappahannock

Invasion of the North
1 June – 1 July 1863

→ Confederate Infantry
movements

⇢ Confederate Cavalry
movements

→ Union Infantry
movements

⇢ Union Cavalry
movements

✕ Battle site

═ Metalled road

— Subsidiary road

Hooker's army had only reached Frederick in Maryland, and he became surly and resentful of Washington's attempts to goad him into what he saw as precipitate action.

George Meade, an irascible man at the best of times, was not amused to be woken at three o'clock in the morning of 28 June by a courier bearing a dispatch from general-in-chief Henry Halleck. Assuming the worst following several recent disagreements with Hooker, Meade snarled that he had done nothing to deserve dismissal and was stunned to find that the envelope contained not a request but an order to assume command of the Army of the Potomac. With the exception of his chief of staff, nobody else in the army knew that Hooker

John Reynolds

had submitted his resignation, conditional upon being given much broader authority than he was likely to be granted. He may have miscalculated the degree to which the military crisis had strengthened his hand, but a more probable explanation for the ultimatum is that he sought a face-saving way to avoid another encounter with Lee.

Meade was likewise unaware that fellow Pennsylvanian and corps commander Major General John Reynolds, whom he knew to be better connected politically and considered the most likely candidate, had pre-empted the possibility in a private interview with Lincoln. As well as declaring his lack of confidence in both the leadership of Hooker and the strategic direction of Halleck (which, they both knew, meant Lincoln himself), Reynolds told the President that only Meade enjoyed the confidence of his peers and would also accept the appointment without preconditions. When signing the order Lincoln said he supposed Meade would fight well 'on his own dunghill' – Pennsylvania please note – but the letter of appointment gave him authority to appoint and dismiss officers at his discretion and the right to give orders directly to adjacent army commands, powers previously denied to Hooker. Given the incandescent heat of the potato being dropped in Meade's lap these provisions are less a mark of confidence in him than of Washington's fear that he might after all refuse the appointment, leaving them with no choice but to accept Hooker's ultimatum. Lincoln/Halleck continued to tug on the reins, but the terms of Meade's appointment were a significant softening of the bit at which previous army commanders had chafed in vain.

In a tense interview with Hooker, camped nearby, Meade learned the location of the rest of the army for the first time and discussed various possibilities. Ideally he wanted to gather the army for a review: the seven infantry corps could all have passed through Frederick on their way north and the troops would have benefited from an opportunity to see the face and bearing of the man who now held their lives in his hands. There are a number of reports of junior officers and soldiers making an effort just to set eyes on Meade during battle lulls at Gettysburg, so his instinct in this matter was sound. But the idea was quickly abandoned because there was no time for this or any other of the usual niceties, nor indeed for more than a few hours of sleep over the next week.

A similarly impersonal change of commander would have been unthinkable in the opposing Army of Northern Virginia, where Lee's entourage was little more than a secretariat, but the Army of the Potomac had a large headquarters staff and Meade's assumption was akin to a change in the chief executive officer of a large corporation. Still, he was acutely aware of the need to instil confidence in his troops, both in him and in themselves. Instead of the review he issued a cleverly worded proclamation: 'The country looks to this army to relieve it from the devastation and disgrace of foreign invasion. Whatever fatigues and sacrifices we may be called upon to undergo ... let each man determine to do his duty. ... I rely upon the hearty support of my companions in arms to assist me.' No nonsense here about erring brothers – the 'other' was properly demonized and the need to redeem past defeats subtly emphasized, a refreshing change from the bombast of some previous army commanders.

Reynolds told Lincoln that Meade was the only senior officer who could be depended upon to obey orders unquestioningly and so it proved down the chain of command. Several officers refused Meade's invitation to become his chief of staff, to replace Hooker's crony Major General Daniel Butterfield in whom he had no confidence. Not only did Butterfield fully live down to his new commanding officer's opinion of him, he also devoted himself to collecting or fabricating evidence against him, which he was to lay before a partisan Joint Committee of Congress eight months later. The austere Meade's distaste was personal as well as professional – prostitutes became known as 'hookers' because Fighting Joe and his cronies kept so many of them on retainer for their own entertainment and as part of the lavish hospitality that bought them abiding popularity with journalists and visiting politicians. Much has been written about the failure of Lee's corps commanders to act in the spirit of his general instructions, but his problems in this respect were less than Meade's, whose very authority was tenuous.

Ambrose Hill

To a significant degree Lee's campaign plan was posited on his opponent being the mercurial Hooker and when he heard of his replacement he commented, 'General Meade will commit no blunders in my front and if I make one he will make haste to take advantage of it.' This was a more favourable assessment than he made of either Ambrose Hill or Richard Ewell, his new corps commanders, when recommending their promotion to the rank of lieutenant general. Much later he mused that he might have won if Stonewall Jackson had been there, but at Gettysburg he refused to divide his army even once, let alone twice as he had at Chancellorsville, and the high opinion he had of Meade must have influenced his decision to fight a conservative battle. Of course the feeling was entirely mutual and Meade was similarly inhibited, but Lee's judgement that he faced an alert and dangerous opponent has not been afforded the attention it deserves.

He was right to be cautious: Meade was a professional whose explosive rages were a product of frustration that the army to which he had devoted his life had so far made a poor showing because of clumsy or tentative leadership. Unfortunately he had only a superficial acquaintance with Lincoln, who enjoyed plain speaking, and it is poignant to note the contrast between his stilted dispatches to Washington and the ferocious determination revealed in a letter to his wife:

> We are marching as fast as we can to relieve Harrisburg [the capital of Pennsylvania, threatened by Ewell] but have to keep a sharp lookout that the rebels don't turn around and get at Washington and Baltimore in our rear. They have a cavalry force in our rear, destroying railroads, etc., with a view to getting me to turn back, but I shall not do it. I am going straight at them and will settle this thing one way or another.

His dismissive reference to the Confederate cavalry force under Major General 'Jeb' Stuart, currently between him and Washington, is typical. However excited the civilians might become, Meade knew that Stuart's ride was just a distraction, similar to the flawed stratagem upon which Hooker had based his Chancellorsville campaign. Brigadier General John Gregg's cavalry brigade was sent to locate Stuart, but nobody seems to have cared that he failed to do so. The morale of the well-equipped and -mounted Union cavalry corps was soaring after what it believed were victories over Stuart at Brandy Station on 9 June and around Aldie eight days later, and while the Confederate cavalry élite was tiring out its horses to no great effect, Union cavalry divisions under Brigadier Generals John Buford and Judson Kilpatrick were competently screening the movement of their own infantry. Unfortunately, although they sent back accurate and timely reports, when these did not coincide with his own opinions they were disregarded by Major General Alfred Pleasonton, the Union cavalry corps commander.

'Jeb' Stuart

The reborn cavalry was not the only trump recently dealt to the Union commander. After nearly being killed by Confederate round shot at Chancellorsville, a chastened Hooker abandoned an experiment in dispersing

his guns among the infantry divisions and restored the large Artillery Reserve that had done such execution at Antietam. Each corps still had its own endowment, but every cannon in the army was directly or indirectly under the overall command of the dedicated and competent Brigadier General Henry Hunt, just in time for the greatest artillery battle of the war. By contrast Lee retained the dog-like but useless Brigadier General William Pendleton as titular artillery commander, with all the guns under the control of the corps commanders. Union batteries were larger and their ordnance standardized, but it was Hunt's ability to mass them where and when needed that was to provide the decisive difference at Gettysburg.

Richard Ewell

There is however little evidence that Meade appreciated how important the support arms would be. He was mainly concerned with the correct distribution of his infantry corps both to cause the Confederates to pull back from Harrisburg and Columbia and to cover Washington and Baltimore against a foray by the main Confederate force under Lee at Chambersburg in the Cumberland Valley. Union corps were under half the size of the Confederates' and after suffering 12 per cent casualties at Chancellorsville, a further 20 per cent, including a high proportion of two-year veterans, left the army before Gettysburg. Compounding Meade's difficulties, during this period new recruits joined as discrete units instead of filling out the veteran regiments, even when others from their own states were depleted. Only the regiments withdrawn from garrison duty (Brigadier General George Stannard's from Washington in I Corps and Brigadier General Henry Lockwood's from Baltimore in XII Corps) had even half their notional full strength of 1,000 men and some entire brigades were well below this total (Colonel Patrick Kelly's in II Corps and Brigadier General Thomas Kane's in XII Corps). Meade also knew that Major General Oliver Howard's corps was still shaky after breaking at Chancellorsville, where Major General Henry

Slocum's and Desperate Dan Sickles's corps had also been severely mauled. Finally, although Slocum and Major General John Sedgwick had gracefully accepted the promotion of Meade, to whom they were senior, they could not be subordinated to anyone else.

After weighing all these factors, the corps deployment Meade decided upon after close consultation with Reynolds, whom he made area commander of the left wing closest to Lee's known concentration around Chambersburg, was a necessarily broad net. The dependable Sedgwick and Meade's old corps under Major General George Sykes were sent east to Manchester and Union Mills, screened by Kilpatrick's cavalry division, while Reynolds with Howard under his direct command thrust westwards towards Emmitsburg, screened by Buford. In the centre Meade sent the trusted Major General Winfield Hancock to nearby Uniontown and himself rode with Sickles's and Slocum's divisions towards Taneytown, where he established his headquarters. After Reynolds's corps advanced towards Gettysburg, followed by Howard's, Meade ordered Sickles to the left flank via Emmitsburg and sent Slocum forward to Littlestown, equidistant from both wings.

Major General Darius Couch, the commander of the 10,000-man Union garrison at Harrisburg, kept Meade informed about the Confederates (Ewell's corps) massing across the Susquehanna from him, while on 30 June Kilpatrick reported a brisk engagement with part of Stuart's force at Hanover. Meade could not, therefore, focus on the main enemy force in the Cumberland Valley to the exclusion of a possible sweep around his right. In fact Stuart's orders were to join up with Ewell, which argues that Lee had just such a manoeuvre in mind when he began the campaign. It does not require the eye of a great commander to see that all roads led to Gettysburg, but the same can be said of Hanover, Littlestown or Taneytown – and even more so of the crucial choke point on the Baltimore Turnpike at Westminster, towards which Meade sent the army's baggage train. Even if he had not circulated a contingency plan for a stand along Pipe Creek (see Appendix A), Meade's dispositions announced that it was his fallback position.

There may be room for doubt in other spheres of human activity, but in pre-battle manoeuvres it is more blessed to give than to receive. The enemy had the initiative and Meade perforce could only narrow his opponent's options and guard against the danger of any part of his army being defeated in detail, something he knew Lee would seek to achieve. Nearly 7,000 men and abundant stores had already fallen to Ewell around Winchester in mid June and with intelligence estimates indicating that he was outnumbered, Meade could not afford another such loss. He could not have imagined what poor reconnaissance the cavalry retained by Lee was performing, so he had to prepare for any of several possible thrusts accurately aimed at his weakest points. The strong left wing under Reynolds was tasked with a spoiling role against a sudden Confederate debouchment in strength from the Cashtown Gap, but the distribution of the Union army was far from optimum for a concentration around Gettysburg.

Thus despite lacking his 'eyes', Lee accomplished the ideal of getting there first with the most men, only to be thwarted by the unexpectedly robust resistance put up by the first Union forces on the field. But behind them was the aggressive will of Meade to close with the enemy, casting aside the more prudent Pipe Creek alternative and confident in his army and in himself. From top to bottom, the Army of the Potomac was to fight as though retreat was not an option, its determination coming as a shock to the Rebels, who were surprised to discover that the despised Yankees were capable of fighting as fiercely as they in defence of their homeland.

2

BUFORD'S AND DOUBLEDAY'S BATTLE (DAY 1)

A key theme at Gettysburg was the progressive dislocation of Confederate expectations. This began as soon as the leading corps of Lee's army under Ambrose Hill ran into Buford's cavalry screen north-west of the town. Pleasonton, well to the rear, had the advantage of eleven days' seniority, Hooker's favour and consequently good publicity from the press corps, but by any measure of personal and professional quality Buford should have had command of the Union cavalry corps. He scarcely put a foot wrong throughout the campaign and drove himself so relentlessly that exposure and exhaustion fatally weakened his resistance to typhoid six months later. By contrast Hill, exercising corps command for the first time but with a record for extreme boldness at brigade level, was suffering from gonorrhoea and was mentally absent throughout the battle.

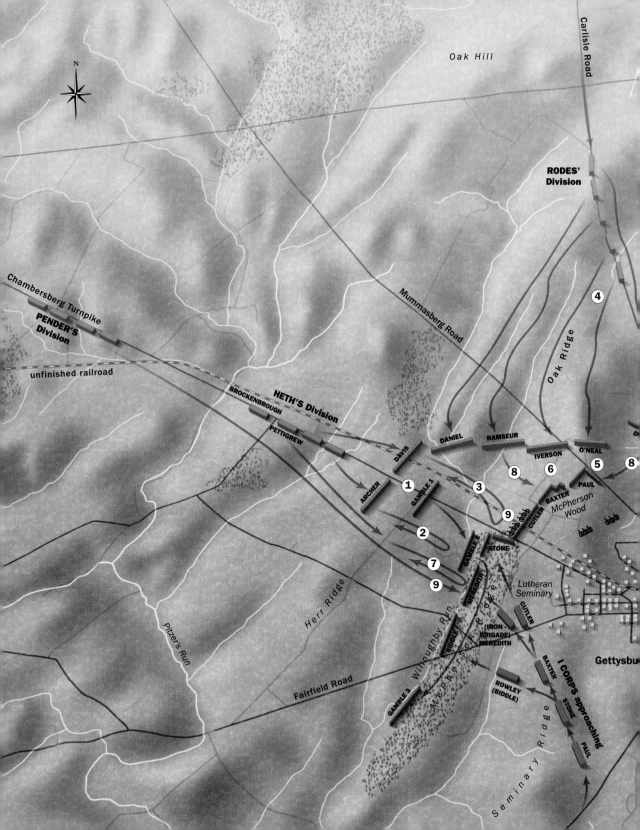

Carlisle Road

Oak Hill

RODES'
Division

④

Mummasberg Road

Oak Ridge

Chambersberg Turnpike

PENDER'S
Division

unfinished railroad

BROCKENBROUGH

HETH'S Division

PETTIGREW

DAVIS

DANIEL

RAMSEUR

IVERSON

O'NEAL

⑧

⑥

⑤

⑧

ARCHER

GAMBLE 1

①

③

PAUL

⑨

CUTLER

BAXTER

McPherson
Wood

②

GAMBLE 2

STONE

⑦

⑨

MEREDITH

Lutheran
Seminary

Herr Ridge

Willoughby Run

McPherson Ridge

CUTLER

(IRON-
BRIGADE)
MEREDITH

BAXTER

I CORPS approaching

Pitzer's Run

BIDDLE

Gettysbu

GAMBLE 3

STONE

ROWLEY
(BIDDLE)

Fairfield Road

PAUL

Seminary Ridge

N

The canonical version of the way the battle began is that the leading Confederate division under Major General Harry Heth marched on Gettysburg in search of a cache of shoes, but this is unlikely: Heth knew that Major General Jubal Early's division of Ewell's corps had passed through the town four days previously and, footwear being much in demand in the ragged Confederate army, could be depended upon to be wearing any shoes there might have been in the town. Heth's advance was rather a reconnaissance in force and although it was seriously mismanaged this does not detract from Buford's achievement in buying time for the lead elements of Reynolds's corps to come up. The cavalryman had the inestimable advantage of a bird's-eye view of the battlefield from the tower of the Lutheran Seminary, from whence he directed his part of the battle. His reserve brigade was elsewhere and Colonel Thomas Devin's depleted brigade was spread in a wide arc covering the northern approaches to Gettysburg, so he had only Colonel William Gamble's 1,600 troopers with whom to oppose Heth's division of 7,000 men.

Even though a quarter of Gamble's men had to tend to the horses while the rest fought dismounted, they were equipped with the Sharps breech-loading carbine and supported by a battery of regular-army horse artillery under Lieutenant John Calef. The volume of fire they laid down forced the leading Confederate brigades under Brigadier Generals James Archer and Joseph Davis, the latter a nephew of the Confederate President, to deploy in front of Herr's Ridge and imposed further delays on them by conducting a fighting retreat in the finest dragoon tradition through farms, orchards and woods, before making another stand along the tree-lined banks of Willoughby Run. This diagonal feature, combined with the domination of the Chambersburg Turnpike and a nearby unfinished railway line by Calef's battery, unbalanced the

Day 1 – Buford's and Doubleday's battle

1 Leading brigades of Heth's division (Hill's Corps) engaged by Gamble's troopers from Herr's Ridge to McPherson's Ridge, directed by Buford in the Lutheran Seminary tower.

2 Archer's brigade charges across Willoughby Run and is shattered by Meredith's Iron Brigade directed by I Corps commander Reynolds, who is killed. Doubleday takes over.

3 Davis's brigade hooks around Union line but is repulsed by Cutler's brigade and Meredith's reserve regiment. Biddle takes over brigade command from the drunken Rowley.

4 Leading elements of Rodes' division (Ewell's Corps) arrive at the northern extension of Oak Ridge. Rodes and his staff driven off Oak Hill by Union shell fire.

5 Three regiments of O'Neal's brigade make a half-hearted attack on the Union right in McPherson's Wood, met by intense fire from the batteries that shelled Rodes off Oak Hill.

6 Iverson's brigade attacks McPherson's Wood without reconnaissance and is shattered by crossfires from Baxter's brigade deployed in a 'saw tooth' line with artillery firing across its front.

7 Pettigrew's and Brockenbrough's brigades with the remnant of Archer's brigade on the right and Davis' brigade on the left make second assault across Willoughby Run and are repulsed.

8 Part of Doles' and Ramseur's brigades make converging attacks on McPherson's Wood, Daniel's brigade distracts Cutler's brigade and Union artillery in the centre. Union right wing crumbles.

9 General assault by Pender's division forces the McPherson's Ridge line, Stone's brigade and Union artillery hold the centre long enough to permit orderly retreat.

Lutheran Seminary

Confederate advance such that the two brigades fought separate battles and were defeated in detail.

Seventy years earlier, the citizen armies of France revolutionized combat with swarms of skirmishers sent ahead to confuse, attrite and exasperate the enemy. Although in America, as in Europe, specialist regiments as well as flank companies of riflemen were designated for the role, an oddity about the Civil War was that neither army of a people who in many ways pioneered the tactic was inclined to employ open-order formations on any meaningful scale. The infantry manual employed by both sides defined skirmishing as 'a loose, desultory kind of engagement, generally between light troops thrown forward to test the strength and position of the enemy.' The words 'desultory' and 'between light troops' speak for themselves, but in case there were any doubt, the manual went on to circumscribe the skirmishers' essential freedom of action to the point that they were little more than a weak line, neither fish nor fowl.

The two Confederate brigadiers responded differently to the tactical novelty of skirmishers who put up far from desultory resistance. Archer launched a full-blown assault across Willoughby Run and into the woods on the forward slope of McPherson's Ridge and when Gamble's men gave way the attackers became prematurely exultant, unaware that the cavalrymen were falling back through the leading regiments of Brigadier General James Wadsworth's I Corps division, now arriving at the double to secure the ridge. The Confederates were therefore not psychologically prepared to encounter Brigadier General Solomon Meredith's Iron Brigade, generally regarded as the best infantry in the Union army, which hit them head on and along their right flank. With his left galled by fire from Captain Daniel Hall's battery, which took over Calef's commanding position in the midst of the action, Archer and hundreds of his men surrendered, while the rest fled back to Herr's Ridge. Having bought crucial hours at minimal cost, Gamble's troopers trotted off to cover the southern flank.

Meanwhile Davis's brigade had advanced more cautiously, tending away from the guns on the turnpike and thus to outflank the Union position on McPherson's Ridge. Three regiments of Brigadier General Lysander Cutler's brigade had barely taken up their positions to the north of the turnpike and in support of Hall's battery when the three, considerably larger, regiments Davis had to hand advanced upon them with devastating effect. Firing short-range double-canister loads impartially at Archer's brigade to his left and Davis's to the right, Hall suddenly found himself isolated and lost a gun during his precipitous withdrawal. He had harsh words with Cutler and Wadsworth about this, but they seem to have judged that a sacrificial lamb is entitled to bleat if it is fortunate enough to survive the experience.

Unfortunately Archer's attack had collapsed before Davis drove in the Union right, freeing Cutler's remaining two regiments and the Iron Brigade's

The back of McPherson's Ridge after the battle: tourist pointing to the spot where Reynolds fell

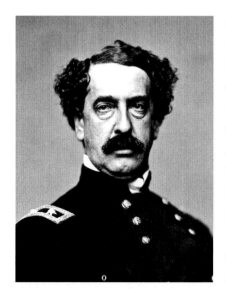

Abner Doubleday

reserve 6th Wisconsin to perform another textbook head-on and flanking counter-attack. Although part of Davis's 2nd Mississippi was caught in a steep-sided railway cut and surrendered, his other regiments withdrew in more or less good order. Ten miles away while this debacle unfolded, Ambrose Hill belatedly hurried to join Heth on Herr's Ridge, where they nervously awaited the arrival of Lee. But he displayed his usual forbearance and refrained from asking them how many shoes they thought were worth the loss of a thousand men.

On the Union side divisional commander Wadsworth, acting corps commander Major General Abner Doubleday and area commander Reynolds had been in the thick of things and the latter was killed. This nearly balanced the scales, because the reverses suffered by the Union later in the day might well have been avoided had he lived. The 'speak no ill of the dead' rule tends to spare fallen heroes from criticism, but this is often unfair to those left to pick up the pieces. Reynolds's first sight of the battlefield was from Buford's eyrie atop the Lutheran Seminary, but instead of directing his forces from there he took Buford with him to perform staff-officer tasks and was killed while urging on veteran regiments led by proven officers. While undoubtedly there are times when a senior officer must be seen by his men to share their fortunes unhesitatingly, this was not one of them. Having committed two corps to battle immediately, and the whole army eventually, he should not have thrown away his life doing the work of a colonel.

The timing of his death was particularly unfortunate because Oliver Howard, who replaced him as area commander and whose battle we shall consider next, felt bound by Reynolds's order to secure the I Corps' right flank even though it had been given in ignorance of the imminent arrival of Major Generals Robert Rodes's and Jubal Early's divisions of Richard Ewell's corps from the north. It has been suggested that Doubleday could have held

Seminary Ridge if he had been allowed to fall back sooner, but as he and Howard discussed when the latter briefly visited him, both lines were enfiladable from their parent Oak Ridge, and neither position could be held if the saddle at McPherson's Wood were lost. Sorely missed was Stannard's brigade, which arrived in the evening after a seven-day forced march from garrison duty around Washington, but the splendidly handled corps artillery under Colonel Charles Wainwright partly compensated. As well as continuing to command the vital turnpike and railway lines, the guns posted to cover the right flank did so to such good effect that the first Confederate attacks from the north were channelled away from the vulnerable rear of the McPherson's Wood position.

John Buford pictured with members of his staff

The gods of war bestowed another wintry smile on the Unionists, for at about 1400 hours this crucial position was attacked by two brigades that had suffered heavy officer losses at Chancellorsvile, commanded by men in whom Rodes, their divisional commander, had no confidence. Brigadier General Alfred Iverson, who owed his rank to the political influence of his father, and Colonel Edward O'Neal, of whom in particular Rodes had earlier expressed the strongest reservations, this day failed to practise the vigorous 'follow me' leadership that characterized the Confederate officer corps. With Rodes impatiently giving orders over his head, only three of O'Neal's five regiments attacked, while Iverson sent his brigade to be massacred in a killing ground that even desultory skirmishing would have detected and then abandoned his command for the next two days, possibly aware that one of his colonels had expressed a dying wish for someone to do away with 'that imbecile'.

The Union position at the time of these assaults consisted of a long line formed by Gamble's troopers south of the Fairfield Road, with Colonel Champman Biddle's brigade and the Iron Brigade, under the command of Colonel James Robinson after Meredith was crippled by a shell immediately following the repulse of Archer's attack, continuing the line along the woods in front of McPherson's Ridge overlooking Willoughby Run. This was followed by a refused flank formed by Colonel Roy Stone's brigade along the Chambersburg Turnpike, connecting to another line along the treeline in front of the Oak Ridge saddle, from which Cutler's brigade and part of Baxter's destroyed Iverson's clumsy assault. O'Neal's half-hearted advance was stopped by the rest of Baxter's men on another refused flank along a stone wall parallel to the Mummasburg Road, where they were later joined by Brigadier General Gabriel Paul's brigade.

Rodes rushed his first attacks because, from his vantage point on Oak Knoll, he could see at a glance the imperative need to get between Doubleday's right and the approaching left wing of Howard's corps, but it was not only haste and the inadequacy of the instruments to hand that caused them to fail so completely. When he tried to bring up his guns to enfilade the Union line, Wainwright's batteries plastered them with shells and drove them and Rodes himself off Oak Knoll. Also the Union position along the Oak Ridge saddle was itself further echeloned to create vicious crossfires, as Iverson's hapless brigade soon discovered, and most of Union infantry enjoyed tree cover and the gently sloping, unobstructed lines of fire that are so pleasing to a rifleman's eye. Heth and Rodes certainly blundered, but they were up against first-class troops, skilfully deployed. The Union stand here was an epic of arms marred only by the antics of Brigadier General Thomas Rowley, who briefly took over Doubleday's division, rode about shouting drunken and fortunately ignored orders, fell off his horse and was finally removed from the scene by the Provost Guard.

The beginning of the end came when Heth's remaining brigades led by Brigadier General James Pettigrew and Colonel John Brockenbrough, with the remnants of Archer's and Davis's brigades on the wings, made another frontal assault across Willoughby Run and were repulsed with difficulty. A little later Heth was knocked unconscious by a bullet (the thickness of his skull was much commented upon) and command of his division passed to Pettigrew. Simultaneously Rodes's right-wing brigade under Brigadier General Junius Daniel launched a converging attack against Stone's brigade on the refused Union flank, but it was enfiladed by Wainwright's guns and also fell back.

The lull ended when Major General William Pender's fresh division advanced against McPherson's Ridge and by now the defenders, in particular the resolute Iron Brigade, were too thin to hold. Stone was wounded and captured fighting the rearguard while the rest fell back on Seminary Ridge, Wainwright's guns pulling out only after hammering Pender's left under Brigadier General Alfred Scales, severely wounding Scales himself. The carnage as the Confederates surged into double-canister range was gruesome and Augustus Buell, boy cannoneer with Battery B, 4th US Artillery, later wrote a gripping account of the moment when the Confederates finally prevailed:

Up and down the line men reeling and falling; splinters flying from wheels and axles where bullets hit; in rear, horses tearing and plunging, mad with wounds or terror; drivers yelling, shells bursting, shot shrieking overhead, howling about our ears or throwing up great clouds of dust where they struck; the musketry crashing on three sides of us; bullets hissing, humming and whistling everywhere; cannon roaring; all crash on crash and peal on peal, smoke, dust, splinters, blood, wreck and carnage indescribable; but the brass guns of Old B still bellowed and not a man or boy flinched or faltered!

Rodes finally launched properly prepared pincer attacks by Brigadier General Stephen Ramseur's and part of Brigadier General George Doles's brigades against the Union bastion in McPherson's Wood. Paul's brigade was overwhelmed, its elegant commander shot through the eyes and the colonels who replaced him falling in rapid succession until there were none left. What followed was a reasonably orderly retreat, not a rout, although two of Wainwright's hard-working guns were lost at this stage. Doubleday had filled Reynolds's shoes as well as anyone could have and I Corps had significantly eroded the combat effectiveness of three Confederate divisions, yet Major General John Newton was promoted over him that evening and he was later discarded. In part because he needed a scapegoat for Reynolds's and Howard's decisions but also because of personal dislike, Meade committed an injustice that resonates to this day.

No other would have done much better when hit in the flank by over twice its number of screaming Confederates; nonetheless Oliver Howard's XI Corps carried the stigma of having broken before Stonewall Jackson's surprise attack at Chancellorsville. The work ethic and perceived aloofness of the German-Americans ('Dutchmen') who were concentrated in this corps did not endear them to their Anglo-Scots countrymen, although the insults heaped upon them were as nothing beside the vitriol expended upon their fellow immigrants from Ireland (a contemporary joke told of a slave complaining that his master treated him like an Irishman). Many of the 'Dutchmen' had joined to serve under Major General Franz Sigel, promoted above the level of his competence by Lincoln precisely to encourage German enlistment, and felt betrayed when he resigned because he perceived that his appointment to a small corps (at

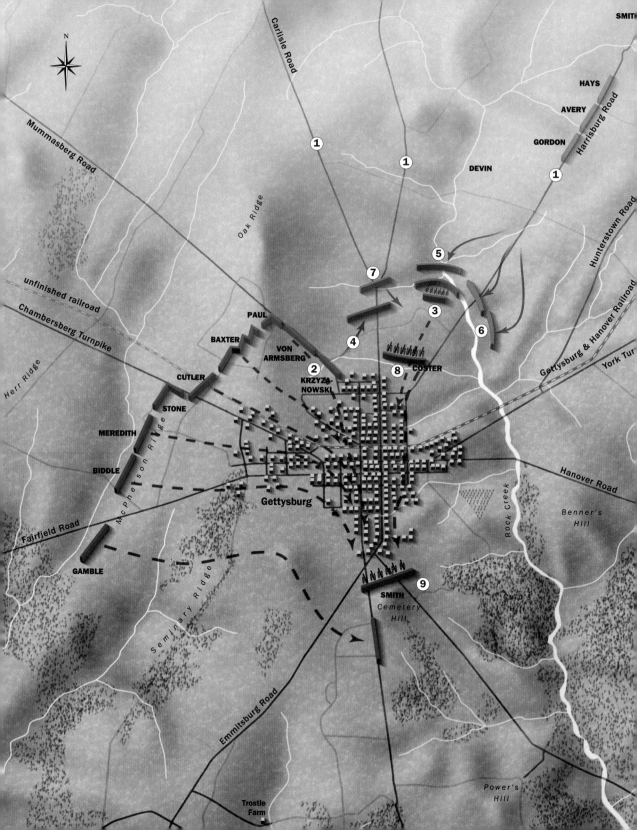

just over 9,000 men) was a rebuke for his mishandling of an independent command in 1862.

His one-armed replacement, the 32-year-old Howard, was the youngest corps commander in the army and also the most devout, having trained for the ministry while teaching at West Point. He had adequate warning to refuse the right flank of the Union army at Chancellorsville but failed to do so, without reducing the esteem in which Meade and others held him. He was widely thought to be a gentleman and this counted for much in the post-Hooker army. Whether a Christian gentleman should have been quite so adept at acquitting himself of the consequences of his own actions and blaming others is another matter, but his combination of personal qualities meant that Doubleday and the 'Dutchmen' were to bear the blame for Howard's errors this day.

Not the least of these was a belief that his demoralized and resentful corps needed the stick, not the carrot. As chief stick wielder he imported the 28-year-old Brigadier General Francis Barlow to take over command of the first division to crumple at Chancellorsville. Slovenly in appearance and with the usual non-West Pointer's chip on his shoulder, this unpleasant young man carried a heavy cavalry sabre and used the flat of it on his men. When we consider that many of the Germans had immigrated to get away from this sort of treatment in their native land, we can only wonder at his brutal arrogance. One of his brigades was mostly non-German and commanded by Brigadier General Adelbert Ames, another 28-year-old imported by Howard, while the other was wholly Dutch and commanded by the Prussian Colonel Leopold von Gilsa. Barlow's animosity towards the latter drove a wedge between the two brigades, although the soldiers of the whole division remained united in their hatred of him.

Day 1 – Howard's battle

1 Devin's thin cavalry screen across the northern approaches to Gettysburg. Falls back to Rock Creek, then joins Gamble on Cemetery Ridge.

2 Schimmelfennig's division (Schurz promoted to corps command) advances to support the right flank of I Corps.

3 Barlow advances his division from the Alms House Ridge to Blocher's Knoll without authority.

4 Krzyzanowski's brigade scrambles to cover Barlow's flank, grossly over-extending to try and remain in contact with von Armsberg's brigade.

5 Gordon's brigade makes frontal attack on Barlow's position through the woods in front of Blocher's Knoll.

6 Hays' and Avery's brigades outflank Barlow's position.

7 Part of Doles' brigade attacks into the gap between Krzyzanowski's right and Barlow's left.

8 Three regiments of Coster's brigade and Wilkeson's battery sacrifice themselves holding the Alms House Ridge to cover Barlow's retreat.

9 Smith's brigade and Wiedrich's battery retained by Howard at Cemetery Hill, provide rallying point for I Corps and XI Corps remnants.

The other two divisions had put up a somewhat better fight at Chancellorsville and were commanded by Major General Carl Schurz, over-promoted for the same reasons as Sigel, and the more competent Brigadier General Baron Adolph von Steinwehr. All in all a motley crew and Howard would have been well advised to keep them in close mutual support. Perhaps he intended to do so, but the last order he received from Reynolds was to protect the right flank of the I Corps' position along McPherson's Ridge and he chose not to reconsider this when, along with news of Reynolds's death, he received accurate reports from Devin's cavalry screen to the north of the town of the arrival of Ewell's corps in strength. This is not to deny how extremely hazardous it is to conduct a withdrawal under pressure, but after the first failed Confederate attacks there was a protracted lull during which Howard could have ordered Doubleday to begin a phased withdrawal.

Against this, the ease with which the assaults by Iverson and O'Neal were shattered and the dominance established by Union artillery led both Doubleday and Howard to overestimate the strength of the McPherson's Wood redoubt. Doctrine in both armies was shaped by an obsession with 'key points' peculiar to West Point training and this also helps to explain why the position was held even when outflanked. To close up to it, Howard's own corps had to occupy a largely featureless front while reshuffling its command structure. When Reynolds's death promoted Howard to area command, in theory Schurz became corps commander and Brigadier General Alexander Schimmelfennig took over his division, leaving all the brigades except Ames's under the command of colonels. Even in a more cohesive corps this would have caused problems, but the lack of mutual confidence within XI Corps meant that Howard did not formally relinquish command, a circumstance promptly exploited by Barlow.

Howard's orders, faithfully relayed by Schurz, were for Schimmelfennig to continue the line of the refused I Corps' right flank, diverging from the Mummasburg Road at about a 35-degree angle until joining with Barlow's division on the Almshouse Ridge on the eastern side of the Carlisle Road. But because they came from Schurz, Barlow ignored these instructions and marched his division forward to Blocher Knoll. He had ridden there earlier with Howard, but whatever they may have discussed is immaterial beside the fact that he deliberately disobeyed Schurz's order and took up a position with both flanks in the air, forcing Colonel Wladimir Krzyzanowski's already overextended brigade on his left into a desperate scramble to conform to his movement. As to his exposed right, perhaps Barlow thought Devin's troopers would cover it along the line of Rock Creek, but the evidence points to his not having given it any thought at all.

Oliver Howard

Barlow was not inexperienced and his intention may have been to establish a strong artillery position from which to flank any attack by Doles's brigade of Rodes's division against Schimmelfennig. If so it was an extreme case of tunnel vision, for he was fully informed of Early's division coming down the Harrisburg Road and, while one Confederate brigade under Brigadier General John Gordon peeled off to assault the knoll frontally (through woods that negated the topographical advantage of the position), two more under Colonel Isaac Avery and Brigadier General Harry Hays swept across Rock Creek virtually unopposed. Lieutenant Bayard Wilkeson's battery of six Napoleons fired all its ammunition during the stand, but once the assault began it could not be spared to lay down the supporting fire across Schimmelfennig's over-extended front that was presumably the whole point of this rash advance.

Part of Doles's brigade was indeed distracted by Barlow's initiative, but only to drive behind Blocher Knoll and between Barlow's division and Krzyzanowski's brigade in what, but for the skill with which von Gilsa's and Ames's brigades retreated, would have been a double envelopment. Barlow was shot after riding to the rear in the hope of turning the division around and it is entirely possible that the bullet came from one of his own men. Two reserve

Heckman's battery on the Almshouse Ridge

regiments kept the jaws of the trap open long enough for the guns and most of their comrades to escape and the division did well to fight its way out of an impossible situation. Historians have been unduly kind to Barlow, generally concurring in the bizarre conclusion that the Germans were poor soldiers. Private Nichols of 61st Georgia would not have agreed: 'We advanced with our accustomed yell, but they stood firm until we got near them. They then began to retreat in fine order, shooting at us as they retreated. They were harder to drive than we had ever known them before.'

Stretched thin and without artillery or any natural feature that might have stiffened it, Krzyzanowski's brigade did not stand for long against the advance of Doles's men, who were supported by enfilading artillery fire from the direction of Oak Knoll and now threatened the line of retreat for the rest of Schimmelfennig's division. It escaped because Howard had earlier deployed Colonel Charles Coster's brigade with Captain Lewis Heckman's battery close to the town, to cover the arc between the Harrisburg and York roads, and well before the collapse at Blocher Knoll he ordered it to move to the Almshouse line spurned by Barlow. Leaving one regiment behind, Coster placed the other three on a reverse slope to protect them from Confederate artillery at Oak Knoll, with Heckman's guns on his left. This deployment briefly deterred Doles, but it proved fatally vulnerable to a flank attack by Hays's and Avery's brigades from the right. The 134th New York suffered 50 per cent killed and wounded in a matter of minutes, the line collapsed and Heckman lost two guns and his life as Doles's newly emboldened men swarmed over his position.

> 'We advanced with our accustomed yell, but they stood firm until we got near them. They then began to retreat in fine order, shooting at us as they retreated. They were harder to drive than we had ever known them before.'
>
> Private Nichols, 61st Georgia

Coster's stand covered the retreat of Barlow's division and bought time for Schimmelfennig's men and guns to escape by forcing the Confederates to regroup and robbing them of momentum, but this was scant return for disabling losses. Unlike I Corps, which finally gave way when outnumbered nearly two to one and still made the enemy pay dearly, XI Corps succumbed to slightly inferior numbers and does not appear to have significantly eroded the combat effectiveness of any Confederate unit. It slowed the Confederate

advance long enough for reinforcements to arrive, but there is little doubt that properly handled – during but even more so before the battle – it could have achieved as much at far less cost.

No systematic effort was made to defend the town through which two Union corps with most of their artillery intact now fell back. The retreating units held together reasonably well until they entered the town and it was the absence of leadership thereafter that resulted in disorder. This odd lapse seems to have been another doctrinal blind spot, with minds that could appreciate the tactical advantages of mere folds in open fields being closed to the possibility of using a human settlement as a bastion. Perhaps because of fastidiousness about fighting among the civilian population, most of the senior Union officers spurned the opportunity to conduct a house-to-house rearguard action in a town with a grid layout that begged for artillery to be set up to scour the streets. The Confederate pursuit was tentative, but Union resistance was mostly directed by company commanders and Schimmelfennig, the one general who tried to organize resistance, was cut off and had to spend the next two days in hiding.

The best and the worst: Barlow, Birney and Gibbon pose behind a seated Hancock later in the war

In *On the Psychology of Military Incompetence*, Norman Dixon argues persuasively that certain types of insecure male are irresistibly drawn to military life and that their overcompensation is a common denominator in military catastrophes. For them, to advance even to probable defeat is assertive and virile, while to fall back and entrench is not. Ironically the action for which Howard was praised in the formal Congressional Vote of Thanks (the only corps commander at Gettysburg so honoured) was his sole act of prudence in retaining Colonel Orland Smith's brigade and Captain Michael Wiedrich's battery to hold Cemetery Hill. Although it was a strong position in itself, what made it crucial was that it controlled the point where the Baltimore Turnpike met the roads from the south, along which the two Union corps under Slocum and Sickles respectively were converging on the battlefield. 'This seems to be a good position, Colonel', Howard commented to his adjutant upon first arriving at the feature. 'It is the only position, General', came the categorical reply.

The sight of Smith's men and Wiedrich's guns around Cemetery Hill steadied the troops streaming out of Gettysburg, but the crucial factor was the arrival of Hancock, another Pennsylvanian, with orders from Meade to take over as area commander. Not only did his presence confirm the imminent arrival of reinforcements, it also put an exceptionally imposing officer in charge of a chaotic situation. We should also consider the matter of self-selection among the retreating soldiers: the retreat through the town gave any man without the stomach for further fighting a golden opportunity to drop out, thus those who now formed up on their colours around Cemetery Hill were a stronger force than mere numbers suggest. Lastly there is the compressed-spring factor of a defence concentrating under pressure and the corresponding slackening of the attack through exhaustion, disorganization and dispersion.

In sum and contradicting Lost Cause partisans, it is doubtful that victory was within the Confederates' grasp at this point. Ewell's corps was not easily going to take Cemetery Hill that evening by frontal assault, while without a substantial force of cavalry there was no way to exploit a vanishingly small opportunity to sweep around it before Slocum's corps finally came up and reinforced the right flank of the Union position by occupying Culp's Hill. Likewise, even if Lee had not specifically ruled it out, Ambrose Hill's corps was in no condition to mount an assault against the left flank of the position along Cemetery Ridge before night fell. Devin's cavalry screen had withdrawn from the north of Gettysburg and rejoined Gamble's men under the direct command of Buford on this front, confronting Hill's battered leading units with 2,500 well-armed and well-led troopers, bursting with confidence after more than holding their own all day.

But what defined the Confederates' failure to exploit their success on the first day was that Lee specifically ordered Ewell not to become too much involved in a struggle for the hills because, at that point, he was not committed to further battle at Gettysburg, even after Ewell's third division and Lieutenant General James Longstreet's corps had come up. A member of Ewell's staff and no fan of Longstreet's recorded that it was Lee who first voiced the alternative that his senior corps commander was later to make his own (my italics): 'I have not decided to fight here, and *may probably draw off by my right flank … so as to get between the enemy & Washington & Baltimore, &* force them to attack us in position.' Since Lost Cause historiography was virtually created by Jubal Early, it is of extreme importance to the understanding of how the battle developed, both on the field in July 1863 and for a generation thereafter in print, to note that the main reason why Lee abandoned this plan was Early's argument that morale would be adversely affected by abandoning ground they (he) had won in battle. This must be borne in mind when we examine Early's further contributions to the Confederate defeat in Chapter 11, for it sheds light on his subsequent efforts to paint Longstreet and Stuart as the culprits.

The Early legacy still hangs over Jeb Stuart's delayed arrival, often cited as the reason why the main force advancing from Chambersburg 'stumbled into' a battle Lee did not want. The trouble with this Lee-absolving explanation is that Stuart's ride around the Union army was authorized by Lee himself, and that not only the main force under Lee but also Ewell's corps and even the detached division commanded by Early himself retained adequate cavalry to perform reconnaissance. That it did not was their responsibility, not Stuart's. What hindsight permits us to see is that it was in the combat role, specifically on Ewell's front where Lee had hoped he would be by this time, that the late arrival of the main cavalry force may have made all the difference.

Had Stuart performed his usual forward screening he might have been able to impose the same delays on Slocum's corps closing from the south-east as Buford's men had done so successfully on Ambrose Hill's advance from the north-west, thereby calling into question the viability of the Cemetery Hill position. At the very least Early would not have felt obliged to detach Brigadier General 'Extra Billy' Smith's brigade to cover his left flank and then to send

Gordon's as well in response to reports of a Union advance along the Hanover Road. Early might then have urged Ewell, over whom he exercised considerable influence, to launch an evening assault on the Cemetery Hill position after all, with Stuart poised to exploit a further collapse by Howard's now thoroughly shaken XI Corps. His absence negated all these possibilities, by contrast with what was, even when measured against the thousands of infantry casualties and the dominant thunder of cannon, the decisive contribution of Buford.

While the celebrated Union 'fishhook' was taking shape as the remains of I and IX Corps were hammered into place around Cemetery Hill, Slocum's unharassed XII Corps was advancing to join them along the Baltimore Turnpike with what might best be described as due deliberation. The activities of Slocum's corps received little attention either at the time or later, until Harry Pfanz's *Gettysburg: Culp's Hill and Cemetery Hill* came to clear the fog of war. This was mainly because the Union right was a complex front and, being the most altered area of the battlefield, one that remains impossible to interpret without Pfanz's intimate knowledge of the historical topography. But there was also a thick polemical smog to cut through, the void left by uninformative Confederate documentation being filled by speculation about what might have been achieved if Ewell's corps had still been commanded by the late Stonewall Jackson.

Harrisburg Road

Huntterstown Turnpike

York Turnpike

Gettysburg

GORDON

3

Hanover Road

Brinkerhoff's Ridge

WALKER

SMITH

Benner's Hill

8

SYKES CORPS (approaching)

Cemetery Hill

1

Spangler's spring

6

Culp's Hill

Wolf Hill

Low Dutch Road

9

4

McAllister's Hill

Taneytown Road

McDOUGALL

RUGER

2

Power's Hill

5

7

GREENE CANDY KANE

Wheatfield Road

Rock Creek

SLOCUM'S CORPS (approaching)

Little Round Top

Baltimore Pike

Although only 36, Henry Slocum was the senior major general in the army and, as we have seen, Meade took pains to avoid ruffling his feathers in the move northwards. The same consideration may explain the ambiguity of the role assigned to him in the Pipe Creek Circular, which left Slocum under the impression that he was to command the right wing of the army, an affirmation of status he clung to despite the entirely different and unforeseen circumstances at Gettysburg. He was a stickler for protocol and although both before and after this battle he showed himself to be an effective and aggressive officer, his slow approach to Gettysburg and refusal to take local command on the first day stemmed from unwillingness to assume responsibility for an inchoate situation created by others. The following (my italics) from his report written in late August is revealing:

> On the morning of July 1, the corps was moved to Two Taverns, and remained at that place until information was received that the First and Eleventh Corps were engaged at Gettysburg, when the march was at once resumed, and, *agreeably to suggestion from General Howard*, the First Division [Williams] was put in position on the right of our line, near Rock Creek. The Second Division [Geary] was moved forward as rapidly as possible, and placed, *pursuant to orders from General Hancock*, on the extreme left of the line [on Cemetery Ridge].

Here, with wonderful economy of language, Slocum subtly registered his disapproval of the divided command at Cemetery Hill when he arrived, where Hancock was handling deployment on the left and Howard on the right. This came about because although they were both given their second stars on the same day, Howard was twenty days senior at brigadier-general level and fretted about taking orders from Hancock. By contrast Slocum, significantly senior to both, nonetheless recognized

Slocum's front

1 Day 1: Remnants of Cutler's and Meredith's brigades posted on northern Culp's Hill to support Steven's battery, construct fieldworks.

2 Day 1: Slocum orders Williams's division to assault Benner's Hill, recalls it before the attack is made.

3 Day 1: Gordon's brigade sent to reinforce Smith on Benner's Hill in response to Williams's aborted assault, later recalled to Gettysburg.

4 Day 1: After being recalled from Benner's Hill, Williams's division posted to lower Culp's Hill overnight.

5 Day 1: Geary's division sent to hold the left of the Union line on Cemetery Ridge overnight.

6 Day 2: Geary's division withdrawn from Cemetery Ridge, posted to upper Culp's Hill, continues line of fieldworks begun by Meredith's brigade.

7 Day 2: Williams's division sent to demonstrate in front of Brinkerhoff's Ridge, pinning Walker's Stonewall Brigade and covering arrival of Sykes's corps.

8 Day 2: Sykes's corps arriving along the Hanover Road, leaves 9th Massachussetts to screen Brinkerhoff's Ridge and bivouacs near Power's Hill.

9 Day 2: Slocum and Warren reconnoitre Rock Creek, report back to Meade that it is unsuitable for assault – in either direction.

Henry Slocum

that Hancock was Meade's appointed deputy and that therefore he could accept *orders* from him without loss of face, whereas Howard was only entitled to make *suggestions*.

We cannot fault Slocum for assuming that defeat was imminent when he learned that Doubleday and Howard were locked in combat with two Confederate corps – another small Union corps was not enough to balance, let alone reverse, the outcome of a battle he had to assume was being fought at odds of two to one. Seen in this light it was a sound precaution on his part to send Brigadier General Alpheus Williams's division to occupy Benner's Hill during the XII Corps approach to Gettysburg, at once making a demonstration against the Confederate left and also well placed to cover any eventual retreat by the other two corps along the Baltimore Turnpike. Once he was sure the defeat had been contained he recalled Williams and came up quickly, agreeing without demur to the unorthodox division of his corps to protect the left and right flanks of the Union position.

Meade sent the stentorian and legendarily profane Hancock racing to assume command because, with Reynolds dead, Hancock was the senior officer in whom he had the greatest confidence and also, presumably, because he did not consider either Howard or Slocum to be the sort of inspirational officer the situation demanded. We have seen, and will see again, indiscipline among general officers that would have earned court martial for privates, so it is fair to note the positive side of Slocum's concern with hierarchy: he obeyed legitimate orders promptly, even when they compromised his own immediate situation. In reply to a post-war query concerning his failure to protest one of Meade's less fortunate orders, he replied in words that damn a remarkably large number of his peers on both sides of this conflict:

The first duty of a subordinate is to obey the orders of his superior; and this is particularly true when an army is engaged, and is in the very crisis of a great struggle. Under such circumstances I can hardly conceive of any excuse that would justify a subordinate in remonstrating, protesting or even delaying for an instant any order for the transfer of troops from one point of danger to another, when directed to do so by his commander.

Slocum's decision to send Williams's division towards Benner's Hill was probably what caused 'Extra Billy' Smith, guarding Early's flank on the left of the Confederate army, to report a substantial enemy force approaching on the Hanover Road. As we have seen, this led to Gordon's brigade being detached to reinforce him, which in turn may have tipped the balance against an evening assault. The sector remained active through the night, with Ewell's third division under Major General Edward Johnson extending the left of the Confederate line and Sykes's Union V Corps arriving along the Hanover Road and skirting Benner's Hill prior to forming on the right of the Union line in front of Power's Hill. The next day Slocum sent Williams's division once more to make a demonstration towards the Hanover Road, and infantry skirmishing in front of Brinkerhoff's Ridge maintained the threat to the Confederate left.

Slocum may have had more than a demonstration in mind. When Meade arrived in the evening of the first day he was mainly concerned with the right wing and the security of the Baltimore Turnpike. Should the Confederates break through there, not only would it render Cemetery Hill untenable, it would also force the army to retreat down the Emmitsburg and Taneytown roads, away from Sykes's corps approaching along the Hanover Road and Sedgwick's pounding along the turnpike. But once these arrived the situation would be transformed, with three Union corps in a position to attack the Confederate left, which Slocum would have been well placed to direct from his headquarters on Power's Hill. Alas, a side-by-side examination of their reports of the campaign shows that Meade was unaware of Slocum's new

John Geary

incarnation as commander of the right wing of the Union army, although it is easy to see why Slocum believed it was what Meade intended. Tending to confirm this belief was that after Sykes's corps arrived, Meade requested Slocum to explore the possibility of launching an attack across Rock Creek. Along with Brigadier General Gouverneur Warren, Meade's chief of engineers, Slocum reconnoitred the creek and concluded that it was unsuitable for offensive action in either direction, although this did not rule out a wide hook towards Benner's Hill.

While for the Unionists the memory of their bloodily repulsed assaults on the entrenched Confederates on Marye's Heights at Fredericksburg was only six months old, their opponents had not yet learned the same lesson. To the contrary, the Army of Northern Virginia was characterized by violence in attack that Hooker described as 'savage blows' and treated the storming of defended hills as all in a day's work. Thus Slocum was unduly sanguine about how impregnable the XII Corps position on upper and lower Culp's Hill would seem from the other side of Rock Creek. The result was that when the Confederates unexpectedly attacked here in force during the evening of the second day, Meade had ordered all except one of Slocum's brigades to reinforce the hard-pressed Union left. Many battles have been decided by such imbalanced perceptions, but this was not, because most unusually for the Union army at this stage of the war, the hills were crowned by extensive field fortifications.

A legacy of the scramble to reform the Union line in the evening of the first day was that Wadsworth's battered I Corps division became anomalously sandwiched between Howard's and Slocum's corps. Hancock placed it in support of Captain Greenleaf Stevens' battery of Napoleons, located to fire across the front of Howard's line at the base of Cemetery Hill, but Wadsworth had good reason to be very uneasy about the dark mass of Culp's Hill looming over him. The division was now so weak that he had to divide it, with the remains of the Iron Brigade supporting the battery while Cutler's took position further up the hill where, lacking the men to do otherwise, he placed his right flank above the steepest slope, ordered his men to dig in and prayed. So it was that when Geary's division of Slocum's corps marched back from the Union left in the morning of the second day, he found himself obliged to continue the line along the crest of Culp's Hill.

A steeply uphill position negates the advantage of a rifle's flat trajectory and after two years of war no commander would willingly silhouette his men against the sky, so Geary followed Cutler's example and set his men to creating earth, rock and timber breastworks, topped by logs propped up to provide gun slits and head cover. As trees to the front were cleared and incorporated into the works, their crowns were trimmed and left pointing downhill, the time-honoured *abatis* of siege warfare. By more or less following a common contour line, a crossfire was created at the re-entrant between upper and lower Culp's Hills. Perhaps unimpressed by the fact that the position was assigned to Kane's seriously understrength brigade, Brigadier General George Greene, commanding the front-line brigade on the upper hill, ordered his men to build an internal traverse overlooking this re-entrant.

Brigadier General Thomas Ruger's division formed on lower Culp's Hill to the right of Kane, but from Greene's traverse southwards the line of breast-works ceased to follow the contour line and ran parallel to a stone wall over the top of the lower hill and down to Rock Creek. The usual murderous eche-loning was omitted but Ruger did post three regiments to bring the banks of Rock Creek under fire from a detached position on the other side of the clearing around Spangler's Spring, while the whole line had a strong forward line of skirmishers to make the river crossing even more hazardous. The clearing itself was dominated by a concentration of Union artillery along the

George 'Pop' Greene

Baltimore Turnpike and, with Sykes's corps in reserve, Slocum had good reason for complacency.

He deserves more generous consideration than he has received. In all the literature of this much-chronicled battle, no weight has been attached to what was probably the key to his behaviour, namely that he would become the army commander should Meade be killed or incapacitated. Through this prism much that otherwise seems to be pedantic concern with seniority begins to look like hard-headed realism, and the misunderstanding with Meade can be seen to have been very much more the fault of the latter. Even with all the advances in communications that have taken place since, modern experiments with a flattened command pyramid have failed, because clear and unequivocal lines of authority remain essential to military effectiveness. Victory spreads a forgiving mantle over the errors of the winning side, but some of those committed by the Army of the Potomac at Gettysburg stem from Meade's lack of 'shakedown' time in command, compounded by a surprisingly cavalier approach to the chain of command. The success of Hancock's temporary appointment on the first day should be weighed against the proverbial 'order, counter-order, disorder' on the left in the afternoon of the second day, and virtual command chaos in the centre on the third.

Howard, who might have harboured a grievance for being left hung out to dry by him on the first day, penned the following eulogy when Slocum died in 1894: '[His] resolute insistence the afternoon of July 2nd and his organized work and battle the ensuing morning, in my judgement prevented Meade's losing the battle of Gettysburg. It was a grand judgement and action, a step all-important and essential to victory.' If to this we add appreciation of the dynamic prudence of his approach, his readiness to take the battle to the enemy, his meticulous preparation to defend Culp's Hill and the manner in which he discreetly held himself in readiness to assume command of the army, it is clear that Slocum was another general done less than justice in Meade's post-battle report.

At the end of the first day's fighting the option of enticing Lee further away from the security of the Cumberland Valley was still open and Hancock's instructions from Meade were not only to make the best of a bad situation, but also to decide whether the strength of the Gettysburg position merited abandoning the Pipe Creek alternative. Not surprisingly Hancock hedged and, while consolidating the position around Cemetery Hill, he ordered his own corps to halt 3 miles south of Gettysburg on the Taneytown Road. He may have thought thereby to leave the final decision to Meade, but by the time the latter arrived around midnight, four of his seven infantry-corps commanders were present (Hancock had returned to his, but Sickles had arrived from the south) and when they assured him that it was a strong position he replied, 'I am glad to hear you say so, gentlemen, for it is too late to leave it.'

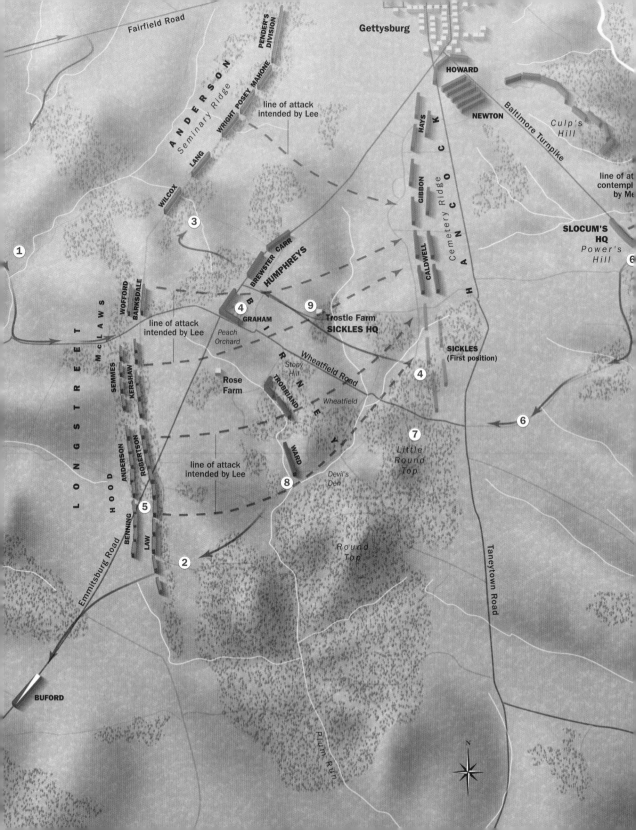

Fairfield Road

Gettysburg

HOWARD

NEWTON

Culp's
Hill

Baltimore Turnpike

PENDER'S
DIVISION

A N D E R S O N
Seminary Ridge

MAHONE

POSEY

WRIGHT

line of attack
intended by Lee

HAYS

H A N C O C K

GIBBON

line of at
contempl
by Me

LANG

WILCOX

SLOCUM'S
HQ

Power's
Hill

3

BREWSTER

CARR

HUMPHREYS

CALDWELL

Cemetery Ridge

1

6

WOFFORD

BARKSDALE

line of attack
intended by Lee

B

GRAHAM

9

Trostle Farm
SICKLES HQ

Peach
Orchard

4

M c L A W S

Rose
Farm

Stony
Hill

Wheatfield Road

SICKLES
(First position)

SEMMES

KERSHAW

TROBRIAND

B R A N N E Y

Wheatfield

4

L O N G S T R E E T

ANDERSON

ROBERTSON

H O O D

line of attack
intended by Lee

WARD

Little
Round
Top

6

7

BENNING

LAW

8

Devil's
Den

5

Emmitsburg Road

2

Round
Top

Taneytown Road

BUFORD

Plum Run

N

While the Union corps commanders were agreeing that the Cemetery Hill position could not well be taken, on the other side Lee was tolerably sure it could, but ran into collective dysfunctionality among his own corps commanders. Lee himself was debilitated by diarrhoea and by the early symptoms of congestive heart failure, while as we have noted Ambrose Hill had his own deeply demoralizing problems. It is less easy to explain why the usually aggressive Richard Ewell was so tentative after easily routing XI Corps, save to observe that the advice given to him by Early was not as robust as he was to imply post-war. Lastly James Longstreet, according to his own later accounts, chose this occasion to decide that he was a better general than Lee and to drag his feet when his advice was rejected. In fairness, he was merely echoing Lee's own initial statement of intent to manoeuvre in order to force the Union army to attack him, but that was not how he presented it after Lee's death, prompting this killing riposte from Confederate Lieutenant General Richard Taylor: 'That any subject involving the possession and exercise of intellect should be clear to Longstreet and concealed from Lee, is a startling proposition to those having knowledge of the two men.'

Thus when we come to consider the sequence of events that nearly brought the Union to defeat on the second day, we must not fall into a reverse of the Lost Cause fallacy and refight the battle with only one side refraining from committing its more egregious blunders. Hindsight makes Wellingtons of us all, but if we exercise it to make a balance of the opportunities missed by each side, the only fair conclusion is that they cancelled each other out. Meade failed to organize his army as well as he might for defence, but Lee failed to co-ordinate his to best advantage in attack. Lee had the prestige to issue detailed orders with reasonable certainty that they would be obeyed, but experience and personal inclination caused him to refrain from doing so and to trust to the discretion of his corps

Day 2 – Meade's and Lee's deployments

1 Circuitous route taken by Hood's and McLaws's divisions to confederate right wing.

2 Buford's cavalry division withdrawn by Pleasonton leaving Union left flank unguarded.

3 Preliminary reconnaissance by Sickles finds only Anderson's right.

4 Sickles advances nearly two miles without authority.

5 Further Confederate delay as Longstreet over-extends his right.

6 Learning of Sickles's advance, Meade orders Sykes's corp to march to support him.

7 Warren rides to signal station on Little Round Top.

8 Hunt inspects Smith's battery above Devil's Den.

9 Meade arrives at Sickles's HQ as Longstreet's guns open fire.

**James
Longstreet**

commanders. By contrast, although lacking familiarity with army command, the impatient Meade tried to direct matters in person or through a small number of trusted subordinates to whom he delegated authority.

Both were to be disappointed and the reason is not hard to identify. The great Confederate artilleryman and chronicler Colonel Porter Alexander put his finger on it when he wrote, 'scarcely any of our generals had half [the staff officers] they needed to *keep a constant & close supervision on the execution of important orders.* An army is like a great machine, and in putting it into battle it is not enough for its commander to merely issue the necessary orders. He should have a staff ample to supervise the execution of each step & to promptly report any difficulty or misunderstanding' [italics as original]. As commented earlier, Lee had no staff worthy of the name and surrounded himself with the sort of well-born young men the English call 'chinless wonders', but things were little better on the Union side. We have seen how Reynolds died while performing duties he should have delegated to others and Meade's activism also betrays lack of confidence that instructions conveyed by his staff officers would necessarily be obeyed.

In the matter of overall senior-officer competence the balance comes down more in favour of the Confederates because of political appointees and the related but not identical problem of the degree of politicization prevailing in the two armies. Lee enjoyed a relationship of the utmost mutual regard with President Jefferson Davis, who in turn dominated his cabinet to a degree that his opposite number could only dream of. Further, Davis had been a regular army officer in the Mexican War and later War Secretary under President James Buchanan, and so enjoyed professional military standing. In contrast Lincoln had no military and very little government experience and started the war as little more than the chairman of a cabinet of independently powerful politicians. There was little respect and less loyalty in either direction at the summit of the Union war effort and generals played at politics while complaining about 'political interference'.

It is however not wise to draw too rigid a line between professional officers and political appointees in either army, still less to assume that the former were necessarily more able. Appointment to West Point itself was by political patronage and the pre-war army was so small (approximately 16,000) and promotion so glacial that not many men of talent made it a career. Nonetheless, during the forced draft creation of mass armies, promotion to the higher ranks was almost automatic in the South for those with military training or experience, whereas in the North political pull was definitive. The flatter Union command pyramid was in part a result of pressure to find commands for political placemen and this diluted the proportion of formally trained officers in the higher ranks. Excluding the artillery, at Gettysburg 40 of 178 Union brigade commanders or above were West Pointers, by comparison with 24 (plus 7 from other military academies) of 57 on the Confederate side. Before the battle Union Colonel Lucius Fairchild commented upon this when he observed, 'many Generals under whom I may chance to be thrown – political generals who are perfect failures – Generals who are drunkards – Generals who are not fit for the places they hold, I get a big disgust on – When I see the reputation of a good regiment resting on the reports of popinjay staff officers who would not make first class corporals – then I get mad as the devil and *swear* some.'

> 'When I see the reputation of a good regiment resting on the reports of popinjay staff officers who would not make first class corporals – then I get mad as the devil and swear some.'
>
> Colonel Lucius Fairchild

Against this, the Confederate army contained a number of extremely influential politicians who had to be treated with circumspection, most notably William Smith, the 66-year-old governor elect of Virginia known as 'Extra Billy' for his habit of taking commissions on the public contracts he awarded, who commanded a brigade in Early's division and was probably the oldest man on the field. By contrast with Smith, who knew little of military science, cared less and led his brigade indifferently, the no less political William

**Lafayette
McLaws**

Barksdale led his Mississippians in the most effective brigade charge not only of this battle but of the whole war, so even here it is impossible to generalize. When an enraged Ambrose Hill wished to dismiss Brigadier General 'Rans' Wright at Spotsylvania in 1864, Lee dissuaded him in revealing words:

These men are not an army, they are citizens defending their country. General Wright is not a soldier, he is a lawyer. The soldiers know their duties better than the general officers do and they have fought magnificently. ... You understand all this, but if you humiliated General Wright, the people of Georgia would not understand. Besides, whom would you put in his place? You will have to do as I do: when a man makes a mistake, I call him to my tent, talk to him, and use the authority of my position to make him do the right thing the next time.

Although promotion in the Union army was more subject to political calculation detached from military merit, this is not to argue that the Confederate army was more meritocratic, for Lee's favouritism towards impoverished 'old family' Virginians was notorious. But even the famously dim cousins Harry Heth and George Pickett, both resoundingly last in their respective classes at West Point, derived a right to lead in the eyes of their peers and subordinates from both their military training and their genteel background. Lee's resistance to the appointment of non-professionals to divisional command was partly posited on this aristocratic notion but mainly designed to preserve a minimum shared vocabulary of command. Only after they had proved themselves over time did he permit promotion to major general of three officers who lacked formal military training: Gordon, Hampton and Kershaw, all of whom led brigades into combat at Gettysburg. The fact that Hampton was the richest man in the South and maintained a 'legion' at his own expense was not, by itself, enough to obtain the rank.

The strange events that took place during the second day at Gettysburg can best be understood in the light of these essential differences in the ethos of the two armies, but they also reflect each commander's misunderstanding of the situation he faced. Meade's attention was focused to the north, the area of his greatest perceived vulnerability should Lee send Longstreet's corps beyond Ewell's. It was kept there by a sustained artillery duel and infantry skirmishing around Cemetery Hill throughout the day. Given this preoccupation it is odd that the remnant XI Corps, in whom nobody had much reason to be confident, should have been left holding the elbow of the Union fishhook, and that instead of replacing Howard's corps with his own, Hancock took over the

Daniel Sickles

position previously held by Doubleday's and Robinson's I Corps' divisions along Cemetery Ridge, leaving Wadsworth's division still anomalously deployed on western Culp's Hill.

The collective mindset of the entire Union high command seems to have been closed to the possibility that Lee might send Longstreet to extend Hill's line, thence to attack the Union left. Consequently little attention was paid to what was happening south of Hancock's position, where Sickles had been assigned to the position held overnight by Geary's division, a long frontage where the ridge became undifferentiated prior to rising again to the two hills known as the Round Tops. After chivvying Sickles mercilessly during the march north, it is astonishing that Meade now left him unsupervised. Perhaps he just preferred not to think about him, but perhaps also he believed that with Hancock on one flank and Buford on the other, Sickles was unlikely to get into trouble in what Meade regarded as a backwater. He could not have been more wrong.

The rot began when Pleasonton requested permission to withdraw Buford's division from the left wing and send it to faraway Westminster. His given

John Hood

reason – that Buford's men and horses needed relief – was manifestly false: the division had suffered only light casualties, had done little hard riding and was in fine fettle. His most likely motives were jealousy of the glory won by Buford during the first day and alarm at learning that Reynolds, Hancock and Meade had all sought his subordinate's counsel. Pleasonton owed his promotion to largely fictional battlefield prowess at Chancellorsville and he now moved to protect himself from being further outshone. That Meade agreed to the move, assuming but not ensuring that Buford's men would be replaced when they pulled out at midday, simply confirms that he was not much concerned about his left.

Sickles had already, correctly, ignored orders by marching to the sound of the guns (although the march itself was a shambles, with the officer he sent to guide Brigadier General Andrew Humphreys's division nearly leading it into the Confederate army during the night), and he was not one to react conservatively upon finding his flank in the air. He was the highest-ranking political appointee in the army despite being, by the standards of any age, a shameless scoundrel. A notorious womanizer himself, in 1859 he murdered his wife's lover and then walked free after his lawyers, including future Secretary of War Edwin Stanton, pioneered the plea of temporary insanity. Even for a New York Democrat this was excessive, but the war offered a way to revitalize his political career and he recruited the 'Excelsior' Brigade, thus ensuring his appointment to brigadier general. He then had the good fortune to be put under the similarly dissolute Hooker and rose in his wake to corps command. Because he was more usually tending to his political fences in Washington, his first serious experience of battle was at Chancellorsville, where his corps had to retreat precipitately when Jackson shattered Howard's corps to his rear and suffered heavily after abandoning what proved to be a vital artillery position at Hazel Grove.

Thus on finding that the position allotted to him at Gettysburg was akin to Howard's in the earlier battle, with the added threat of what seemed to him another Hazel Grove to his front, he tried several times without success to get his orders changed and then advanced three-quarters of a mile without the permission or even the knowledge of his commanding officer. Although he was later to claim that the move was a refusal of the Union left in anticipation of the Confederate attack that followed, in fact he was trying single-handedly to alter the axis of the Union army so that it faced north-west. If Longstreet's corps had indeed been sent to the Confederate left, his peers and posterity would have applauded Sickles for pinning Hill's corps. But it was not, and his unauthorized advance proved to be an appalling blunder that very nearly destroyed the Union army.

George Sykes

Lee sent out scouts in the early morning, who somehow failed to notice either Buford's pickets or Hancock's corps coming up from the south and reported that the Union flank was both short and unguarded, as it had been at Chancellorsville. But lacking both Stonewall Jackson and Jeb Stuart, Lee chose not to repeat the long outflanking manoeuvre they had performed so successfully during the previous battle, despite Longstreet's repeated pleas. Instead his plan was for simultaneous assaults to be made by Ewell's three divisions against Cemetery and Culp's Hills, and by Major General John Hood and Major General Lafayette McLaws's divisions of Longstreet's corps from the south-west on a diagonal directed at the (then) junction of Hancock's and Sickles's corps. This was to culminate in a frontal assault by Major General Richard Anderson's division of Hill's corps, placed under Longstreet's command in the absence of his own third division under Pickett. What enabled Meade to salvage the Union left this day was Longstreet's mulish insistence on extending his line further than necessary to execute Lee's plan, but not far enough to make a success of his own outflanking scheme.

Still, Longstreet must be given credit for achieving operational surprise, even though the circuitous route he chose to disguise the advance of Hood's and McLaws's divisions delayed proceedings until 1600 hours. The Union signals group on Little Round Top misinterpreted the Confederate troop movements and Meade was still not aware that an attack was imminent when he learned of Sickles's initiative at a conference with his corps commanders at 1500 hours. Flabbergasted, he ordered George Sykes to march his corps from Power's Hill to the Union left at the double and sent Gouverneur Warren to Little Round Top to obtain an overview of the situation, while he rode forward himself to inspect Sickles's position. His visit coincided with the cannonade announcing the beginning of Longstreet's assault, so when a chastened Sickles offered to withdraw, Meade replied that he wished to God he could, but the enemy would not let him.

It is mildly ironic that Little Round Top should have come to be regarded as the key to Cemetery Ridge, because in Lee's scheme it was not supposed to be attacked at all. Even if the Confederates had captured it as part of the major outflanking attack he specifically chose not to make and had then muscled a few guns to the summit, the Union Reserve Artillery park was nearby and would have made the previous day's experience of the Confederate gunners on Oak Hill seem delightful by comparison. The true significance of the hill in the battle was that it commanded the extreme left of the new III Corps' position, held by Brigadier General John Ward's brigade of Major General David Birney's division, anchored by Captain James Smith's battery sited above the boulders around the cave known as Devil's Den. This was the stopper in the mouth of the Plum Run valley, with only a small detachment of 2nd US Sharpshooters guarding (Big) Round Top on the other side.

Hood was no Sickles and Lee's orders, clearly if unenthusiastically conveyed to him by Longstreet, were that he was to attack *parallel to the Emmitsburg Road*. Bearing in mind that Hood's start line was dictated by the line of Biesecker's Woods, this would have involved the whole division wheeling through 45 degrees, with the far right marching nearly 1,000 yards before those on the left even left the woods. But Hood was a secretive general who did not share his thoughts with his brigade commanders and his arm was nearly torn off by a shell fragment at the start of the attack. As a result, Brigadier General Evander Law's Alabama brigade and Brigadier General Jerome Robertson's Texas brigade marched out of Biesecker's Woods together and kept going directly to their front. The advance turned even further from the correct line when half of Robertson's brigade bore right, pushing Law's men towards Round Top. Law withdrew two regiments from his own right wing and sent them around behind the Texans to follow the line of Plum Creek, but news of Hood's wounding reached him at this critical moment and he left his brigade in order to take command of the division. Not surprisingly he was able to exercise little control over the first wave, which had already fragmented into unco-ordinated regimental initiatives.

Longstreet's grand assault was launched one division at a time and a degree of petulance seems to have been involved: Lee had ordered an echeloned advance and an echeloned advance he would get, although the unforeseen opportunity to envelop Sickles's salient by launching simultaneous attacks against its flanks was evident. Nonetheless Hood's division nearly unhinged the Union left on its own. Even before the second wave of two Georgia brigades under Brigadier Generals Henry 'Rock' Benning and George 'Tige' Anderson came forward to support them, 1st Texas and its sister regiment 3rd Arkansas had driven in the Union skirmishers on their side of Plum Creek and were well

Day 2 – Plum Run valley

1 Texas brigade divides during the advance, two regiments push Law's brigade to the right.

2 Law withdraws two regiments from his right, sends them behind the Texans.

3 Texas and Arkansas regiments assault Stone Wall Triangle.

4 Vincent's brigade forms halfway up Little Round Top; Hazlett's battery arrives at crest.

5 Benning's brigade charges the mouth of the valley.

6 Trobriand's 40th New York charges into the valley.

7 Houck's Ridge taken by Texans and part of Benning's brigade.

8 Texans drive in Vincent's right; downhill charge by Weed's 140th New York restores the line.

9 Oates's and Chamberlain's duel on Vincent's left flank.

Position held
by Strong
Vincent on
Little Round Top

up into Rose Woods. 'Texans always move them', said Lee at the Wilderness, and if Robertson's four regiments had stayed together it is fair to assume they would have cleared Ward's brigade out of the woods and occupied Houck's Ridge quite smartly, with untold consequences for the development of the battle.

Union artillery commander Hunt was with Smith's four 10-pounder Parrotts above Devil's Den when they came under fire from sixteen assorted Confederate guns, presaging Hood's assault, and as soon as he saw the mass of Confederates emerging from Biesecker's Woods he realized the position had been outflanked and would probably soon be taken, despite the protection provided by Smith's two other guns placed further back to fire along the Plum Run valley. A herd of cows arrived at the same conclusion and stampeded over him on his way back to his horse, but he picked himself out of the mud and rode to advise David Birney, the now hopelessly wrong-footed divisional commander, of the urgent need to send reinforcements to a sector he had thought so distant from where combat was likely to occur that he had not yet bothered to visit it.

On the other side of the valley, after the now intermingled Texans and Alabamians had brushed aside the sharpshooters on Round Top they could still have attacked across the Plum Run, where only the small 4th Maine stood in their way. Instead they diverged further from the valley and fought their own separate battle with a brigade from George Sykes's V Corps that took up position on the southern slope of Little Round Top before their eyes. This was commanded by a 26-year-old volunteer colonel aptly named Strong Vincent and his timely arrival became one of the best-known incidents of the battle.

Chief of Engineers Warren had been sent by Meade to check the situation on the left and, from the signal station on Little Round Top, he saw the vulnerability of the sector even more clearly than Hunt did at about the same time from the other side of the valley. He dispatched an aide to Sykes, whose corps was approaching from the north of the hill, with an urgent plea to send a brigade, which Vincent intercepted and responded to on his own authority.

Neither Vincent's approach nor the position his brigade occupied were visible from the summit, where Warren remained unaware of his presence and believed the first Union unit to arrive was Lieutenant Charles Hazlett's V Corps battery. In an illuminating incident, *General* Gouverneur Warren declared the hill unsuited for artillery, but V Corps artillery commander *Captain* Augustus Martin overruled him, saying that the noise of his guns would reassure the infantry.

To anticipate events, when Hazlett's battery came under rifle fire from across the valley, Warren rode north himself to fetch infantry support and encountered the V Corps' Zouaves of the 140th New York, whom he had once commanded. The colonel knew Warren, so he also marched to the hill without further ado while the rest of his parent brigade marched to and fro in response to conflicting orders. Sykes was at last obliged to recall its commander, the youthful Brigadier General Stephen Weed, from attendance on Sickles (where Meade had sent him) and ordered him to lead his remaining three regiments at the double to join the 140th on the western slope of Little Round Top.

Thus although their own plans were in disarray thanks to the early crippling of Hood, the first phase of the Confederate assault had caused all semblance of unified command on the Union left to collapse, with corps, divisions and brigades being broken up and sent into battle piecemeal. Sykes brought his corps from the barb of the Union fishhook to the shank with admirable dispatch, while thanks to heroic marching the leading elements of Sedgwick's corps also arrived in time to be fed into the battle – but what the impetuous lunge forward by Barlow's division had done to XI Corps the day before, Sickles's unauthorized advance had now done to the whole army. The result was the sort of small unit brawl that favoured the more opportunistic Confederate style of combat.

Fortunately for the Union, much of the Confederate impetus was wasted in a struggle for the Plum Run valley, where hell's portals gaped. 1st Texas and 124th New York fought a vicious duel in and around the triangle of stone

The Slaughter
Pen immediately
after the battle

walls to the west of Devil's Den, where 4th Maine and 99th Pennsylvania, the latter rushed across from his right wing by Ward, were locked in combat with 44th and 48th Alabama. As the valley gradually filled with smoke the fire of the Confederate batteries in Biesecker's Woods and the Union guns in the valley and on Little Round Top became indiscriminate, but did not for that reason slacken. Shot and shell ricocheted wickedly on the stony ground, in particular the rocky slope across the Plum Run from Devil's Den, soon to be known as the Slaughter Pen.

The 124th New York did not finally give way until the second Confederate wave commanded by Benning came up and both 15th and 20th Georgia crunched in on either side of 1st Texas, the regiments becoming intermingled after a suicidal competition among their colour sergeants over which should lead. The New Yorkers had suffered 40 per cent casualties at Chancellorsville and now lost a similar proportion, most of their field officers paying the price of exemplary leadership. The guns above Devil's Den were not finally abandoned until after 4th Maine and 99th Pennsylvania turned from the valley to launch separate counter-attacks in support of the 124th and were beaten back. It is instructive to note that 1st Texas, which was in action the longest and whose relentless aggression was commented on by friend and foe alike, suffered significantly fewer casualties than any other regiment engaged here, on either side.

At this point the 'Mozart Regiment' 40th New York, drawn from Colonel Philippe de Trobriand's brigade on the right of Rose Woods, arrived and attacked into what had truly become the valley of the shadow of death. This was a very recent amalgamation of remnant regiments chewed up at Chancellorsville, with a core contingent made up of hardbitten mercenaries hired by Mozart Hall, part of the extraordinarily corrupt New York City Democratic Party machine. One is reminded that Wellington once deplored that his own highly effective troops were 'the scum of the earth, enlisted for drink'. Whether or not the Mozarts had fortified themselves on the march, they now charged across the Plum Run like men possessed and drove the

Confederates across the Slaughter Pen, re-forming and attacking seven times until the collapse of the Union position above Devil's Den plus heavy flanking fire from the woods to their left cooled their fury.

Thanks to the sinister names and the evocative post-battle photographs taken by Mathew Brady and Alexander Gardner, the struggle in the valley has received the most attention, but equally intense combat took place in Rose Woods, where the right wing of Ward's brigade, weakened by the removal of 99th Pennsylvania, was pushed in by 3rd Arkansas, here also in competition with 15th Georgia. Ward's regiments were small and his command had been further depleted by the detachment of 3rd Maine to the Peach Orchard (the feature that reminded Sickles of Hazel Grove at Chancellorsville). This meant that divisional commander Birney had to rob Trobriand's brigade to reinforce Ward's. The progressive weakening of the defenders' line is the whole point of an echeloned attack, but there was not much Birney could do about it, other than to place a battery in the open field behind the gap that soon opened between the two brigades.

> 'In great deeds something abides. On great fields something stays. Forms change and pass; bodies disappear; but spirits linger, to consecrate the ground for the vision-place of souls.'
>
> Lt. Col. Joshua Chamberlain

While Ward's men were being pushed back along Houck's Ridge, on the other side of the valley the intermingled Texans and Alabamians attacked Strong Vincent's four regiments on Little Round Top. The Confederates were exhausted from marching all day just to reach Biesecker's Woods, followed by an advance uphill over very broken terrain while being sniped by the US Sharpshooters, who killed several officers. Above all, they had run out of water and were not only tormented by thirst but also unable to clean their rifles, fouled from firing at the will o' the wisp Union skirmishers. More by accident than design the two straying Texas regiments, flanked by Alabamians, engaged the attention of Vincent's brigade to the front, while acting Colonel William Oates led the two Alabama regiments furthest up the hill in an attempt to sweep around the flank, where he ran into 20th Maine under the command of Lieutenant Colonel Joshua Chamberlain.

Chamberlain's subsequent apotheosis owed much to tireless self-promotion, but we can surely be indulgent of the man who wrote, 'In great deeds something abides. On great fields something stays. Forms change and pass; bodies disappear; but spirits linger, to consecrate the ground for the vision-place of souls.' There is no doubt that he earned the Congressional Medal of Honor finally awarded to him in 1893 and, since it was not at that time awarded posthumously, we can surmise that it also belatedly honoured Strong Vincent. The vicious duel between Oates's and Chamberlain's commands in the saddle between the Round Tops was certainly important, but arguably less so than the struggle on Vincent's right flank where the Texans nearly broke through. Vincent died rallying his men at this point, as did the colonel of the 140th New York Zouaves who came cascading down the hill to restore the situation in the nick of time.

While Chamberlain on the left was containing, outflanking and finally scattering Oates's men in a desperate struggle culminating in a bayonet charge, the crest of Little Round Top came under fire from 1st Texas across the valley. Earlier one of their bullets had grazed the throat of Warren and now they added a Union general to the long list of casualties attributable to their deadly marksmanship. Stephen Weed reached Little Round Top after the 140th but before his other three regiments came into line, and he was looking out over the Plum Run when a bullet shattered his spine. His friend the gunner Hazlett rode over and knelt by his side, only to be killed instantly by a bullet in the head. For a feature that neither side had valued beforehand, Little Round Top had become a brutally expensive piece of real estate.

Probably the most dapper Union officer at Gettysburg, certainly the one with the longest name and the only officer on either side whose father had been one of Napoleon's generals, Colonel Philippe Régis Dénis de Keredern de Trobriand accepted the depletion of his brigade with remarkable aplomb, possibly because the sector entrusted to him was more defensible than Ward's on his left. On the Rose Woods flank Trobriand's men held a low stone wall running uphill from the western branch of the Plum Run, while his right was covered by one of the Union army's trademark artillery traps. Additionally the far side of the creek to his front had been cleared, enabling him to mount a forward defence of the crossing from tree cover. Nonetheless, 3rd Michigan had already been taken from him to provide skirmishers around the Rose Farm and, after his reserve Mozart Regiment was sent to assist Ward, Trobriand was left with only 700 men to confront

Peach
Orchard

Trostle
Farm

Plum Run

8

Trostle's
Woods

Stony
Hill

Wheatfield Road

5

6

WINSLOW

KERSHAW

7

3

9

4   Stone wall

Wheatfield

Rose
Farm

Rose's

1

ANDERSON

2

Woods

Biesecker
Woods

ANDERSON

Devil's
Den

L
R

Emmitsburg Road

Round
Top

Bushman's
Woods

N

Plum Run

'Tige' Anderson's Georgia brigade when the second wave of Hood's division attacked. Trobriand was fortunate that one of Anderson's regiments remained behind to guard the Confederate rear and that another diverged to join the attack on Ward's command in Rose Woods.

David Birney's division had suffered the highest loss of any in the Union army at Chancellorsville and he had been instrumental in persuading Dan Sickles that the Peach Orchard was another Hazel Grove. Now, as the enormity of his miscalculation crashed in upon him, Birney's generalship lost all coherence and nowhere was it more apparent than in his handling of this sector. Without informing Trobriand he sent two regiments from Colonel George Burling's reserve brigade to reinforce the line facing the Plum Run, but in the midst of the first push by Anderson's brigade they lost their colonels and unilaterally pulled back across the Wheatfield, exposing the flank of Trobriand's 17th Maine. Cut off from support on either side and in one of the finest performances by any Union regiment at Gettysburg, the 17th not only continued to hold the stone wall but also coolly refused its own right flank and helped to hold the creek crossing as well.

Trobriand was likewise not informed that Brigadier General James Barnes, on whom more below, had come up to reinforce his right flank. Having just survived one hour-long attack and being tolerably certain the next one would succeed, when Birney asked him to give up another regiment he politely declined. Meanwhile, after trying to comply with the conflicting demands of overexcited staff officers sent by both Birney and Sickles, George Burling ordered the last regiment remaining under his command to report to the former and rode off in disgust to rejoin Humphreys, his own divisional commander. A further illustration of Birney's loss of composure is that he ordered the battery he had placed in the Wheatfield to fire round shot into the tree tops over the heads

Stony Hill

1 Anderson's brigade attacks through western Rose Woods, held at the creek by Trobriand.

2 11th Georgia helps to break contact between Ward's and Trobriand's commands.

3 Two of Burling's regiments abandoned the creek line.

4 17th Maine holds the stone wall against 11th Georgia and covers the gap in the creek line.

5 Tilton's brigade, Barnes's II Corps division, extends Trobriand's right.

6 Sweitzer's brigade, Barnes's division occupies the Stony Hill.

7 Kershaw attacks through Rose Farm and orchard.

8 Barnes retreats to Trostle Wood without advising Trobriand.

9 Trobriand's men beat fighting retreat.

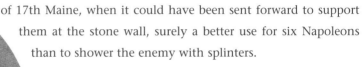

George 'Tige'
Anderson

of 17th Maine, when it could have been sent forward to support them at the stone wall, surely a better use for six Napoleons than to shower the enemy with splinters.

For the Confederates, Benning and Anderson made a slightly better effort than Hood's first wave to wheel and attack parallel to the Emmitsburg Road, but a strict alignment would have sent Anderson's men in the open into the teeth of the heavy concentration of Union artillery at the Peach Orchard, so from the start they veered away from the line of the road, moving further to their right as they came under flanking fire from 3rd Michigan in the Rose Farm orchard. The southern extension of Rose Woods provided only a brief respite before they emerged into the clearing along the Plum Run and were mowed down by Trobriand's men from the trees on the other side. More men were killed and wounded here than in the infamous Slaughter Pen, grim witness to the determination of the Georgians and the matching steadiness of Trobriand's command. Although two of his regiments had achieved a lodgement on the far bank and another was hotly contesting the line at the stone wall, Anderson pulled them back across the creek to regroup and rode back to Brigadier General Joseph Kershaw's brigade on Seminary Ridge to request support. On his return he was wounded and it seems unlikely that anyone exercised effective command of the brigade for the rest of the day.

Sometime during the first attack two Union brigades of Barnes's V Corps division (the third was Strong Vincent's, already in action on Little Round Top) were brought forward by corps commander Sykes himself and took up position on Trobriand's right. With only 654 men Colonel William Tilton's was a brigade in name only, but even with one regiment miles away in front of Brinkerhoff's Ridge and half of another guarding the artillery train, Colonel Jacob Sweitzer brought over 1,000 men to the field. With thirty guns placed to fire across their front, these should certainly have been sufficient to stand against the third stage of Longstreet's echeloned assault by Lafayette McLaws's division.

The fatal weakness of the position was organizational, because Barnes answered to Sykes, not to Sickles and still less to Birney, even though he was now placed in the middle of the latter's division. The crucial gun line was also semi-independent, because Sickles had parcelled out his own guns across the whole corps' front, so most of the batteries now facing the direction from which the next attack was expected were belatedly brought forward from the Artillery Reserve by Lieutenant Colonel Freeman McGilvery. Although Birney had asked for the guns, their massed deployment to refuse this flank was the work of McGilvery and of artillery commander Hunt himself.

The importance of the position was fully appreciated by the Confederates facing it and Porter Alexander, Longstreet's acting chief of artillery, brought up four batteries from the corps' reserve to reinforce the four commanded by McLaws's artillery chief, for a total of thirty-two assorted guns firing from the Seminary Ridge treeline, here known as Pitzer's Woods. The distances were not great and Alexander judged what followed to be the most intense artillery duel of the war. The gunners on both sides suffered nearly 20 per cent killed and wounded, but the Confederate casualties all came from counter-battery fire, whereas the Union batteries also suffered heavily at the hands of the infantry. The disparity reflects that Confederate fuses for shell and case-shot had become cripplingly unreliable since their main Richmond munitions factory blew up some months earlier.

They were to pay a high price for their inability to silence the Union batteries. Even today the message 'infantry in the open' from forward observers brings exultation to gunners' breasts and their great-grandfathers must have felt the same when more than 2,000 South Carolinians of Kershaw's brigade emerged from Pitzer's Woods, followed closely by Brigadier General Paul Semmes's 1,300 Georgians, and marched down the treeless slope towards them. Once again their orders were to advance parallel to the Emmitsburg Road and once again the regiments on the left sensibly declined to charge in

Young
Confederate
killed in
Devil's Den

Posed photograph of a Union battery cleared for action

the open against massed batteries. Lee had little confidence in McLaws and ordered Longstreet to supervise this division personally, so the failure to hit the Peach Orchard strongpoint from two sides at once is the latter's alone. It has been suggested that William Barksdale was slow in making his brigade ready, but everything we know about him tells us that he was straining at the leash. Incomprehensibly Longstreet *chose* not to launch Kershaw's and Barksdale's brigade attacks simultaneously.

There is also reason to doubt Kershaw's assertion that only a misunderstood order prevented the regiments on his left from successfully storming the gun line. He himself reported the 'clatter of grape' against the Rose Farm buildings and it was a good 500 yards of open if smoke-shrouded ground from there to the gun line, whereas the swale of the Plum Run provided at least some cover for an oblique advance towards the western finger of Rose Woods. It is far more likely that the South Carolinians sidled steadily to the right and charged Tilton and Sweitzer's brigades with the pent-up fury of men too long under fire without the possibility of hitting back.

Unfortunately the deployment of the two Union brigades betrayed divisional commander Barnes's failure to anticipate the direction from which the attack came. He had been a contemporary of Lee at West Point but had not pursued a military career and was out of his depth. He placed his men as though the only threat was from the south, with two of Sweitzer's regiments in column in the treeline at the base of Stony Hill, while the third was deployed in line behind the junction of Trobriand's line and Tilton's extension of it along the creek. As a tactical aside we should note that some of Tilton's men awaited the Confederate attack lying down, with ammunition spread out before them, and sprang up to fire their first volley at close range. Wellington would have approved but Trobriand did not, echoing the complaints of his disgruntled countrymen half a century earlier.

Barnes was chief among those subsequently blamed by Dan Sickles and David Birney for the collapse of this sector, although neither of them anticipated the angle of Kershaw's attack, any more than Longstreet intended it. But Barnes himself admitted that once it became apparent he had been wrong-footed, he ordered a withdrawal on his own authority to Trostle Woods behind the Wheatfield Road. What he failed to mention was that he did this without warning Trobriand, who was still holding off Anderson's men along the creek. The low casualty figures for Tilton's brigade argue that he was ordered to retreat before the full impact of Kershaw's attack was felt, which means that Sweitzer's brigade can scarcely have been engaged at all before abandoning the hill.

With Ward's division driven away from his left and Barnes's having vanished from his right, even the imperturbable Trobriand recognized that it was time to leave. His three regiments fell back by sections, hammering the enemy at every stage and even covering the withdrawal of the battery in the

**Philippe de
Trobriand**

Wheatfield to the road behind it. Even now the work of this remarkable brigade was not done, because when Anderson's men ventured over the stone wall Birney asked 17th Maine to march back into the field and the sight of them alone was enough to drive the Georgians back. He then asked 5th Michigan to do the same against Kershaw's men entering the field from the west and the Michiganders held that front also until Brigadier General John Caldwell's division arrived to relieve them, as we shall examine in the next chapter.

Every Confederate unit that came up against Trobriand's three regiments suffered above-average casualties, particularly in Anderson's brigade. If we also consider the courage of 3rd Michigan in its lonely outpost around the Rose Farm and the Mozarts' performance in the Plum Run valley, it is clear this brigade had exceptional élan. With regiments from Maine, Michigan, New York and Pennsylvania, some recently amalgamated with others and containing both long- and short-service volunteers and conscripts, the only thing they had in common was that their commanding officer was a jaunty little French adventurer with no formal military training but who, like his father before him, had found his true calling in the service of a grand imperial cause.

The implacable demands of countering an echeloned attack now began to weaken the Union centre on Cemetery Ridge. As the left of his salient gradually gave way Dan Sickles, now sincerely desperate, implored Meade for further reinforcements and the army commander instructed Winfield Hancock to send a division from his own II Corps, although he stressed that it was to report to Sykes, not Sickles. Hancock sent his old division, now under the command of his hand-picked successor John Caldwell. It was the only Union division with four brigades, but these were much depleted and Colonel Patrick Kelly's Irish Brigade was a mere remnant, with four of its five regiments reduced to two companies each, all armed with smooth-bore muskets.

Lines of authority were by now almost comically scrambled, to the point that Sykes's chief of artillery warned his battery commanders not to let

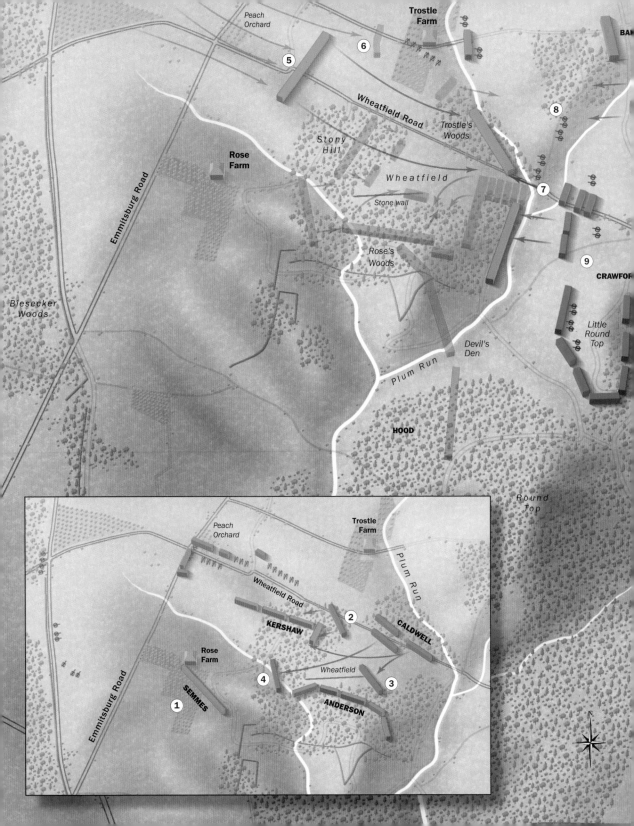

Peach
Orchard

Trostle
Farm

5

6

Wheatfield Road

8

Stony
Hill

Trostle's
Woods

Rose
Farm

Wheatfield

7

Stone wall

Biesecker
Woods

Rose's
Woods

9

CRAWFOR

Little
Round
Top

Plum Run

Devil's
Den

HOOD

Round
Top

Emmitsburg Road

BA

Peach
Orchard

Trostle
Farm

Wheatfield Road

KERSHAW

2

CALDWELL

Plum Run

Rose
Farm

4

Wheatfield

3

SEMMES

1

ANDERSON

Emmitsburg Road

N

themselves be commandeered by Sickles. As Caldwell rode at the head of his division towards Sykes at Little Round Top, an aide approached Brigadier General Samuel Zook, commanding the rear brigade, and asked him to ride forward to consult with Sickles at Trostle Farm. He persuaded Zook to break formation and march directly to Trostle Woods, correctly anticipating that Sykes would order Caldwell to launch a counter-attack into the Wheatfield. Whether the only divisional assault made by the Union army at Gettysburg should have been made here is less easy to say. Sykes was a professional with a good combat record and he had a better view of the situation than the embattled Sickles, but in his otherwise boastful post-battle report he pointedly admitted no responsibility for it.

Zook's men passed through Barnes's two brigades, now in Trostle Woods, and assaulted the Stony Hill position they had abandoned, in time to distract Kershaw from falling on the massed batteries along the Wheatfield Road. A brigade staff officer recalled 'a close encounter when the firing became terrific and the slaughter frightful. We were enveloped in smoke and fire, not only in front, but on our left, and even at times on the right. ... Our men fired promiscuously, steadily pressing forward, but the fighting was so mixed, rebel and Union lines so close together, and in some places intermingled, that a clear idea of what was going on was not readily obtainable.' Zook himself was mortally wounded at the start and by the end of the battle his brigade was to be under the command of the second-in-command of 140th Pennsylvania, all officers senior to him having fallen.

On the other side of the Wheatfield, the hated martinet Colonel Edward Cross was also fatally stricken leading his brigade against the Texans and Georgians now holding all of Houck's Ridge as well as the stone wall defended so long and honourably by 17th Maine. Zook's and Cross's attacks drew nearly the full attention of the Confederates on their respective sides of the

The Wheatfield

1 Semmes advances to support Kershaw, killed at Rose Farm.

2 Zook's brigade counter attacks Stony Hill. Zook killed.

3 Cross's brigade recovers the stone wall, Kelly's advances to Stony Hill. Cross killed.

4 Brooke's brigade charges across the Plum Run, met by Semmes in Rose Wood.

5 Wofford's brigade advances along Wheatfield Road, disperses Union gun line.

6 Barksdale's 21st Mississippi becomes detached, takes Trostle Farm.

7 Costly advance by Ayres's division into the Wheatfield.

8 Nevin's VI Corps brigade appears on ridge, Wofford withdraws.

9 Crawford's division counter attacks across the Plum Run.

John Caldwell

field, permitting Kelly's little brigade to advance in the open to join the push to recover Stony Hill. The Irish were lucky to reach the treeline almost unscathed and thereafter they enjoyed the advantage of attacking uphill (until now enjoyed only by the Confederates), and at such close range that their muskets, faster to reload and slower to foul, enabled them to drive one wing of Kershaw's brigade back upon the other. Kershaw's men were obliged to expose their upper bodies, whereas their opponents could rest their muskets on the rocks behind which they sheltered. Much the same reversal of roles was being visited upon the Texans on the other side of the Wheatfield, where Cross's men drove them from the low hill at the end of the stone wall.

To this point, Caldwell's division had done everything required of it and more. On the right it had relieved pressure on the gun line, on the left it had drawn on itself the flanking fire from across the Plum Run valley that had just claimed the life of Stephen Weed, and as a bonus it had driven Anderson's and Kershaw's brigades apart, opening the way to recover Trobriand's old position along the banks of the western Plum Run. When Caldwell sent in his reserve brigade under 25-year-old Colonel John Brooke to relieve Cross's men, it charged instead into the space prised open by the other brigades and continued across the Plum Run and through the woods on the other side. What followed was to prove a disaster for the division, but it may also have been the final straw that irrevocably altered the axis of the Confederate assault as a whole, which had begun to conform to the north-easterly direction it was supposed to take.

Until Brooke, flag in hand with all the pride and folly of youth, led his cheering men across the Plum Run, it had been a textbook counter-attack, catching the enemy overextended and exhausted; but he now had the misfortune of running into part of Paul Semmes's brigade, moving to the cover

Trostle Farm after the battle

of the woods after Semmes himself was killed at the Rose Farm while preparing to make a frontal assault on the Union gun line. These were men with a score to settle and they fell on Brooke's disordered brigade and drove it all the way back to the Wheatfield. At the same time Confederate Brigadier General William Wofford's brigade surged along the Wheatfield Road gun line that had always provided the real strength of the Stony Hill position, and Zook's and Kelly's brigades collapsed. A lieutenant with 140th Pennsylvania asserted that 'neither valor nor discipline could withstand such a fire and such odds', but Lieutenant Colonel Charles Morgan of Winfield Hancock's staff censoriously recorded that the remnants of Caldwell's division were now 'flying to the rear with no shadow of an organization. All attempt to rally them … within reach of the enemy's bullets was useless.'

Edward Cross

Jacob Sweitzer's men now bravely emerged from Trostle Woods to try to hold the Wheatfield against converging attacks, with Stony Hill and the stone wall once more in Confederate hands. Pathetically, their gallant sacrifice to cover the rout of Caldwell's division was not considered to be sufficient expiation for their earlier withdrawal, although once it became apparent that Sickles's salient was doomed there was much to be said for an orderly withdrawal to Trostle Woods – the battle for the Wheatfield only assumed the importance it did because Sickles and Birney were obsessed with holding the Peach Orchard long after their original assumptions had been proved wrong.

But its greater significance is that it drew Wofford away from following in the wake of Barksdale's charge, which we shall examine in the next chapter. Wofford was a scrapper and it was too much to hope that he would resist the temptation of sweeping along the gun line to outflank Stony Hill, but had he then regrouped and turned north-east, he might perhaps have drawn Kershaw and Semmes with him and the grand assault would have retained conceptual unity. Instead they all fell on Caldwell's and Sweitzer's commands and pursued them along the Wheatfield Road, a change of axis which rendered what followed in this sector operationally irrelevant.

Lee's plan was for persistent right hooks to be followed by a straight left, and Sickles's advance to the Peach Orchard demanded only an adjustment in the sequence of attacks. Unco-ordinated though they were, the first stages of the grand assault had achieved the desired effect: the Union command system was in disorder, its reserves were committed and Confederate intentions were still so well concealed that an entire division had been drawn away from the centre, the place where the breakthrough attempt was to be made. The brigades of Lafayette McLaws's division could have made a limited assault to take out the Peach Orchard and then regrouped to advance with the Emmitsburg Road on their left. That they did not was Longstreet's fault and

his post-war collaboration with Sickles to rewrite the history of this battle was born of the fact that the errors of the other provided each with an alibi for his dubious generalship.

After the battle: a wrecked caisson

Brigadier General Romeyn Ayres's division of Sykes's corps contained the bulk of the regular-army infantry, two brigades (the third, non-regular brigade was Weed's, now on Little Round Top) under the command of elderly colonels whose lack of advancement tells us all we need to know of their abilities. The bluff Sidney Burbank was another of Lee's West Point contemporaries, while the cadaverous Hannibal Day graduated the following year, and their contribution to the battle on this front was to be brought under galling fire by the Confederates without doing much damage in return. Sykes was to claim that their advance was made to cover the collapse of Caldwell's division, but in fact they were sent to clear Houck's Ridge of the Confederate snipers who had brought Little Round Top under such deadly fire. The regulars were taken in the flank as the Confederates swept across the Wheatfield and driven back across the Plum Run, suffering a staggering number of casualties for such a short engagement.

North of the Wheatfield Road, the retreat of the Union artillery was exemplary, with the Confederates at times so close that the following dialogue took place. 'Halt, you Yankee sons of bitches, we want those guns!' – 'Go to hell! We want to use them yet awhile.' The casualty returns do not, of course, record the dreadful execution among the horses and several guns had to be towed back by their own men. Pfanz singles out for special mention the fighting retreat of Captain John Bigelow's six Napoleons from the left of the Wheatfield gun line to the Trostle Farm, achieved in part by using the guns' recoil to gain ground, under pressure from both Wofford's brigade and Barksdale's straying 21st Mississippi. The battery was only overrun when the Mississippians worked around it, demonstrating yet again that experienced soldiers did not charge artillery from the front. Bigelow lost eight men killed, eighteen wounded, two missing, forty-five horses and four guns. The battery had fired 3 tons of ammunition, including ninety-two short-range canister loads, but to what effect is impossible to establish.

The 21st Mississippi continued its solitary advance, crossing the Plum Run to capture an isolated Union battery on the left of a new gun line, like the first assembled by the Reserve Artillery's McGilvery, which was all that was covering a wide gap in the Union line. Well to the right of the 21st, Wofford's brigade was delayed by Tilton's men at the line of Trostle Woods but then advanced rapidly to the fork of two tributaries of the upper Plum Run, where it also captured an isolated battery. Wofford had his brigade well in hand and when Unionist reinforcements appeared on the ridge above him (Colonel

David Nevin's brigade, the first of Sedgwick's VI Corps to arrive), he pulled back to Trostle Woods, where he received orders from Longstreet to withdraw all the way to the Peach Orchard.

Further downstream the Confederate advance was much less orderly, the absence of Semmes and Anderson being felt as three intermingled brigades advanced into the Plum Run valley to assault Little Round Top. We must presume they were out of control, because Kershaw would obviously have ordered them to regroup on Houck's Ridge if he could. But they had already broken three divisions from three separate corps and the sight of Ayres's regulars falling back was an irresistible lure. Counter-attacked by Colonel 'Buck' McCandless's brigade of Brigadier General Samuel Crawford's V Corps' division, the Confederates were driven back across the Plum Run and over the corpse-littered Wheatfield to Stony Hill.

At some point during this poorly documented action volunteers from 6th Pennsylvania Reserves took out a nest of enemy sharpshooters near Devil's Den in an engagement judged to have been so remarkable that all six of them were awarded the Congressional Medal of Honor in 1897. There remained only a night advance by Crawford's other brigade under Colonel Joseph Fisher, which went forward with Joshua Chamberlain's 20th Maine to occupy Round Top virtually unopposed, and the Union line was now far stronger than it had been before the battle began.

On the Confederate side, Hood's and McLaws's divisions were spent and by now it may have dawned on the survivors that theirs had never been the main thrust of the grand assault. Even if they realized it, it would not have been much consolation to know that they had performed their assigned task admirably. Along and south of the Wheatfield Road, approximately 11,670 Confederates in seven brigades had fully occupied sixteen Federal brigades and about 18,745 men. In return for 3,795 casualties they inflicted 5,255 and overran several batteries, although only the guns captured above Devil's Den remained in their possession at the end of the day. But above all they drew the reserves upon themselves, such that a mile-wide gap opened in the Union centre. All this between 1600 and 1900 hours, almost meriting Longstreet's self-serving hyperbole in claiming that it was 'the best three hours' fighting done by any troops on any battlefield'.

Even given that the strength and extent of Longstreet's assault caught the Union high command with its preconceptions around its ankles, with the exception of Strong Vincent's and Philippe de Trobriand's brigades the Unionists did not match the tenacity of the Confederates, although the latter lost the leadership of Hood (and by extension Law), Anderson and Semmes comparatively early. What the fighting on the Union left proved was probably no news to either side: in a swirling battle where regimental and company leadership was at a premium, the Confederates usually prevailed.

The charge by William Barksdale's Mississippians is considered the finest infantry-brigade assault by either side during the entire war and it does not detract from their achievement to observe that the first troops they encountered had the misfortune of belonging to a division commanded by David Birney and a brigade commanded by Brigadier General Charles Graham, Dan Sickles's closest cronies. Four regiments were deployed in an arc around the elbow at the crossroads: Trobriand's 3rd Michigan was at the Rose Farm, Ward's 3rd Maine was to its right and Berdan's 1st US Sharpshooters was in front of Pitzer's Woods, but when Graham's own 63rd Pennsylvania ran out of ammunition he unaccountably withdrew it not only from the skirmish line but from the sector before the battle began. Companies from the front-line regiments at the Peach Orchard were also deployed as skirmishers and it remains a mystery how four Confederate brigades and

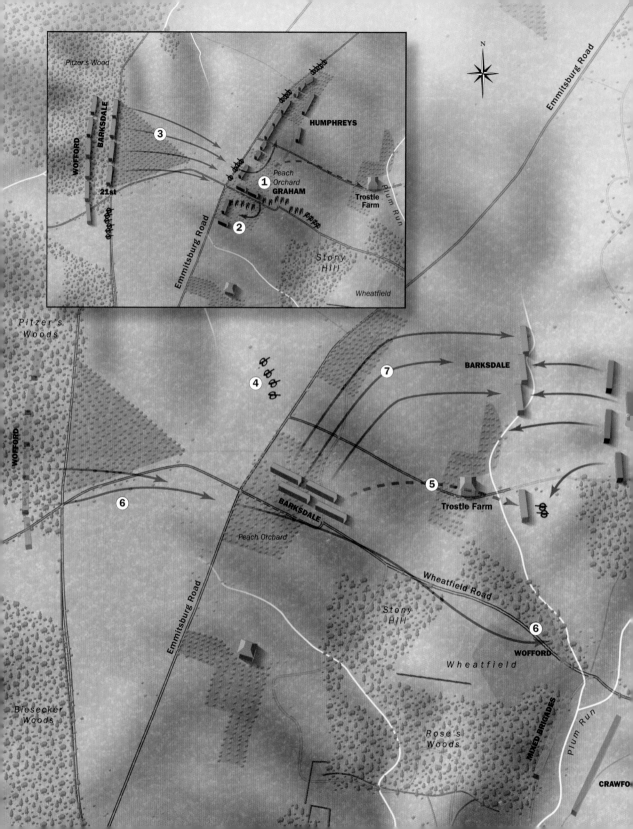

Pitzer's Wood

BARKSDALE

WOFFORD

21st

HUMPHREYS

③

① Peach Orchard

GRAHAM

②

Trostle Farm

Plum Run

N

Emmitsburg Road

Stony Hill

Wheatfield

Pitzer's Woods

WOFFORD

④

⑦ BARKSDALE

⑤ Trostle Farm

⑥ BARKSDALE

Peach Orchard

Wheatfield Road

Emmitsburg Road

Stony Hill

⑥ WOFFORD

Wheatfield

Biesecker Woods

Rose's Woods

MIXED BRIGADES

Plum Run

CRAWFO

eight batteries could have formed for attack under the nose of this probing line without Birney and Graham awakening to their peril until it was far too late.

Soon to be severely wounded and captured, Graham was belatedly reinforced by three regiments taken from Brigadier General Andrew Humphreys's division on his right. The echeloned Confederate attacks concentrated his attention to the south, and when Kershaw's brigade debouched from Biesecker's Woods and crossed the Emmitsburg Road towards the artillery trap on that front, Graham must have shared the gunners' moment of exultation. But when Barksdale's brigade charged out of Pitzer's Woods from the west, the inadequacy of his dispositions became apparent. He rushed the infantry support from behind the Wheatfield Road gun line to the part of Peach Orchard to the south of the crossroads, but Barksdale's attack pushed between them and three Pennsylvania regiments whose substantial Chancellorsville losses had not been made good, which were formed behind ten guns along the Emmitsburg Road. These had been the particular target of the batteries directed by Porter Alexander himself and since Confederate shells and case-shot tended to burst long, the Pennsylvanians were understandably shaky.

To belabour the point about relative firepower, Kershaw's 2,000 men turned away from thirty massed guns with minimal infantry support, whereas Barksdale's 1,400 punched through about 3,000 infantry whose guns were dispersed across their front. The high ground that Birney and Sickles had thought so important at this point was no higher than Seminary Ridge, here only 700 yards away across a slight hollow, and Barksdale's men had the Wheatfield Road to use as a guideline and an arrow of fruit trees on either side of it to provide some cover for half the distance. The Mississippians charged shoulder to shoulder, accepting a high initial casualty rate to maximize shock at the notional point of impact – notional because, as Richard

Peach Orchard

1 Graham adjusts his line to face threat of Kershaw's advance from the south.

2 Belated attempt by Graham to prepare for an attack from the west.

3 Barksdale's brigade smashes Graham's position then turns left.

4 Alexander brings up batteries in close support.

5 21st Mississippi becomes detached, takes Trostle Farm and battery beyond.

6 Wofford's brigade also follows Wheatfield road.

7 Barksdale's three regiments disperse Excelsior Brigade, turn right.

8 Willard's and Lockwood's brigades counter attack.

**Fanciful representation of the
battle at the Peach Orchard**

Holmes cogently puts it, hand-to-hand fighting very seldom occurs on these occasions, one side or the other suddenly remembering an urgent appointment elsewhere. Here the regiments at the crossroads paid the usual high price for breaking in the immediate presence of the enemy.

As we saw in the last chapter, 21st Mississippi became detached and went on to perform a creditable charge on its own under the leadership of Colonel Benjamin Humphreys, whose vivid memoirs fill a hole in the Confederate narrative almost as large as the one Barksdale's brigade had now made in the Union line. The other three regiments regrouped, made a 90-degree turn and drove along the line of the Emmitsburg Road and into Andrew Humphreys's division like a malevolent lawnmower, losing contact with Wofford's brigade which had moved up smartly behind them but which swept on along the Wheatfield Road.

At about this time Longstreet himself rode ahead of his fellow Georgians and Lafayette McLaws was to recall that he went forward because he was not happy with the way the attack was progressing. What is not clear is whether this personal intervention was an attempt to turn Wofford's brigade north, or if at this late stage Longstreet despaired of the original scheme and decided to settle for the destruction of the III Corps' salient. It all depends on exactly when he rode forward and what he said, and that is impossible to establish. The almost insanely brave Wofford never shrank from combat, but on this occasion he may have been seduced by the prospect of easy victory and he was pointedly not commended in Longstreet's post-battle report. Whether he was at fault or a scapegoat we cannot know.

The last-recorded attempt by Sickles to salvage the position was to beg Colonel Henry Madill of 141st Pennsylvania to hold. Madill replied for all of Graham's shattered brigade: 'Where are my men?' he asked tearfully. Sickles certainly could not answer and rode back to the Trostle Farm, where a cannonball mangled his knee. To digress briefly, personal courage of the highest order was a commonplace in both armies, from grizzled generals to the little drummer boys who could have been their grandchildren. Some officers were esteemed to be exceptionally brave by their men, the only people whose opinion matters, and Sickles was one of them. But as the history of warfare repeatedly illustrates, fearlessness can be at odds with sound judgement and it is by the latter quality that an officer must be judged. Sickles was very brave, but so were the thousands of men who fell this day because he chose to disobey orders, and it is ironic that today tourists drive past the places where most of them died on roads that bear his name.

One Confederate officer who did not lose sight of the operational objective was Porter Alexander, who brought up two more batteries from his reserve battalion and sent them forward alongside Barksdale's brigade to enfilade Andrew Humphreys's division, which may have contributed considerably to the further success of the Mississippians. Alexander himself remained behind to assemble a massed battery of twenty-six assorted cannon on the Peach Orchard rise. They certainly added to the misery of the retreating Unionists, but it was no Hazel Grove. Alexander was not impressed, because Cemetery Ridge 'loomed up near 1,000 yards beyond us, a ridge giving good cover behind it and endless fine positions for batteries. And batteries were showing up and troops too seemed to be marching and fighting everywhere – there was plenty to shoot at.'

Charles Graham

Indeed there was, but one may fairly wonder how much damage he could do with his unreliable ammunition. Captain George Moody's 24-pounder howitzers and Captain Pichegru Woolfolk's 20-pounder Parrotts were the heaviest ordnance employed by either side at Gettysburg and after they moved up to the Peach Orchard they should have been able to silence McGilvery's new gun line, composed in the main of batteries that had already been badly shot up in the retreat from the Peach Orchard and now a mere 800 yards away in front of Cemetery Ridge. Porter Alexander was an exceptionally able officer and the batteries under his command were boldly handled, but even at this moment of greatest Union disarray and with heavier ordnance to hand there is no evidence that the Confederates won artillery superiority.

The infantry were another matter. The superlatives mount up around Barksdale's three remaining regiments, less than 1,000 men by now, who charged the Sickles-recruited Excelsior Brigade, about 1,800 men under the personal direction of divisional commander Humphreys, a competent professional newly posted to III Corps, whose 'distinguished and brilliant profanity' (the words are Charles Dana's, later Lincoln's Assistant Secretary of War) had been much in evidence during the few weeks he had served under Sickles. Humphreys had several advantages against an attack from the west: the treeline on Seminary Ridge, here called Spangler's Woods, was further away from his position than from the luckless Graham's; the Emmitsburg Road ran along a slight ridge that gave his men some reverse slope protection; and he had two full batteries of Napoleons ready to sweep his front and a third came up in time to cover his draughty right flank.

In sum, Humphreys's position was strong before Barksdale's brigade attacked from the flank and not untenable even then against ordinary men, given reasonable steadiness among his own. Neither condition prevailed and the Excelsiors dissolved in the face of the howling Mississippians, who came at them 'like devils incarnate', in the words of one of Humphreys's staff. After the battle Humphreys blamed it all on the earlier removal of Burling's brigade, but methinks he protested too much – failure to hold in an open field engagement with a two to one numerical advantage argues that lack of reserves was the least of his problems. We shall return to Humphreys's division in the next chapter, because it moved – or rather was pushed – out of the sector we are considering, now a void in the fronts of both armies where the only sizeable body of troops was Barksdale's.

This remarkable brigade had by now broken or driven off fifteen Union infantry regiments totalling about 4,200 men, inflicting the bulk of their 1,800 casualties, as well as causing the precipitate retreat of eight batteries with forty-four guns and over 800 men. Bearing in mind that many of the Mississippians' 141 killed and 470 wounded – and most of their 178 missing – must have been lost when they were counter-attacked at the end of their long advance, the phenomenon we noted with reference to 1st Texas is even more starkly illustrated: a resolute attack *reduces* overall casualties. Military training has always stressed this, but it is a bone that persistently sticks in civilian throats, probably because of distaste for what happens once the two sides can see each other and begin to read body language. The less determined side begins to make subconsciously placatory gestures such as firing high and 'shrinking', a visual clue and not a literary trope, but this has the opposite effect. The attackers may become feral and carnage can ensue among men who may have virtually ceased trying to defend themselves.

This is the reason why a fighting retreat in the face of an enemy who pursues closely is so very difficult: it is a psychological contradiction that tests discipline, morale and leadership to the limit. Here the amateur Barksdale showed a better instinctive understanding than his professional colonels, who begged him to give them time to regroup after smashing the Excelsiors. 'No, crowd them', he replied fiercely. 'We have them on the run. Move your regiments.' Riding ahead to turn his command hard right, he flourished his sword towards Cemetery Ridge and shouted 'Brave Mississippians, one more charge and the day is ours.' Like wolves they howled their approval and drew on unfathomable reserves of energy to charge what was, in effect, the whole Union army.

It should be noted that Barksdale and his staff were the only men in the brigade who rode into battle (he ordered his regimental commanders to advance on foot) and that he also led from the front. At some point not far from the furthest point of the brigade's advance, at about the line of the Plum Run north of McGilvery's gun line, his luck ran out. The Union surgeon who examined him reported two wounds, one a sucking chest wound too large to have been made by a Minié bullet, so he was another high-ranking casualty of the Union artillery. Left behind when the brigade fell back he died that night, kindly treated but alone, in a Union forward-aid station. But such was the impression his charge had made that even now his exhausted men rendered one last service to the grand assault by drawing a further 3,300 Union troops upon themselves.

The first of these were the four regiments of Colonel George Willard's brigade, the largest in Winfield Hancock's corps and about a quarter of the troops left under his command since the detachment of Caldwell's division. Meade, his attention now fixed to the south as firmly as it had been in the other direction three long hours earlier, appointed Hancock in overall command of the left when he learned that Sickles was wounded – not, we may suspect, entirely unwelcome news. Thus Meade's most trusted subordinate and yet more troops had been drawn away from the point where Lee's last, shortest and supposedly strongest punch was supposed to land with concentrated fury. Its chances of success were improved when Willard's brigade was drawn away from the Union centre and then hotly engaged for an hour or more. Willard himself was killed by a shell as his brigade charged across the Plum Run, while in one last ostentation of pride and endurance the Mississippians gave way grudgingly and Porter Alexander's massed guns helped to make their retreat back to the Emmitsburg Road another heavy entry against the Union in the attrition ledger.

Finally, two of the largest Union regiments under Brigadier General Henry Lockwood had marched across from Slocum's wing and also charged across the Plum Run as far as the Trostle Farm, a tremendous compliment to 21st Mississippi, which had already abandoned one captured battery to Willard's advance and now also had to leave Bigelow's as it fell back to the shelter of Alexander's new gun line. In the gloom the fresh Union troops recovered all the cannon lost to Barksdale's command as well as the dying brigadier himself, but if every Confederate brigade had performed as well as his, this day's battle would have ended with Meade's army split in two and retreating along the diverging axes of the Taneytown Road and the Baltimore Turnpike.

The final stage of the grand assault was entrusted to Major General Richard Anderson, in command of the only division in Hill's corps not involved in the previous day's fighting. Longstreet's third division was only 3 miles away after a leisurely march along the Chambersburg Turnpike, but when George Pickett reported his arrival to Lee he was ordered to bivouac where he stood. By contrast Meade fed the leading brigades of John Sedgwick's corps, which had marched further than Pickett's, into battle as they arrived. The lack of urgency on the Confederate side is striking and the standing down of Pickett suggests that Lee no longer believed a decision likely in the few daylight hours remaining. The most obvious reason was Ewell's failure to attack in synchrony with Longstreet, with consequences we shall examine in the next chapter, but another may have been Lee's vantage point on Seminary Ridge opposite Cemetery Hill, with a discouraging view of the fresh regiments and batteries that kept appearing over the opposing ridge.

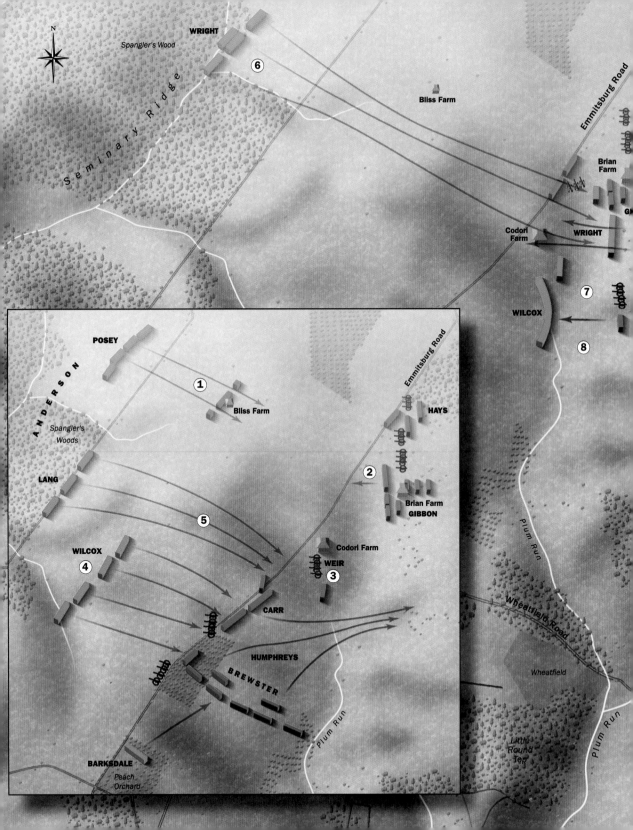

WRIGHT

Spangler's Wood

Seminary Ridge

⑥

Bliss Farm

Emmitsburg Road

Brian
Farm

Codori
Farm

WRIGHT

⑦

WILCOX

⑧

POSEY

①

Bliss Farm

ANDERSON

Spangler's
Woods

HAYS

②

LANG

Brian Farm
GIBBON

⑤

Codori Farm

WEIR

③

WILCOX

④

CARR

HUMPHREYS

BREWSTER

Plum Run

Plum Run

Wheatfield Road

Wheatfield

Little
Round
Top

BARKSDALE

Peach
Orchard

Plum Run

Emmitsburg Road

Longstreet was fully occupied with his own corps and may have presumed that with Lee accompanying the suffering Hill, and with both located close to Anderson's division, it would be adequately supervised. The logic of the whole assault dictated that by now it should have been massed, ready to charge a depleted II Corps on Cemetery Ridge. But it was not concentrated, Anderson himself was well back on Seminary Ridge and his brigadiers had only general instructions about how to advance relative to one another. The most probable explanation of how Lee could have let this happen illustrates the central paradox of his nature: although an extremely aggressive general, in person he was non-confrontational to the point of diffidence. As a result Anderson's attack was not a knock-out punch but a futile if vigorous slap.

It was doubly fortunate for the Union that Richard Anderson was a general of whom Longstreet's chief of staff commented 'his capacity and intelligence were excellent, but it was hard to get him to use them.' He commanded over 6,700 men in five brigades, the largest being Brigadier General Cadmus Wilcox's 1,712 Alabamians, while at 739 men the Florida Brigade under its temporary commander Colonel David Lang was the smallest in the army. Anderson may have wanted Wilcox to command both his own and the inexperienced Lang's brigades, but his orders did not make this explicit and he also employed the words 'advance in unison', perhaps intended to mean together but understood to mean side by side. Wilcox had received instructions from Longstreet himself to charge across the 600 open yards then separating the two ridges, but there were two problems with this. The first was that Wilcox had no confidence in Longstreet – immediately after the war he wrote 'I never had any respect for Longstreet's ability for I always knew he had but a small amount.' The second was that Longstreet's order was given before Andrew Humphreys's division occupied the Emmitsburg Road to Wilcox's front. With

Day 2 –
Cemetery Ridge

1 Posey's brigade advances to drive Union skirmishers out of the Bliss Farm.

2 Hancock orders 82nd New York and 15th Massachusetts to the Emmitsburg Road.

3 Weir's battery and 19th Maine placed by Hancock to cover Humphrey's flank.

4 Wilcox advances in a single line against the left and centre of Humphrey's division.

5 Lang engages the right of Humphrey's division, drives back Hancock's flank guard.

6 Wright's division advances to Cemetery Ridge.

7 Approximate position of the stand by Meade and his staff.

8 Death charge of 1st Minnesota.

9 Stannard's brigade counter attacks.

Longstreet away on the right it was up to Anderson to make the necessary adjustment, and he did not.

Almost perversely, he further diminished the shock power of the attack by sending Brigadier General Carnot Posey's 1,300 men forward to act as a flank guard around the Bliss Farm well before the other brigades advanced, while Brigadier General William Mahone's 1,500 men did not advance at all, either this day or the next. Because his career did not suffer, indeed later prospered, there has been speculation that he was held back by order of the army commander, but given Lee's punctiliousness about hierarchy this seems unlikely. When one of Anderson's staff officers tried to persuade Mahone to advance in support of Brigadier General 'Rans' Wright's attack, which went forward last, he declared that Anderson himself had ordered him to stay where he was. At a guess, it may be that Longstreet privately shared his doubts about the entire assault with Anderson, with whom he had worked closely in the past, and instructed him only to throw the full weight of his division into the attack if he judged success likely. Aware that Ewell's corps had not attacked as intended, Anderson may well have concluded that he should hold back Posey's and Mahone's brigades against a possible counter-attack.

Less comprehensible is that no corps or even divisional artillery was assigned to Wilcox's front. Hill's artillery commander Colonel Lindsay Walker lacked Alexander's flair and missed (or was forbidden) a clear opportunity to run guns forward in support of a further advance once Humphreys's ridge was taken. Left to his own devices and obviously not anticipating that Barksdale would crush Humphreys's left, Wilcox overextended his brigade front to achieve an overlap on that side, while the Floridians were placed to outflank the other. Unlike Barksdale Wilcox was not prepared to march his men in close order into artillery fire. Had he massed the two brigades in Spangler's Woods, it might have proved impossible for Humphreys to salvage as much of his command as he did.

By the law of averages something had to go right for the Union and Andrew Humphreys received a blessing in disguise. Extremely well disguised, he must have thought as he repeatedly tried to rally his men during their painful retreat, but it was not the double envelopment it could easily have been. Although he claimed to have regrouped the Excelsiors and to have fallen back in good order, and finally to have counter-attacked and won back the ground, this was mainly the doing of his second, unbroken brigade under Brigadier General Joseph Carr. Humphreys nonetheless constantly exposed himself to enemy fire to set an example to his men, and beyond that he deserved honour for refusing Meade's invitation to become his chief of staff, choosing to remain in a corps which outraged his professionalism in order to see his division through the battle. Duty done, after it was over he felt free to accept the post and promotion to major general.

Andrew Humphreys

Wilcox's and in particular Lang's men also suffered heavily the next day, but their joint casualties for the two days were not much greater than those of Carr's brigade in this engagement alone. Lang outflanked Carr's position but to do so had to charge a battery of six Napoleons, which he blamed for most of this day's losses. Even if this was no more than an impression, it argues that the retreating Union infantry did little damage to their pursuers, by contrast with the heavy casualties inflicted by Doubleday's mangled I Corps as it fell back from McPherson's Ridge the day before. That Humphreys emerged with his reputation enhanced while Doubleday was discarded has much to do with Meade's prejudice, but may also have reflected an awareness that the former was working with much poorer material.

When Sickles advanced his corps to the Emmitsburg Road Winfield Hancock commented that it would soon come tumbling back, but he still moved elements of Brigadier General John Gibbon's division forward to protect its right flank. Two regiments of Brigadier General William Harrow's brigade advanced 200–300 yards from their position behind a stone wall in front of Cemetery Ridge and formed along the Emmitsburg Road north of

Codori Farm, where they set about building inadequate breastworks with railings. When Humphreys's last reserves were drawn off to support Graham's brigade at the Peach Orchard, he sent a staff officer to beg for reinforcements, and Hancock responded with two of the five understrength regiments in Colonel Norman Hall's brigade. When Humphreys's division gave way these were approaching his right and helped to stiffen Carr's brigade during the retreat. On their right Lieutenant Gulian Weir's Reserve Artillery battery had also gone forward – these being the guns that victimized Lang's Floridians – with Harrow's 19th Maine personally placed by Hancock in close support.

Having gone the extra mile to support III Corps, Hancock made adjustments to consolidate his own position. Behind Harrow's men on the Emmitsburg Road, in a now familiar deployment, he placed Lieutenant Fred Brown's battery of six Napoleons on a slight rise facing north-north-west to create a crossfire with the batteries on Cemetery Ridge. To the left of these, the rest of Hall's brigade held their section of the stone wall while Brigadier General Alexander Webb's was formed in a column of regiments behind the crest. Far behind Weir's guns, on the axis along which Humphreys's men were soon to fall back, Hancock placed a battery of Napoleons from the Reserve Artillery supported by 1st Minnesota, the last of Harrow's regiments, together holding the section of the ridge once held by Caldwell's whole division. Lastly, after the Peach Orchard caved in, Hancock sent one of his own batteries, Captain James Rorty's six 10-pounder Parrotts, to strengthen McGilvery's ragged gun line, by this time all that was defending the section of the ridge beyond the Minnesotans.

Hancock did all of this while most of Ambrose Hill's corps' artillery and some of Richard Ewell's was shelling Cemetery Hill and his own right wing. About half of these, some thirty guns, shifted fire to his front when Posey advanced in brigade strength to drive the Union skirmishers out of the Bliss Farm. Unlike most Union commanders engaged this day he remained serene and gutted his own corps to assist others without protest or profanity, a mark of great self-restraint on the part of this usually vehement officer. This was particularly evident when, in the midst of handling the tactical demands of countering attacks by Posey, Wilcox and Lang, and with 'Rans' Wright's assault imminent, he received Meade's orders to detach yet another brigade (Willard's) and then to assume command of the left wing. Had he done nothing else at Gettysburg, his composure at this moment amply repaid the confidence reposed in him by Meade. He delegated local command to Gibbon and obeyed promptly, when every instinct in him must have cried out against it, because the crisis of the battle was still to come on his corps' front.

Although totally inadequate as the climax of the day's proceedings, Richard Anderson's effort makes sense when viewed as a set-piece divisional attack. With their left covered by Posey and their right cleared by Lang, Wright's 1,400 Georgians had a clean shot at Cemetery Ridge, with only Harrow's two uneasy regiments along the Emmitsburg Road to deal with. Some of Posey's men also advanced tentatively from the direction of the Bliss Farm but were discouraged when Brown's battery engaged them with canister, although this seems to have inflicted as many casualties on Harrow's men, who fell back and pointedly left Brown to try to salvage his guns unaided. Nonetheless lack of support by Posey, who had no orders to provide it, caused Wright to stop his brigade on the ridge while he sent couriers back for reinforcements, instead of turning to fall on Gibbon's left as Barksdale would have done in his place.

Wright's imaginative account speaks of 'a mountain ... so precipitous here that my men could with difficulty climb it', and that they 'were now complete masters of the field, having gained the key, as it were, of the enemy's whole line.' So they had, but turning it was another matter. To his right Hancock put in an appearance and ordered the small 1st Minnesota to make the most celebrated bayonet charge of the war. The regiment sacrificed itself to drive Wilcox's disordered Alabamians back to the Plum Run, here not much more than a trickle in a thickety hollow, and then traded rifle fire with them to such good effect that Wilcox ordered his men to fall back. As with the original order to advance, he did not see fit to advise Lang, who although greatly outnumbered was driving Carr's brigade and Hall's

Alexander Webb

regiments before him. Once again the Floridians scrambled to conform and this was seen by Wright as a precipitate retreat, convincing him that his position was untenable just as his left was vigorously counter-attacked by Hall's remaining regiments and most of Webb's brigade.

In an incident 100 yards to the south, prior to the Minnesotans' death charge, Meade and his staff rode up to the ridge and made a front overlooking the darkening Plum Run swale, swarming with Alabamians and Floridians whose yelling was described by an officer nearby as 'more devilish than anything that *could* come from human throats'. How long they stood there, whether or not their presence deterred the enemy and how they were not all shot out of their saddles are among the more piquant unanswered questions of a battle with more than its fair share. They were still there when George Stannard's brigade advanced from the I Corps' position in reserve behind the ridge, nearly 2,000 neophyte Vermonters who had arrived after the first day's battle, but who now advanced like veterans and completed the destruction of Wright's salient.

Behind them came what was left of John Robinson's I Corps' division, which raises the question of why the reserve posted behind the angle of the Union line at Cemetery Hill was available to repulse the last flick of the scorpion's-tail assault from the west, when it was supposed to be fully taken up by pressure from the north. Even more to the point, why were five of six XII Corps' brigades now either engaged on this front or marching towards it from Slocum's right wing? The answer – and the central pillar of Lost Cause revision-ism and recrimination for decades to come – is that only now, with Longstreet and Hill's men falling back across the entire extent of their advance, did Ewell's corps launch its own attack on Cemetery and Culp's Hills.

11

CEMETERY HILL

No less than for a rifleman, an artilleryman's ideal was a position offering cover to fire over, down a gentle and unobstructed slope. Height bought range, but because the guns had to stand on reasonably level ground and could be wrecked if fired with their barrels significantly depressed, an emplacement above a steep incline created what in this context is the decidedly inappropriate term 'dead ground', where attacking forces could regroup before launching their final assault. This was the Achilles' heel of the Union artillery bastion at Cemetery Hill, which was not one hill but two on a south-west to north-east axis, with the Baltimore Turnpike running between them. The long West Hill was an ideal artillery platform and guns were arrayed across it, a dozen rifles facing west, followed by an almost unbroken rank of twenty Napoleons facing north-west and running across the turnpike, under Major Thomas Osborn, the XI Corps artillery chief.

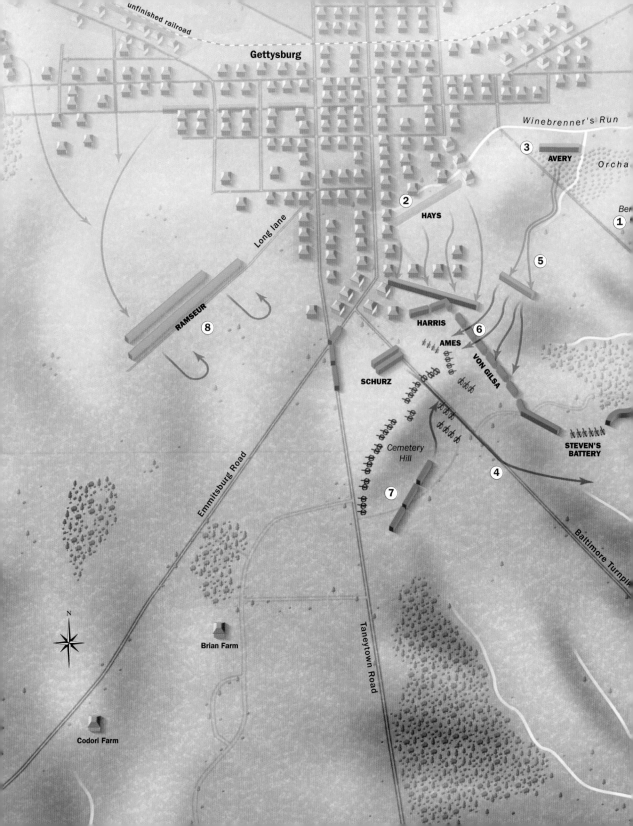

unfinished railroad

Gettysburg

Winebrenner's Run

③ AVERY

Orcha

② HAYS

Ber

①

Long lane

⑤

RAMSEUR

⑧

HARRIS

AMES

⑥

VON GILSA

SCHURZ

STEVEN'S
BATTERY

Emmitsburg Road

Cemetery
Hill

④

⑦

Baltimore Turnpike

N

Brian Farm

Taneytown Road

Codori Farm

There were as many guns facing north-east under the command of Charles Wainwright, hero of the first day, but here the terrain was less suitable for artillery, which had to be deployed on forward slopes and dug in. Three full batteries of 3-inch rifles were placed here, two running slightly downhill from near the crest of East Hill and the third similarly placed on West Hill on the other side of the turnpike. Finally a battery of heavy 20-pounder Parrotts was dug in near the landmark two-storey cemetery gatehouse in between the two hills, with four guns facing north-east and two facing north-west. The placement and choice of guns on this side was optimized for firing across the front of the Union right on Culp's Hill, but this created a considerable area of dead ground immediately in front of them, while only four guns could be sited where the two gun lines intersected, overlooking the town. Five of the batteries on Cemetery Hill came from the Artillery Reserve and more were available, had there been anywhere left to put them.

As we saw in Chapter 5 the dead ground to the north-east was covered by Wadsworth's division in support of Greenleaf Stevens's battery of Napoleons, placed to fire across the front of East Hill. Oliver Howard must have judged the deterrent effect of all the guns on this hill to be greater than it proved to be, because he deployed Barlow's shattered division, now commanded by Adelbert Ames, along the Brickyard Lane running across the base of the hill, a position with a fatally poor field of fire at the centre. Unlike the artillerymen and the commanders on Culp's Hill, Howard and Ames did not order them to create breastworks along the natural contours, perhaps sharing the common belief that entrenchment was bad for morale. How much worse they thought it could get is hard to imagine. Infantry cowered when fired over by their own artillery and it is no coincidence that the place where the men of this division were yet again to break was directly under the muzzles of cannon that had shaken them all day but could not depress enough to help them when the crunch came.

Day 2 –
Cemetery Hill

1 Latimer's counter battery driven from Benner's Hill.

2 Hay's brigade advances to start line along Weinbrenner Run.

3 Avery's brigade forms along Weinbrenner Run behind an orchard.

4 Four of Shurz's reserve regiments sent to support Greene on Culp's Hill.

5 Probable line of attack by Avery's brigade.

6 Point where the attacking brigades overlapped and von Gilsa's brigade gave way.

7 Carroll's brigade counter attack.

8 Ramseur's (Rode's) division advances little beyond the sunken lane.

The view from the other side was nonetheless daunting. The hill dominated the town and apart from Seminary Ridge, occupied by Hill's corps, only Benner's Hill, far to the left and facing Culp's Hill, offered a platform for counter-battery fire. This made discouraging viewing for Richard Ewell and his division commanders, and at the back of their minds there must have been a gnawing certainty that to launch an infantry assault in broad daylight would be so evidently suicidal that their men might balk. Morale in Jubal Early's division was high after its relatively easy victory the day before, but Robert Rodes's division had been severely mauled, mainly by massed Union artillery. Rodes himself was incapacitated by an unidentified illness and his second-in-command Stephen Ramseur may have lacked the authority to motivate the other brigadiers, or else the troops may have felt they had done enough, and when the time came the division collectively declined to make a frontal assault on Osborn's Napoleons.

This is to get out of chronological sequence, for the aborted Rodes/Ramseur attack did not take place until after Early's assault on the other side of Cemetery Hill had fallen back. But working along the concave Confederate line, this sector follows from the events of the last chapter and was very active for most of the day. The three regiments of Orland Smith's brigade of Baron Adolph von Steinwehr's division that had not been involved in the first day's fighting were posted along the Taneytown Road and vigorously contested the ground between the two armies with skirmishers from Dorsey Pender's division of Ambrose Hill's corps while a heavy artillery duel tore the air overhead. In the late afternoon the Union gunners felled another general when a shell fragment ripped into Pender's thigh, a wound that tore open and killed him during the retreat.

Rodes's/Ramseur's men were conspicuous by their absence until the evening. Their overnight bivouacs were close to Lee's headquarters at the Lutheran Seminary, so their dilatory performance was even more directly under his eye than Richard Anderson's had been, and he must have been stunned as all about him previously dependable officers failed even to move

their men into position on time, let alone to perform their allotted tasks in what was not a very complex battle plan. For once we cannot blame Lee's staff: Ewell had unequivocal instructions to await the sound of Longstreet's cannonade announcing the start of his grand assault, then to make a *diversion* against the Union right, 'to be converted into a real attack if an opportunity offered'.

In war as in politics there are few genuine accidents or coincidences; generally if something happens at a particular time, someone willed it. Before attributing anything to happenstance or incompetence we must ask the question that usually clears the mists of history – who benefited? Here, clearly, Ewell's corps had much to lose by obeying Lee's instructions and as

View from the location of Steven's battery: von Gilsa's men held the line marked by trees on the left

Hays' Tigers charging Cemetery Hill

much to gain by waiting until Longstreet's attack had drawn away Union troops. Ewell and Early were competent and experienced generals, and it is far more difficult to believe that they were incapable of mounting a suitably impressive demonstration at 1600 hours, than to accept that from the beginning they intended to make a corps attack at dusk, when it had a better chance of success.

Officers are likely to have tunnel vision about whatever unit is under their command, the best of them because of an intensely personal feeling of responsibility, but all of them because the performance of their men reflects on them professionally. Jubal Early was no heedless butcher but he was ambitious to an unbalanced degree and his version of events reflects the latter over the former quality. The most telling point against him is that his post-war writings were obsessively concerned with attributing blame to others for what went wrong at Gettysburg. The comparison with the role of Dan Sickles on the Union side is compelling, and reasonably exact in terms of the consequences of their actions and their influence on the historiography of the battle. In modern parlance both were passionately 'in denial' for the rest of their lives, unable to admit their heavy responsibility even, indeed especially, to themselves.

Throughout the day the outskirts of Gettysburg witnessed venomous small-scale attacks and counter-attacks, punctuated by the boom of cannon as exasperated gunners let fly. Cemetery Hill and its surrounds were a 'target-rich environment' and XI Corps' skirmishers were constantly in action trying to keep their Confederate counterparts at a distance. Just how distant that could be was shown when an enigmatic squad of Swiss equipped with telescopic sights on their rifles and special tripods made a brief appearance at the crest of East Hill to silence a snipers' nest in a church tower nearly 1,000 yards away. Sharpshooters seem to have been a law unto themselves in the Union army and they vanished from the record as mysteriously as they entered it. Both sides were keen to avoid civilian casualties and this, along with the need to conserve artillery ammunition, meant the town suffered little serious damage.

For narrative convenience the assault by Edward Johnson's division on Culp's Hill is covered in the next chapter, although it preceded and is operationally inseparable from Early's attack on Cemetery Hill, because as we shall see it drew off four regiments of the XI Corps' reserve. In a prelude to both attacks Johnson's young artillery chief Major Joseph Latimer attempted to set up a counter-battery on Benner's Hill, but he was killed and his guns were driven from it by Wainwright's massed batteries on Cemetery Hill, and by another battery hauled to the crest of Culp's Hill for this sole purpose and later withdrawn. With both flanks of Culp's Hill now covered by uncontested

Union artillery, Johnson had no choice but to attack it frontally in what was, operationally, simply a demonstration designed to facilitate the assault by Early and Ramseur on either side of Cemetery Hill. There is a certain grim irony in the fact that Early, probably instrumental in delaying the corps attack until after it might have been useful to Longstreet, was hoist by a similar petard when his own attack at last went forward and was not supported by Ramseur's division, its officers and men equally unenthusiastic about sacrificing themselves for the greater good.

Given the commanding view afforded by the hills in enemy hands, the fact that the outskirts of Gettysburg were thick with Union skirmishers and that just before the attack Ames sent two Union regiments forward to flank Johnson's assault on Culp's Hill (which came within a few hundred yards of Isaac Avery's North Carolina brigade), Early did very well indeed to achieve tactical surprise. This was done by exploiting the topographical indentation marked by Weinbrenner Run to infiltrate Harry Hays's Louisiana brigade north of East Hill, where they had a relatively short distance to cover. Although Avery's men were further along the creek bed, they had the benefit of the only other substantial cover on this front, an orchard that concealed them from Culp's Hill as well as from Ames's late advancing regiments. Even so only the low light conditions made surprise possible.

Harry Pfanz's reconstruction is close to gospel, nonetheless I suspect that both brigades covered the intervening ground faster and in less formal order than he suggests, and regrouped in the dead ground in front of the Union line, overlapping each other opposite the vulnerable centre. These were experienced soldiers led by competent officers who would not have extended their time under artillery fire unnecessarily. Although Avery's men had to cover double the distance, the two brigades arrived together and both brigades' casualties for two days of fighting were below average for the Confederate army as a whole, a further indication that they got under the guns quickly. One who did not was Isaac Avery himself, who decided to ride into this engagement and was mortally wounded as he hurried his men forward, scrawling a last pathetic testament as he died alone: 'Tell my father I died with my face to the enemy'.

Other than the reflection it casts on Howard and Ames for deploying them so badly, there was nothing shameful or even remarkable about little more than 1,000 survivors of a demoralizing defeat twenty-four hours earlier giving way before a determined and well-co-ordinated assault by more than 2,500 of those who had defeated them. When the two regiments that had advanced against Johnson's flank fell back, they may have masked Greenleaf Stevens's Napoleons, the guns of choice for short-range work and the only ones placed to cover the dead ground, but he opened anyway with canister and, when this ran out, with case-shot fused to burst at the muzzle, a desperate recourse he should not have employed when firing so closely across the front of Leopold von Gilsa's much put-upon men. Once again placed in an impossible situation, these performed the combat manoeuvre with which their service in the Union army had made them most familiar.

> Tell my father I died with my face to the enemy.
>
> Col. Isaac Avery

At the other end of the Union line Ames's old brigade, now commanded by Colonel Andrew Harris, did little better, thanks in part to the fact that Ames, having weakened his line by sending two of his strongest regiments forward, tried to remedy this by shuffling troops to the right immediately before the attack. All order – and any hope of a coherent narrative – broke down in the darkness and the thick smoke from guns firing over the heads of the struggling infantry. What appears to have happened is that Hays's right surged over and around the Union left flank, here refused along a low stone wall, and then charged the part-battery at the top of East Hill. The next section of the Union line seems to have held, but where Hays's and Avery's brigades overlapped they met with little immediate resistance and stormed over their side of the hill, overrunning the first gun line and surging to the Baltimore Turnpike. Lit only by the flare of rifle and cannon fire, men could not tell friend from foe until they reached close quarters and 'clubs, knives, stones, fists – anything calculated to inflict pain or death was resorted to'.

Although Early had intended to send John Gordon's brigade in support, when he learned that Rodes's men had not advanced he held it back and Nemesis rapidly closed in on Hays's and Avery's men. Howard was without reserves and appealed to II Corps for help. Since by now he had beaten off Anderson's assault, acting corps commander Gibbon was able to detach Colonel Samuel Carroll and three regiments of his brigade. Two regiments from Webb's brigade were also sent, but played no part in the counter-attack, although one was to play an equivocal role on Culp's Hill. After driving the Confederates from the hill, Carroll received a request from Ames to remain. 'Damn a man who has no confidence in his troops', he snapped and rode off to seek Howard. The XI Corps' commander also asked him to hold the line because 'he had no troops he could trust to his front'. This time Carroll kept his opinion to himself.

Hindsight tells us that Early erred in not sending Gordon's brigade forward, but he could not see how successful the first wave had been. There was also confusion caused by there being two hills and he may have thought his men were still hung up on East Hill when in fact they had advanced to the foot of West Hill. For whatever reasons, another well-executed but unsupported Confederate breakthrough was held up just long enough for the Union's numerical superiority to make itself felt.

12

Although Sykes's corps was soon removed from the right wing and Sedgwick's never joined it, the arrangements made by Slocum to be free to exercise command over two or more corps persisted, so for the rest of the battle XII Corps was commanded by Alpheus Williams, the longest-serving divisional commander in the army, whose ferocious whiskers belied the caring nature that earned him the nickname 'Old Pap' from his men. This promoted Thomas Ruger to command Williams's division and Colonel Silas Colgrove to command his brigade. When the inexperienced Brigadier General Henry Lockwood arrived in the morning of 2 July with two of his big garrison regiments (the third arrived twenty-four hours later), he became the next-highest-ranking officer in the corps and, rather than permit him to take over from the veteran Ruger in the division to which he properly belonged, Williams made Lockwood's brigade a de facto third division.

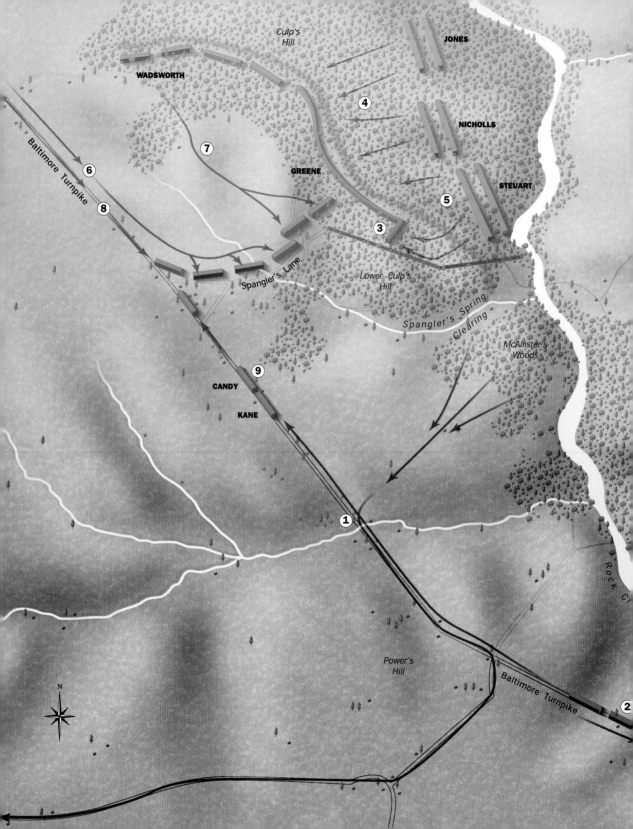

Culp's
Hill

JONES

WADSWORTH

4

NICHOLLS

7

GREENE

STEUART

6

5

8

3

Baltimore Turnpike

Spangler's Lane

Lower Culp's
Hill

Spangler's Spring

Clearing

9

McAllister's
Woods

CANDY

KANE

1

Rock Cr

Power's
Hill

Baltimore Turnpike

2

N

The battle that took place in this sector during the evening of the second day was defined by Meade's decision to strip it in order to send reinforcements to the left and by an extraordinary mix-up that took 2,500 men out of the battle altogether for several crucial hours. After Meade rode to Sickles's command post and saw for himself the disaster now threatening his left he must have suspected another Chancellorsville in the making and switched completely from over-concern with his right to an equally strong conviction that XII Corps faced only a feint. He ordered the entire corps to move to the left wing and although Slocum obtained permission to leave a skeleton force behind, Lockwood's and Ruger's divisions were immediately set in motion, followed a little later by Geary's. All save one brigade left their carefully prepared positions and took the swiftest route to the left, marching down the Baltimore Turnpike and turning right along the Granite Schoolhouse Lane, past Slocum's headquarters on Power's Hill. Williams himself led Lockwood's men along this route and as we saw in the last chapter they had an exhilarating first experience of combat. Ruger's division arrived after the action was over and had the dispiriting experience of a night counter-march.

Meanwhile Geary led Colonel Charles Candy's and Brigadier General Thomas Kane's brigades down the turnpike, leaving only Brigadier General George Greene's brigade of 1,400 men to hold a position previously defended by over 9,000, with the works on Lower Culp's Hill and McAllister Woods abandoned. Geary's orders were to follow Ruger's division, but he lost touch in the gathering darkness and continued south along the turnpike to the Rock Creek bridge, which in the absence of further instructions he deployed to defend. Although it is surprising that he did not send a staff officer to Slocum for confirmation, responsibility for the error lay in Meade's initial failure of appreciation, compounded by poor staff work and by Alpheus

Day 2 – Culp's Hill

1 Acting corps commander Williams leads Lockwood and Ruger's divisions to the Union left.

2 Geary marches two brigades to Rock Creek in error, leaving only Greene's brigade to hold the hill.

3 Greene deploys 137th New York to cover re-entrant.

4 Jones's and Nicholls's brigades assault the upper hill.

5 Steuart's brigade outflanks Greene's right but gets lost in the dark.

6 Schurz's four XI Corps regiments arrive to hold Spangler's Lane.

7 Wadsworth's two I Corps regiments arrive to hold the traverse.

8 71st Pennsylvania arrives from II Corps, departs.

9 Geary's brigades return, probe lower Culp's Hill, replace Schurz and Wadsworth's regiments.

'Old Pap' Williams

Williams's unfamiliarity with corps command, which caused him to lead rather than direct the march to Cemetery Ridge. It was a blunder, but hindsight permits us to see that its consequences were favourable to the Union, because it gave the Confederates a chimerical success on this flank that was heavily reinforced the next day, when it should have been abandoned, their grossly overextended exterior line rationalized and the troops made available for use elsewhere.

Unaware that events were developing so favourably to his front, Ewell's third divisional commander Edward Johnson had to deal with two responsibilities at once. On his left, Brigadier General James Walker's Stonewall Brigade had been occupied all day facing threats from Slocum's early morning manoeuvres near Brinkerhoff's Ridge and the arrival of Sykes's corps along the Hanover Road, while in the afternoon Gregg's cavalry division plodded into place, the horses exhausted and the troopers perforce deployed as infantry. This left Johnson with three brigades and about 4,700 men to assault Culp's Hill in the first phase of Ewell's corps attack. Other factors conditioning his deployment were that his artillery support had been blasted off Benner's Hill and that throughout the day the woods across Rock Creek were held by aggressive Union skirmishers, supported by crossfire from McAllister Woods, which prevented proper reconnaissance.

Johnson was tasked with a holding action to occupy the troops to his front and draw in reinforcements from elsewhere, but if Confederate scouts had been able to penetrate the Union screen to discover the true situation, Early's division might have attacked Culp's and not Cemetery Hill. Johnson's attack was designed to seize the wooded forward slopes of Culp's Hill with Brigadier General John M. Jones's Virginians and Colonel Jesse Williams's Louisianians in order to pin the troops on the upper hill, while Brigadier General George 'Maryland' Steuart's mixed-origin brigade, at 2,100 men Johnson's largest, struck at the lower hill and the vulnerable re-entrant between the two. The aim was to neutralize the enemy's absolute artillery superiority and to cause maximum Union concern for the safety of the Baltimore Turnpike.

George Greene was left in charge on upper Culp's Hill. He was the oldest Union general, affectionately nicknamed 'Old Pop' to differentiate him from 'Old Pap' Alpheus Williams, nine years his junior but both unthinkably elderly to the young men under their command. A West Pointer, he left the army to pursue a successful career as a civil engineer and was not free to rejoin until early 1862. He it was who prevailed on his divisional commander John Geary, who was of the 'entrenchment is bad for morale' persuasion, to order the building of breastworks along the ridgeline and he himself supervised the construction of the traverse above the re-entrant. When the rest of the corps marched off, Greene was ordered to hold the entire line of works but wisely limited himself to placing 137th New York, his largest regiment, on the western slope of the lower hill, where it could fire across the front of the rest of the brigade on the upper hill.

When the Confederates advanced the Union skirmishers put up a brisk resistance before falling back, wounding John Jones and his two senior regimental commanders. To Jones's left, Jesse Williams's men met with less initial opposition but came up to a Union line not masked by retreating skirmishers and were stopped cold. The advantage of attacking uphill negated by Greene's elaborate works, two Confederate brigades were held in check by three small Union regiments, probably suffering few additional casualties but inflicting even fewer amid the smoke-deepened darkness of the woods. Steuart's right was caught in the crossfire of 137th New York, but two regiments on his left gingerly entered the abandoned Union works on the lower hill and only came under fire, probably from other elements of their own brigade, when they ventured over the crest. In daylight the two wings of Steuart's command would have made short work of the New Yorkers, now sandwiched between them, but the troops on the lower hill became disoriented and groped further to their left.

Culp's Hill   They were met by four regiments from Carl Schurz's reserve XI Corps' division, sent by Oliver Howard before the attack on Cemetery Hill, which arrived to extend Greene's right along Spangler's Lane. Once he was sure that Early's assault was not directed at his position, James Wadsworth of the I Corps' remnant on western Culp's Hill also sent two of his reduced regiments, and officers from the two corps found time to exchange insults about each other's performance the day before. The terrifying situation into which the reinforcements sent to Greene's open flank were pitched is illustrated by 71st Pennsylvania, the regiment from Webb's division mentioned in the last chapter. This was a sound regiment under a good colonel that fought well the next

day, but it had no stomach for a fight where one could as easily be killed by friend as by foe and, after losing three officers and eleven men, it pulled out and returned to Cemetery Ridge.

While Steuart's two North Carolina regiments continued to engage the works on the southern slope of the upper hill, his own Maryland Battalion and three Virginia regiments consolidated their hold on the lower hill. Now hit from three sides, 137th New York suffered severely and had to fall back. Where each unit was located relative to the others and who fired on whom was guesswork then and remains so today. The regiments sent by I and XI Corps withdrew during the night when Geary's lost brigades returned, so they never got an accurate fix on the positions they held, but Kane's brigade eventually relieved whoever was holding the traverse, while Candy's men took over the line along Spangler's Lane. 'Eventually' covers several hours of probing by the returning brigadiers, who could not consult with Greene and found out the hard way that their old positions were now firmly in Confederate hands. Kane, almost prostrate with pneumonia, had temporarily ceded command to the aggressive Englishman Colonel George Cobham, who kept the fighting going long after everyone else had decided to call it a day.

Greene's stand deserves to be considered at least on a par with the far more celebrated performance of Strong Vincent's brigade on Little Round Top and owed everything to his insistence on creating substantial breastworks to protect his men. The intrinsic strength of the Culp's Hill position was such that Johnson had little choice but to attack as he did and this meant that he had no reserves to exploit the unexpected success on his left, nor enough light to do so even if the Stonewall Brigade had not been tied down at Brinkerhoff's

Ridge. Although on the map we present a coherent interpretation of what the units involved may have done, we might more frankly have shaded over the re-entrant and the whole of lower Culp's Hill and marked it 'confused small-unit engagements'. It was one of the very few genuine night battles fought during the Civil War and the incidence of friendly fire and of individuals or even entire patrols being captured after losing their way underlines why there were not more.

When Alpheus Williams returned to Culp's Hill after being detained by a council of war summoned by Meade, who was under the impression that the fighting was over for the day, he was astounded to find that the position had been held by only one brigade and that the lower works were in enemy hands. His surprise is revealing: it means that Geary's departure was ordered by Slocum in response to Meade's insistence *after* Williams had set off for Cemetery Ridge, which helps to explain why Geary got lost, and that even at this late stage no member of the Union high command, Slocum included, believed that the hours-long rattle of musketry on the right was anything other than a Confederate demonstration. This puts the whole of Richard Ewell's corps attack into perspective as a failed stratagem, comparable to Jeb Stuart's ride around the Union army.

13

Even after an agitated Alpheus Williams reported the true state of affairs to him, Henry Slocum was unperturbed. 'Well, drive them out at daylight', he said, and left the details to his acting corps commander. Williams went away muttering that this was easier said than done, but during the night he set about making, in the words of his report, 'such arrangements for heavy artillery fire, with infantry feints upon the right, followed by a strong assault by Geary's division from Greene's position on the left, as I judged would speedily dislodge the enemy'. Or, as he put it more succinctly to Thomas Ruger on the newly reclaimed McAllister Woods knoll, 'We will hold the position we now have until morning. Then, from those hills back of us, we will shell hell out of them.'

During the night artillery commander Hunt also took a hand in the matter and by dawn sixteen rifled guns were located around Power's Hill to bring

Gettysburg

Rock Creek

York Turnpike

N

STUART
⑦

⑨

⑧
GREGG

Hanover Road

SMITH

JOHNSON

Culp's
Hill

⑤

③

④

STEUART

Baltimore Turnpike

COLGROVE
①

② RUGER

McDOUGALL

Rock Creek

⑥

SLOCUM
Power's
Hill

the forward slope of Culp's Hill under fire, while ten Napoleons were placed on a rise south-west of the Baltimore Turnpike to cover the clearing around Spangler's Spring and the breastworks and wall held by Steuart's men down the eastern flank of the lower hill.

With Rock Creek once again rendered a no-man's-land by artillery and by Silas Colgrove's men in McAllister Woods, Williams completed the containment of the Confederate penetration by posting Colonel Archibald McDougall's brigade between Colgrove's brigade and Lockwood's two-regiment division, the latter placed on either side of the batteries of Napoleons on the turnpike. The fly in the ointment was that on the other side, now obedient to Lee's orders, Ewell had reinforced Johnson's division with Edward O'Neal's and Junius Daniel's brigades from Robert Rodes's division, plus 'Extra Billy' Smith's small brigade from Early's division, while the arrival of Jeb Stuart's cavalry during the second day had at last freed James Walker's Stonewall Brigade to join in. The losses suffered by O'Neal's and Daniel's brigades on the first day were not separately accounted for and this makes it impossible to be precise, but there was probably little to choose between the two sides numerically.

What followed from dawn to midday was a seven-hour battle among nearly 20,000 men worthy of the extensive consideration in its own right given it by Harry Pfanz, but which we can only summarize here. The last of Johnson's three assaults was repulsed an hour before the attack against the Union centre that he was supposed to support and his division alone suffered what seems to have been a grossly underreported 1,900 casualties in return for Union losses of barely more than 1,000. At the operational level, even though it eventually drew in brigades under Brigadier Generals Alexander Shaler and Thomas Neill from Sedgwick's corps, Meade now had adequate reserves and the battle tied up a much greater proportion of the Confederate army. If we also consider that this diversion kept

Day 3 –
The right wing

1 Colgrove's brigade reoccupies McAllister Woods knoll.

2 McDougall's brigade, Lockwood's division and artillery secure the Baltimore Turnpike.

3 Smith's brigade from Early's division advances to secure Steuart's left flank.

4 Steuart's last assault – civil war among Marylanders.

5 Slocum sends Shaler's brigade to reinforce Geary's line.

6 Slocum sends Neill's brigade to protect Rock Creek crossing.

7 Stuart rides out along the York Turnpike.

8 Gregg shadows Stuart along the Hanover Road.

9 Cavalry battle off map.

the whole of Ewell's corps uselessly extended on this unpromising front instead of consolidating strength at the centre, the continued battle for Culp's Hill was a resounding Confederate defeat even before it was fought.

Although both had suffered heavy casualties at Chancellorsville, the morale and leadership of Slocum's XII Corps was clearly well above the Union average, whereas Johnson's division was much diminished. All of Johnson's brigadiers were new or interim appointments, while he himself was newly returned from a year-long sick leave with a disabling ankle wound. He was regarded as an unimaginative pounder by his men and hated for his custom of striking them with his heavy walking stick. Of the reinforcements, O'Neal's and Daniel's brigades had shown a pronounced lack of desire for further fighting the day before, but the awkwardness of giving orders to 'Extra Billy' Smith, soon to be the governor of Virginia and hence not a man any Confederate officer would wish to offend, was balanced by the keenness of his men to get into a fight that had so far eluded them.

It is worth underlining that in these largely volunteer armies provident motivators such as 'Pop' and 'Pap' always got more out of their men than the hard-driving martinets, and got shot less often to boot. This was not necessarily because of what we now call 'fragging', but also because the latter more often had to pull their men into battle. What is so striking about the battle around Culp's Hill is how well managed it was on the Union side, with regiments firing their ready-use ammunition and then being relieved by others while they moved back out of the line of fire to take a break, during which they cleaned their rifles, restocked their pouches and refilled their canteens. This enabled them to maintain what can accurately be termed a wall of fire, which prevented the Confederates on the upper hill from mounting any meaningful assault and made regrouping or even withdrawal extremely hazardous. Except around the lower hill, where some counter-attacks were mounted, Union casualties were light and came during the periods of handover, when the troops were briefly exposed either entering or leaving the front line.

An illustrative vignette is that during the night Candy's 66th Ohio was ordered to march out of the works at the top of upper Culp's Hill and to form at right angles to the main line, down the steep slope to the right of the Confederate position held by Jones's brigade overnight and by Daniel's the next day. That a single Union regiment was able to harass two Confederate brigades for several hours and suffered only one killed and sixteen wounded tells us much about the whole engagement. The attackers on the slopes of the upper hill were genuinely pinned down behind inadequate cover by accurate fire from above. They shot back, though – the banner of 149th New York had eighty bullet holes at the end of the battle and twice had its staff shot through. Battlefield sketches show that this regiment lacked the much-praised head logs and fired over a simple rampart, which may explain why the Confederates eventually rushed the crest at this point, a sergeant of the Stonewall Brigade being killed as he reached out to seize the tattered flag.

Pfanz's reconstruction bears out the opinion Johnson's men had of him. Since the upper hill could not be taken in an evening assault when held only by Greene's brigade, the attacks he ordered against it the next day when it was held by Geary's whole division deserve consideration in any compendium of brutal military obstinacy. It was not until the final assault that three brigades were at last concentrated where Steuart's men had achieved a lodgement, although even now the lives of the Stonewall Brigaders were wasted in the attack on the upper hill mentioned above, among them John Wesley Culp, grandson of the German immigrants (Kolb) who had given their anglicized name to the hill on which he died. In what may have been a spontaneous development on the Confederate right, flank companies from Steuart's and Walker's brigades brought Colgrove's men in McAllister Woods under fire from across Rock Creek and 'Extra Billy' tried to attack them across the Spangler's Spring clearing. Under blistering artillery fire he withdrew to the section of stone wall running down to Rock Creek.

Daniel's brigade also came across the front of the upper hill to support Steuart's men, who after hours of enfilade fire from Kane's brigade and others entrenched above the re-entrant were now ordered to mount the assault towards Spangler's Lane that nightfall had curtailed the previous day. A 1st North Carolina lieutenant described the situation:

> Then came General Ewell's order to assume the offensive and assail the crest of Culp's Hill, on our right. My diary says that both General Steuart and General Daniel ... strongly disapproved of making the assault. The works to be stormed ran almost at right angles to those we occupied. Moreover there was a double line of entrenchments, one above the other and each filled with troops. In moving to the attack we were exposed to enfilading fire from the woods on our left flank, besides the double row of fire which we had to face in front, and a battery of artillery posted on a hill to our left rear opened upon us at short range.

The attack had no hope of success. Not only was Steuart obliged to send a whole regiment to refuse his left flank against the aggressive 20th Connecticut, but his advance was across the open Pardee Field, so named for the colonel of 147th Pennsylvania, which along with other regiments and the artillery along the Baltimore Turnpike turned it into a killing ground. If it was intended only as a diversion it worked, albeit at dreadful cost, with Steuart's men drawing the fire of more than double their number of Unionists. In an episode of great poignancy, nearly half of Steuart's 1st Maryland Battalion fell before the guns of, among others, the men of Lockwood's 1st Maryland Regiment, Eastern Shore, who then went out to collect wounded friends and relatives from in front of their position and tenderly cared for men they had done their best to kill minutes earlier.

Lopsided though the balance of casualties was, it would have been even more so but for the fact that Colgrove misjudged the situation following the repulse of Steuart's attack and launched two regiments in a counter-attack across the Spangler's Spring clearing. Caught in a crossfire from 'Extra Billy' Smith's fresh brigade and the flank companies on the other side of Rock Creek, nearly a quarter of all the XII Corps killed and wounded fell in a few minutes. To absolutely no avail, because by now the Confederates had received orders to fall back across the creek and when, about half an hour later, two regiments of McDougall's brigade stormed lower Culp's Hill they found it abandoned. There was no time for the survivors to celebrate before the thunder of cannon far to their left announced the day's main event, with poorly fused Confederate shells arcing over Cemetery Ridge to catch a few, deeply unlucky men in the open.

Slocum kept reinforcements sent from Sedgwick's cannibalized corps near to him on Powers' Hill and sent Shaler's brigade to Geary's front in time to help repel the last assault. Only 122nd New York saw serious action and shortly afterwards the brigade was returned to the army reserve. Neill's brigade was sent east along the Baltimore Turnpike across Rock Creek with orders to cover the Union right and did little more than that, although it might more profitably have been ordered to advance along the creek to clear the skirmishers harassing Colgrove's men in McAllister Woods. But Slocum was more concerned to guard his headquarters and the Rock Creek crossing against a possible attack by the large force of enemy cavalry seen riding out of Gettysburg along the York Turnpike, news of which was semaphored to him by Union signallers on Cemetery Hill.

> ... we were exposed to enfilading fire from the woods ... besides the double row of fire which we had to face in front, and a battery of artillery ... opened upon us at short range.
>
> Lieutenant, 1st North Carolina regiment

Jeb Stuart's cavalry division did not arrive at Gettysburg until the afternoon of the second day of battle and the dashing cavalier received one of the few face-to-face rebukes ever delivered by Lee. 'General Stuart, where have you been?' he asked after a long silence. Stuart began to reply but Lee cut him short. 'I have not heard a word from you for days, and you the eyes and ears of my army.' This was the equivalent of a shouted tirade from any other commander and is more significant for the light it sheds on Lee's agitated state of mind than for the justice of his remarks. Stuart had been ordered to make a diversion behind the enemy army and against a less single-minded commander than Meade it might have worked. Lee had retained the cavalry

Wade Hampton

brigades of Brigadier Generals Beverly Robertson and William 'Grumble' Jones for his own use and sent Brigadier General Albert Jenkins's forward with Ewell, ample for reconnaissance, and if this was not performed to his satisfaction the fault was his and Ewell's. Nonetheless, Stuart was humiliated and anxious to redeem himself in Lee's eyes and together they devised what could be a crucial third-day role for the cavalry.

Stuart had been in front of Carlisle when he received news of the battle and immediately sent his three brigades south along all available routes. The one taken by Brigadier General Wade Hampton brought him into contact with Union cavalry under Judson Kilpatrick near Hunterstown, 3 miles north-east of Gettysburg, and a short battle ensued featuring a reckless charge by Brigadier General George Armstrong Custer. Lee may have believed that there were now two Union cavalry divisions on his far-left flank (Gregg's and Kilpatrick's, although the latter had moved on by now), and this lends credibility to Stuart's statement that he was sent to guard the flank. But given Lee's hopes for the third day it cannot be a full explanation for this deployment of virtually all his cavalry, about one-fifth of the troops remaining under his command. Stuart was certainly sent to deal with the Union cavalry and to free up the Stonewall Brigade on Brinkerhoff's Ridge, but probably also to pursue the Union army if it broke and retreated from Cemetery Ridge. Since this did not occur, what happened 3 miles away between the York Turnpike and the Hanover Road was really just an anecdote.

One not without interest and drama, however. How he knew to do so is not apparent, but Gregg shadowed Stuart's progress along the York Turnpike by taking two brigades along the Hanover Road, posting pickets as he went and leaving his cousin's brigade to cover the Wolf Hill–Brinkerhoff's Ridge position. Gregg had 'borrowed' Custer's brigade from Kilpatrick while the latter was withdrawing from his encounter with Hampton towards the Union left

**George
Armstrong Custer**

to fill the gap created by the inopportune withdrawal of Buford. Corps commander Pleasonton was not pleased to discover that yet another cavalry action for which he could claim no credit was about to take place and peremptorily ordered Custer to rejoin Kilpatrick, but although he was one of Pleasonton's protégés the 'boy general' scented battle and asked Gregg to countermand the order, which he did.

At about the same time as the Confederate infantry charged to destruction on Cemetery Ridge, Stuart ordered Brigadier General Fitzhugh Lee's and Hampton's brigades to sweep away Gregg's troopers and they were met head-on by Custer's and Colonel John McIntosh's men in a classic open-field encounter, with about 3,000 on either side. Neither gave way and the crunch was spectacular, with horses and riders knocked end over end. After sabring each other for a while, during which Hampton received a cut to the head that fractured his skull, both withdrew to their original positions. The two most heavily engaged brigades were once again Custer's and Hampton's, and in their battles here and at Hunterstown the former lost 180 killed and wounded of 1,900 engaged and the latter 73 out of 1,700, significant losses by cavalry standards and, unusually in this war, mostly inflicted by the cold steel that more usually contributed only a pleasant jingle at the trot.

Confederate records of everything that took place on their left are probably scarce because not a single substantive achievement crowned the efforts over two days by one-third of their infantry and all of their cavalry. Neither on foot and certainly not on horseback were Yankees supposed to fight like this. This uncomfortable truth could not be denied and so was evaded, not only in the post-battle reports but also and most tellingly in the post-war writings of Lost Cause partisans. They had been outgeneralled and outfought every step of the way and it was too bitter a pill to swallow.

14

As the shattered survivors of Pickett's Charge fell back from their fabled assault on Cemetery Ridge, Lee rode among them, telling them it was his fault. They refused to accept it and so did Lee's post-war apologists and subsequent hagiographers, but the attack was indeed made at his insistence, over the strenuous objections of Longstreet, his senior corps commander. His own final report of January 1864 reads in part (my italics): 'The result of [the second] day's operations induced the belief that, *with proper concert of action*, and with the increased support that the positions gained on the right would enable the artillery to render the assaulting columns, we should ultimately succeed, and it was accordingly determined to continue the attack. *The general plan was unchanged.*'

That is to say, it was to be an echeloned attack by Longstreet's corps after Ewell's corps had drawn off Union reserves. As we have seen, the latter was

minimally successful and Longstreet may have procrastinated in part to return the favour of Ewell's delayed operations the day before. In the end neither Evander Law's (ex-Hood's) nor Lafayette McLaws's divisions advanced against the now heavily reinforced Union left where they would have been massacred, a fate from which Longstreet's reluctance saved them.

Lee nonetheless insisted that Longstreet should proceed with the breakthrough attempt by about 14,600 infantry advancing in two converging assaults. The larger was formed by about 5,400 men from the four brigades of James Pettigrew's division (Heth was still *hors de combat*) and 2,300 from two brigades of the wounded Pender's division, now commanded by Major General Isaac Trimble. Trimble's two other brigades joined the rump of Rodes's division along the sunken lane from which it had failed to advance the night before and were presumably intended to make a demonstration, although if they did so they made no impression on the Union defenders. The other assault was made by a little over 5,000 men of the three brigades of Pickett's fresh division, with the 1,900 men of Wilcox's and Lang's brigades on their right flank. Even the strength of Pickett's division is the subject of endless debate, while the numbers for the previously engaged units must remain speculative. The figures given here have been arrived at by arbitrarily allotting half the casualties for the whole battle to the first and second days' engagements.

The point of attack Lee chose was slightly north of the penetration achieved by 'Rans' Wright the previous evening and was marked by an angle in the low stone wall running in front of Cemetery Ridge, enclosing a copse of trees that made a distinctive aiming point for an arc of guns running from the Peach Orchard around the town. Lee must also have noted two

Day 3 –
The Artillery

Confederate Batteries

1 Nelson's brigade, (Ewell's Corps reserve).

2 Carrington, Garber and Green (Early's Division artillery).

3 Hurt's two Whitworths on Oak Hill (Hill's Corps reserve).

4 Carter's brigade (Rodes's Division artillery).

5 Dance's brigade (Ewell's Corps reserve).

6 McIntosh's brigade (Hill's Corps reserve).

7 Pegram's brigade (Hill's Corps reserve); Two Sumter Artillery batteries (Anderson's Division artillery); Ablemarie battery (Pender's Division artillery).

8 Alexander's and Eshleman's brigades (Longstreet's Corps reserve); Dearing's brigade (Pickett's Division artillery); Garden and Latham from Hood's Division artillery; Manley and Carlton from McLaws's Division artillery.

9 Two of Dearing's batteries run forward to support Pickett's charge.

Union Batteries

10 Walcott, Gibbs and Rittenhouse (ex Hazlett) from V Corps.

11 McGilvery's gun line: Thompson, Philips, Hart, Thomas, Sterling, Dow and Ames from Reserve and Rank from Gregg's Horse Artillery.

12 Hazard's command: Rorty and Cushing from II Corps, Cowan from VI Corps, Wheeler from XI Corps and Parsons late-arriving from the Reserve.

13 Hazard's command: McCrea (ex Woodruff) and Arnold from II Corps, Turnbull and Milton (ex Bigelow) from the Reserve, Weir sent by Hunt at the height of the charge.

14 Osborn's gun line: Edgell, Norton, Hill, Eakin and Taft from the Reserve, Stewart from I Corps and Dilger and Bancroft (ex Wilkeson) from XI Corps.

15 Wainwright's gun line: Breck (ex Reynolds) and Whittier (ex Stevens) from I Corps, Ricketts, Weidrich and Rugg from the Reserve, XI and XII Corps.

16 Best's brigade from Slocum's Corps. In addition Heckman (XI Corps), Rigby (Reserve) and Heaton (Reserve Horse Artillery) were posted on this front.

**Thure de
Thrulstrup's
painting of
'The Battle of
Gettysburg'**

topographical features that favoured an assault on this point, the first being a rise running parallel to the Emmitsburg Road, which provided a modicum of cover along which the right-hand assault force could advance. The second was a slight rise in the ground running out from the stone wall (where Brown's battery had been sited the day before), which would protect Pettigrew's/Trimble's men from artillery to their right and vice versa for Pickett's force. Until Carol Reardon pointed it out in *Pickett's Charge in History and Memory* the significance of this rise had not been underlined, but it explains much of the survivors' mutual recrimination because 'it cut the lines of sight along the lines of command responsibility: Pettigrew and Trimble fought Hays north of it, Pickett fought Gibbon south of it. Only a few soldiers saw much of both clashes.'

General Lee immediately shook hands with him and said cheerfully: 'Never mind, General, all this has been my fault – it is I that have lost this fight, and you must help me out of it in the best way you can.'

Col. James Freemantle

Indeed, but that did not stop them blaming each other for the failure of the charge, whereas the casualty returns confirm the sacrificial heroism of almost all involved. The 'missing' figures here are more than usually suspect and are no indication of morale, because the regiments that drove furthest were the most likely to be cut off. One grim constant across both assault forces is that the commanders, indeed most of the officers of units that achieved penetration of the Union line, were killed or wounded. Reardon skilfully dissects the manner in which Virginia journalists appropriated the glory for their state and conveniently failed to mention the Virginians of Brockenbrough's brigade, who made the weakest effort of any troops involved. For our purposes it suffices to note that Lee admitted he had asked his men to do too much. Captain Justus Scheibert, a Prussian military observer with the Confederates, was blunt: 'Excessive disdain for the enemy … caused the simplest plan of direct attack upon the position at Gettysburg to prevail and deprived the army of victory.' By contrast British Guards Colonel James Freemantle became a hero-worshipper after witnessing Lee's bearing following the repulse:

I saw General Wilcox come up to him and explain, almost crying, the state
of his brigade. General Lee immediately shook hands with him and said
cheerfully: 'Never mind, General, all this has been *my* fault – it is I that have
lost this fight, and you must help me out of it in the best way you can.'

At the very least Lee should have been aware that his artillery ammunition
was not only of suspect quality but also of inadequate quantity to perform its
allotted task. Once the flank attack elements had been stripped from it, the
assault hinged absolutely on winning and maintaining artillery superiority,
and the failure to achieve this is a better choice for the defining moment of
the war than the charge itself. It illustrates the endemic failure in Lee's command structure that kept an incompetent like William Pendleton as Chief of
Artillery; it cruelly underlines the industrial backwardness of the
Confederacy; but above all it reminds us that successful generals are not a
promising cohort among whom to seek the fine human virtues often ascribed
to them. Every benefit later claimed by Lee for the campaign had already been
achieved: military operations had been kept out of ravaged northern Virginia
for the year, abundant stores had been captured and the Army of the Potomac
severely mauled. Longstreet later suggested that Lee was sometimes overcome
by something akin to bloodlust and this remains a plausible explanation why
Pickett's Charge went ahead when the preconditions were not fulfilled.

On the Union side, during Meade's consultation with his corps commanders the previous evening – not a cheerful gathering – Newton stated that Lee
would not be so foolish as to attack Cemetery Ridge because 'they have hammered us into a solid position they cannot whip us out of', and the others
were in general agreement. Several voiced concern about the existing disposi-
tion of the army, although their main worries were for the left flank and that
the army might not be able to remain in place for more than another day
because rations were running out. None of them anticipated what was to
come and the Union centre remained a patchwork of divisions separated from
others of their own corps, holding the positions they had fallen back upon or

rushed to defend during the second day. Although Meade told Gibbon that if an attack were made it would be against his section of the line, the moral ascendancy won by the Confederates was such that the Union army rested where it stood and waited to see what the enemy would do next. At the point of attack this was an irregular, waist-high stone wall along the forward slope of Cemetery Ridge, but the local commanders chose neither to straighten the line nor to order their men to improve the limited cover the wall afforded.

One who did not rest was the ubiquitous Hunt. Through three changes in army command he had systematically requisitioned excess general supplies to build up an off-the-books wagon train in addition to his authorized reserve, itself generous. Whoever else went hungry, his gunners would not, nor did they lack the spares to recondition damaged gun teams. As we have seen, during the night he personally saw to the placing of five batteries to contain the

Confederate cannon

Confederate penetration on lower Culp's Hill. He also visited Cemetery Hill and confirmed the sensible division between Wainwright's mostly rifled guns north of the turnpike and Osborn's, mostly Napoleons, south of it and facing Seminary Ridge. On the far left the late Charles Hazlett's battery on Little Round Top commanded the whole battlefield and a battery of Napoleons was placed at the north-west foot of the hill. Not only was this flank held by the whole of Sykes's corps, but the bulk of Sedgwick's was either in line or in reserve behind the ridge, where the Artillery Reserve park was also located. It seems most unlikely that either the echeloned attack ordered by Lee or Longstreet's preferred option of marching around the Round Tops could possibly have drawn any more Union resources to this front than were already there.

At the centre topography also played a defining role for the Union. The same contour that provided cover for Pickett's advance continued around the Plum Run swale and came back in front of Cemetery Ridge. This rise came to be known as McGilvery's Ridge because he had realized its importance amid the chaos of the previous day's retreat, and Hunt had made it the principal gun line for the left and centre, with ten 3-inch rifles, fourteen Napoleons and an anomalous battery containing four James 14-pounder rifles and two 12-pounder howitzers, all from the Artillery Reserve and under his direct authority. The space between Osborn's guns on Cemetery Hill and McGilvery's Ridge was under the command of Captain John Hazard, Winfield Hancock's artillery chief, with sixteen rifled guns and sixteen Napoleons in six batteries, only one of the latter from the Reserve. This section lacked optimum artillery emplacements, but for Hunt the batteries on either side provided the true strength at the centre:

> It was of the utmost importance to have our line in the best possible condition to meet the assault ... and with that view to subject his troops from the first moment of their advance and whilst beyond musketry range to a heavy concentrated cross fire of artillery.

It cannot be a coincidence that Lee chose a point of attack where Hunt's dead-ly crossfire was partially negated by the terrain, and where the outer guns of Osborn's and McGilvery's gun lines would be masked by the inner batteries. Thanks to the meticulous measurements made by David Shultz and Richard Rollins, we now know that the attack was launched from a base line of 2,700 yards along Seminary Ridge, that both the left of the Pettigrew/Trimble advance and the right of Pickett's covered a straight-line distance of 1,300 yards and that by the time they reached the stone wall they were concentrat-ed on a front of only 540 yards. Since the attacking brigades arrived together thanks to superb discipline under hellish fire, and assuming the outermost regiments employed a quick step of 85 yards per minute (the double-quick for the last 200–300 yards balancing delays caused by fence crossing), the whole advance lasted little more than fifteen minutes in real time. Combat time, when every second drags past shrieking in terror and rage, remains an unquantifiable dimension.

After the battle the Union artillery chiefs were scornful of the siting of the Confederate guns and of their 'practice', pointing out that had they placed more guns to enfilade the Union line from north of Gettysburg, rounds burst-ing long would still have found targets. This is evidently true, but as Latimer had discovered the day before, there were few places from which Richard Ewell's gunners might engage Wainwright's massed rifles with much hope of success. Here the Confederates' preference for mixed batteries also told against them because, of the twenty-two guns they did site to the north and north-east, fourteen were smooth-bore Napoleons of reduced value in the counter-battery role. Nonetheless, possibly because Ewell's corps had captured dependable Union ammunition at Winchester, Osborn's gun line on Cemetery Hill was to be the most ravaged.

With the exception of two long-range Whitworths on Oak Hill, half of Ewell's and all of Hill's and Longstreet's artillery was placed along the Seminary and Peach Orchard ridges. Guns had been placed on Humphreys's Ridge during the night, but dawn revealed how vulnerable these were to fire from the Union left and Alexander rapidly withdrew them. At about 1300 hours, modern time, after a long morning of infantry skirmishing between the ridges accompanied by ranging fire as the Confederate batteries rolled into place, the Whitworths signalled the start of a cannonade by about 180 guns. The next two hours were appalling for the Unionists along Cemetery Ridge, with ammunition caissons blowing up spectacularly, trees being cut down and the inadequacy of the stone wall becoming increasingly apparent during the last half-hour when fire was concentrated upon it. For those on the reverse slope and in particular for the unfortunate artillery team horses it was a nightmare experience.

Hunt rode back and forth telling his battery commanders to conserve ammunition, because however thankful the front-line troops were that much of the bombardment burst long, it did achieve the isolation of the front line,

Union cannon

driving Meade from his headquarters at the Leister House behind the ridge and causing the Artillery Reserve park to move further away from the line. Along with the massacre of the caisson teams this made re-supply difficult, but Hunt's instructions were repeatedly overridden by Hancock, who felt his troops needed the reassurance of hearing their own guns in action. Thus when the infantry assault began Hazard's overheated guns had only canister left and not much of that. Hunt brought forward four full batteries from the Reserve to reinforce and in some cases relieve the guns at the point of attack – leading Hancock to believe erroneously that twelve guns had been removed at the crucial moment – and was firing his revolver at the advancing Rebels when his horse went down and pinned his leg. For the second time in two days he was trampled (he found the cows more alarming) and ever after complained about Hancock's interference.

Hunt believed he could have stopped the Confederate assault with his guns alone, as he had at Malvern Hill the previous year, but for the reasons discussed above this was unlikely and we must give the nod to Hancock. The moral effect of a heavy artillery bombardment was at least as important as the physical damage it did and this was one occasion when even generals had to ride out in front of their men to steady them. Furthermore, during the crucial final moments of the assault most of Osborn's and McGilvery's guns were masked by their own infantry skirmishers and by regiments that marched out from the Union line to flank the attackers. In the end it was men, not machines, who had to turn back Pickett's Charge.

'**M**agnificent, but it's not war', said Maréchal Bosquet as he watched the Light Brigade ride to destruction, and we can say the same of Pickett's Charge with equal justice. It should not have been made, but when indeed shall their glory fade? The most-written-about episode in the most-chronicled battle in history, it remains the case that: 'Many things cannot be described by pen or pencil – such a fight is one. Some hints and incidents may be given but a description, a picture, never. From what is told, the imagination may for itself construct the scene; otherwise he who never saw, can have no adequate idea of what such a battle is.' Not that Lieutenant Frank Haskell, who wrote these words, did not try. Like Chamberlain he blew his own trumpet strenuously, both really trying to understand the sublime madness that overtook them. So millions of less eloquent survivors have felt, after thousands of less celebrated actions, but as a vivid illustration of why more male children are born than female, this one fairly stands for all.

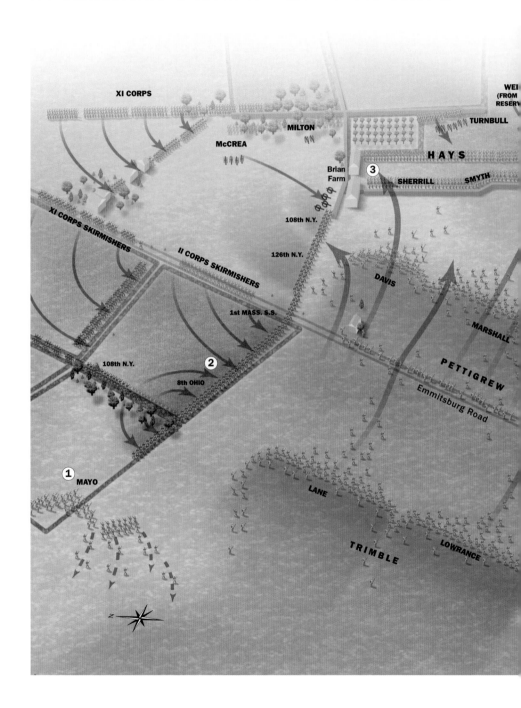

XI CORPS

MILTON

McCREA

WEI
(FROM
RESERV

TURNBULL

HAYS

Brian
Farm

3

SHERRILL   SMYTH

XI CORPS SKIRMISHERS

108th N.Y.

II CORPS SKIRMISHERS

126th N.Y.

DAVIS

1st MASS. S.S.

MARSHALL

108th N.Y.

2

PETTIGREW

8th OHIO

Emmitsburg Road

1   MAYO

LANE

TRIMBLE   LOWRANCE

z

Pickett's Charge

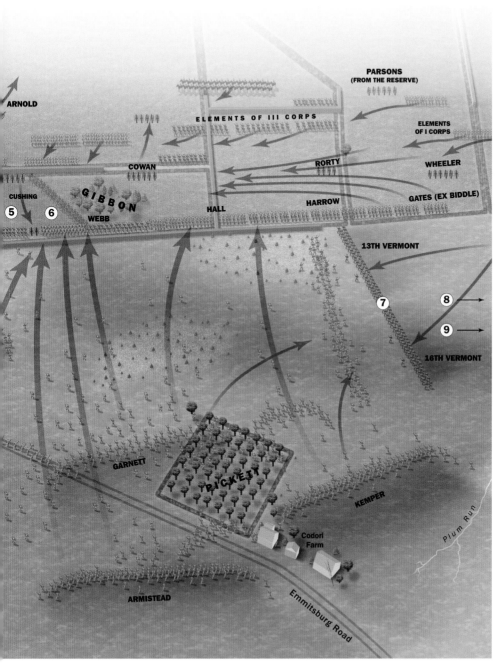

ARNOLD

PARSONS
(FROM THE RESERVE)

ELEMENTS OF III CORPS

ELEMENTS
OF I CORPS

COWAN

RORTY

WHEELER

CUSHING

GIBBON

HALL

HARROW

GATES (EX BIDDLE)

5

6

WEBB

13TH VERMONT

7

8

9

16TH VERMONT

GARNETT

PICKETT

KEMPER

Codori
Farm

Plum Run

ARMISTEAD

Emmitsburg Road

1 8th Ohio and flank companies of 108th New York turn back Mayo's (Brockenbrough's) brigade.

2 These, plus 1st Mass Sharpshooters, 126th NY and McCrea's battery enfilade the charge.

3 11th Mississippi achieves deepest Confederate penetration of the Union line.

4 Weir's fresh battery replaces Arnold's, shatters Marshall's brigade.

5 Junction of Hays's and Gibbon's divisions hit by Fry's, Lowrance's, Garnett's and Armistead's brigades.

6 71st Pennsylvania driven back, Cushing's lead section overrun; 'High Water Mark' - Armistead mortally wounded.

7 13th Vermont joined by 16th to enfilade Kemper's and Garnett's brigades.

8 16th turns and joined by 14th to shatter the late-advancing Florida Brigade.

9 Wilcox's brigade halted by McGilvery's gun line.

George Pickett

If choose one must, the Pettigrew/Trimble advance was the more impressive. Casualties in the preceding forty-eight hours included the commanders of both divisions and four of the six brigades, and now not only the lightly wounded but also cooks, wagon drivers, bandsmen and Provost Guards went forward behind the battle flags of North Carolina, Alabama, Tennessee and Mississippi, in the open and enfiladed from the start by Osborn's guns. John Brockenbrough was absent, mourning the death of his brother, and under Colonel Robert Mayo his small brigade on the Confederate left was turned back by the heavy Union skirmish line in front of the Emmitsburg Road. This left the latter, most prominently 8th Ohio from Carroll's brigade, free to wrap around the left of the Confederate advance, along with four Napoleons run forward to enfilade the last stage of this assault at point-blank range.

Pettigrew's division advanced in two well-spaced ranks and consisted of brigades led by Joseph Davis, Pettigrew's old command now under Colonel James Marshall and Archer's old command under Colonel Burkett Fry. Isaac Trimble's part-division followed in a second wave formed by Brigadier General James Lane's brigade and Scales's old command now under Colonel Lee Lowrance, similarly deployed and about 100 yards behind the first. Davis, Marshall and Lane attacked a section of the stone wall defended by perhaps half the 2,000 Unionists of Colonel Eliakim Sherrill's (ex-Willard's) and Colonel Thomas Smyth's brigades of Brigadier General Alexander Hays's division, with the rest in reserve on the reverse slope of the ridge behind them.

For all their losses during the advance, it is inconceivable that the attackers did not outnumber the defenders, but Bonaparte's dictum held true – the moral is to the physical as three to one. With their officers down, fire pouring in from the flanks but above all with no sign of panic among the troops to their front, the attackers' momentum was spent just reaching the wall. Union firepower was enhanced by Hays's precaution of getting his men to collect abandoned rifles so that most had two or more to hand, and by keeping them from firing prematurely by performing arms drill amid the bombardment. He also rode everywhere in front of his men, laughing and calling out encouragement. 'Hurrah boys', he cried. 'We're giving them hell!' They could see it was true and drew further strength from his exemplary contempt for danger.

> Hurrah boys, we're giving them hell!
>
> Brig. Gen. Alexander Hays

The Confederates preserved their dressing until they reached the Emmitsburg Road and then some, not all, rushed the remaining distance. Spared the debacle on the first day, 11th Mississippi now advanced on the heavily enfiladed left and deserves a special mention for penetrating the Union line around the Bryan Farm, where the gallant Sherrill fell fighting them. But Marshall's brigade paid the highest price when Gulian Weir's battery, as it had the day before, rode up in time to shred a promising Confederate advance with double canister. A surrendering Confederate asked, 'Where can I go to get out of this hellish fire?' With commendable honesty Weir reported pointing him to the rear and saying 'I wish I could go with you', because the Confederate guns on this front reopened as soon as they saw groups of men falling back, without concern for their own wounded and captured. It would be easier to accept this as a logical if heartless action designed to discourage a counter-attack if Hill's artillery commander had earlier run some guns forward, although this was also due to Pendleton having withdrawn some fully replenished batteries intended for use in the close support role both here and on Pickett's front, where Porter Alexander certainly would have made good use of them.

Fry's Tennessee/Alabama brigade and Lowrance's North Carolinians penetrated the angle where the stone wall ran perpendicular from Hays's to Webb's brigades, held by the same 71st Pennsylvania that had found night fighting so little to its taste on Culp's Hill the night before. Hit simultaneously by the Virginians led by Brigadier Generals Richard Garnett and Lewis Armistead,

Armistead
leading his
brigade into
the angle

this regiment and part of Lieutenant Alonzo Cushing's battery stood until the last minute, Cushing falling at the wall, then pulled back through the copse of trees. Webb's second line (the continuation of Alexander Hays's front) was thinly held by 72nd Pennsylvania, reinforced only by Hays's Provost Guard and 99th Pennsylvania from Ward's division of Birney's corps, which had played such an active part in the defence of Devil's Den the day before, but these and Captain Andrew Cowan's late-arriving battery from Sedgwick's VI Corps turned the area within the walls of the angle and around the copse of trees into an abattoir.

Although by this time Trimble, Marshall, Fry, Lowrance, Lane and most of their regimental commanders had fallen, historians have paid far more attention to the doomed officers of Pickett's division. Michael Shaara's *The Killer Angels* and the TV special based on it made much of Garnett riding into battle because of a foot injury, but Brigadier General James Kemper also rode, as did several of their regimental commanders, and all paid the penalty. The abiding image is of Armistead, who wisely advanced on foot and made his officers do likewise, putting his hat on the end of his sword and leading the brigade in the rush to the 'high water mark'. In fact Pettigrew's men penetrated further, but the place where Armistead was mortally wounded and, as he lay dying, was distressed to learn that his good friend Winfield Hancock had also been hit, is where the first of many monuments was placed, when the charge was beginning its metamorphosis from a savage struggle for supremacy into a symbol of reconciliation.

The lines of advance taken by both Pettigrew/Trimble and Pickett pinned down Union troops respectively to the left and right of their aiming point. Although the obliqueness of the northern advance was more immediately apparent it still seemed menacing to those on Cemetery Hill and panicked one of Osborn's gun captains into a precipitate retreat. The first part of Pickett's dog-leg advance aimed directly at the line behind and to the north of McGilvery's gun line, held by units that had been routed the day before (Caldwell's division and elements of Birney's corps). These remained rooted to the spot well after Pickett's men turned to the oblique along the line of the Emmitsburg Road, a manoeuvre performed with such cool precision that it elicited the admiration of both sides.

The advance of Pickett's division to the diagonal of the Emmitsburg Road was not immediately brought under heavy artillery fire, McGilvery's gun line having a less clear line of fire and being further away from the Virginians' start line than Osborn's from Pettigrew's/ Trimble's. The first wave consisted of Garnett's and Kemper's brigades in two well-spaced lines, with Armistead's formed in a single line close behind them, so that observers saw the advance as three equally spaced

Alexander Hays

lines of two ranks each. Because he was the only general officer in either attack to survive the campaign intact (Pettigrew was killed during the retreat while Davis nearly died of typhoid), doubts have occasionally been cast on Pickett's leadership, but in truth his division performed as well as any in the entire war and he and his staff rode forward of the Codori Farm and about 200 yards from the stone wall, the same distance as the other divisional commanders and their staffs. All of these mounted groups made inviting targets well within range of dozens of guns and thousands of rifles, and Pickett was lucky not to share the fate of Pettigrew and Trimble.

They had done their duty well and the two main infantry advances were nearly perfectly co-ordinated, but the essential element of combined assault failed. As noted, the guns supporting Pettigrew and Trimble were not run forward, although well enough supplied to fire on friend and foe alike after the charge failed. The reverse occurred to the south, where Porter Alexander briskly advanced Major James Dearing's brigade and some others to the Emmitsburg Road in support of Pickett's division, but here they rapidly exhausted their ammunition. The blame for this ultimately rests with Longstreet, who could have pulled rank on Pendleton. Instead he attempted to delegate responsibility for launching the attack onto Alexander, a colonel and not even his senior artillery officer. The first of two notes he sent him speaks volumes:

> If the artillery fire does not have the effect to drive off the enemy or greatly demoralize him so as to make our efforts pretty certain, I would prefer that you should not advise General Pickett to make the charge. I shall rely a great deal on your good judgement to determine the matter, and shall expect you to let General Pickett know when the moment offers.

Longstreet also delegated responsibility for ordering Wilcox and Lang forward to Pickett, without stressing that they should all advance together and without rescinding the order after he decided the advance had become pointless. He later said that Lee asked him why he had not cancelled the whole charge and he replied that he had no authority to do so. This rings false on two counts: Lee was too punctilious to ask such a leading question and Longstreet did in fact override Richard Anderson's order for Wright and Posey to advance in support of Pettigrew and Trimble, saying it would be a useless sacrifice. But who knows what effect the sight of them coming up might have had upon the first wave, in particular those who stuck at the Emmitsburg Road?

The delayed Wilcox/Lang advance meant that the Union skirmishers wrapped around Pickett's right as they had Pettigrew's/Trimble's left. The 16th Vermont was joined by the 13th, two of the largest regiments in the Union army with their morale sky-high after their pursuit of Wright's brigade the evening before. Two of Kemper's and one of Garnett's regiments were compelled to wheel away from the assault to counter their galling fire and the attacking brigades finally lost alignment.

The intervention of the Vermonters was so decisive that Hancock sought to take the credit for it, but that belongs to George Stannard, who had drilled them for five hours a day while on garrison duty around Washington. While other units collapsed into struggling knots of men firing at will, the 'Paper Collar Brigade' formed perfect lines in the open field and fired volley after crashing volley. When Pickett's men fell back Stannard left the 13th to collect prisoners, turned the 16th around and marched it along with the 14th to serve Lang's luckless Floridians the same. Of the units known to have been engaged by the metronomic 16th Vermont, 8th Virginia was literally annihilated and the Florida Brigade did not have enough men left to form a viable regiment.

Even so, Pickett's division had also achieved numerical superiority at the point of attack. The bulk of Sedgwick's corps was too far away to affect the outcome and there simply were no substantial reserves positioned behind Gibbon's division to contain a breakthrough. There is abundant evidence that despite leadership quite as heroic as Hays's, the men of Webb's brigade nearly broke – indeed he himself reported that at one moment he feared disgrace. But while admittedly the fighting quality of the defenders was higher than the troops shattered by Barksdale's Mississippians the day before, the attackers were not devils incarnate either. The moment passed, the Confederates wavered and suddenly every Union regiment within range piled into the struggle, as Hancock recalled:

> The situation was now very peculiar. The men of all the brigades [plus elements of I, III and VI Corps] had in some measure lost their regimental organization, but individually they were firm. The ambition of individual commanders to promptly cover the point penetrated by the enemy, the smoke of battle, and the intensity of the close engagement, caused this confusion.

Not really. What caused the confusion was Union command failure, directly attributable to Meade's over-reliance on Hancock and indifference to hierarchy. Sedgwick was second in seniority to Slocum and could have been put in charge of the left wing, freeing Hancock to tidy up and consolidate the centre. Meade had expressed a vague hope of counter-attacking on the left, but he ignored Sedgwick and cannibalized his corps, the only force under his command that might have been able to exploit the repulse of Pickett's

Charge. Probably not, however, because although some of the retreating Confederates reached Seminary Ridge and kept going, across the army discipline held, as Kilpatrick soon discovered on the far left when he sent Brigadier General Elon Farnsworth's cavalry brigade into what he seems to have believed would be a pursuit.

Given a choice of what unbroken infantry they would least like to charge, probably the Union cavalry would have selected the dead-eyed 1st Texas, and it was they who killed Farnsworth and stopped his charge. Still later that day 'Grumble' Jones's Virginia cavalry brigade at Fairfield, a crucial crossroads behind Lee's army, trounced 6th US Cavalry. Had Buford been there instead of Brigadier General Wesley Merritt, he would probably have committed the entire Reserve Brigade and cut Lee's main line of retreat, however temporarily. But because these two disasters were the result of his orders, Pleasonton claimed victory and heaped praise upon Kilpatrick and Merritt, thereby in his mind balancing the earlier initiatives of his two other over-competent brigadiers. Once again demonstrating poor character judgement, Meade accepted his cavalry commander's self-serving reports at face value and recommended him for promotion, something he was to regret when Pleasonton traduced him to the Joint Committee of Congress in early 1864.

L incoln, whose entire military experience had been to collect a militia stipend during the Black Hawk War thirty years previously, was convinced that Meade should now have destroyed Lee's army and his opinion was shared by Halleck, whose crawl from Pittsburgh Landing to Corinth after the battle of Shiloh set a record for slow pursuit that still stands. Presuming on acquaintanceship from their days together at West Point, Union transportation chief Herman Haupt paid a brief visit to Meade to tell him what he should do and when his advice was not heeded rushed to Washington to add his carping to the wounded-hero posturing of Dan Sickles. If any of these had performed their own duties to the exacting standards they set for Meade, he might have been in a position to do more than follow Lee back to the Potomac. It is absurd to think that he could have done in eleven days what it took Grant over a year to achieve with greater resources against

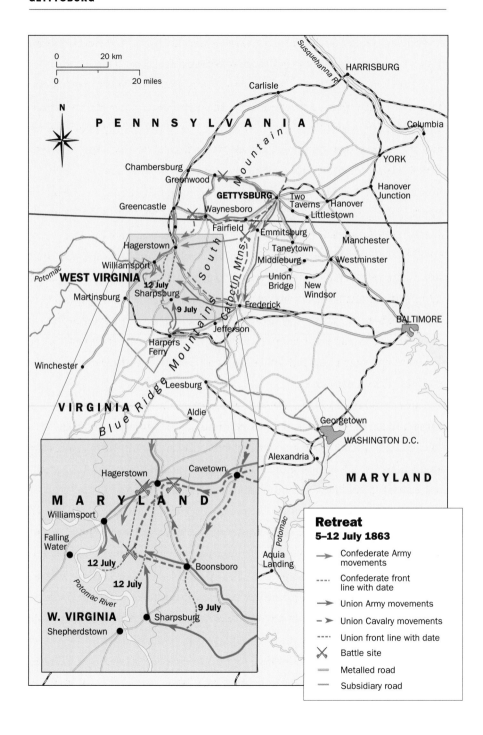

Susquehanna R.

HARRISBURG

Carlisle

Columbia

P E N N S Y L V A N I A

Mountain

YORK

Chambersburg

Hanover
Junction

Greenwood

GETTYSBURG

Two
Taverns

Hanover

Greencastle

Waynesboro

Littlestown

Fairfield

Emmitsburg

Manchester

Hagerstown

South

Taneytown

Williamsport

Middleburg

Westminster

WEST VIRGINIA

Potomac

Union
Bridge

New
Windsor

12 July

Catoctin Mtns

Sharpsburg

Martinsburg

9 July

Frederick

BALTIMORE

Mountains

Jefferson

Harpers
Ferry

Winchester

Blue Ridge Mountains

Leesburg

V I R G I N I A

Aldie

Georgetown

WASHINGTON D.C.

Alexandria

M A R Y L A N D

Hagerstown

Cavetown

M A R Y L A N D

Williamsport

Falling
Water

Potomac

12 July

Aquia
Landing

Boonsboro

12 July

9 July

Potomac River

W. VIRGINIA

Sharpsburg

Shepherdstown

Retreat
5–12 July 1863

→ Confederate Army
movements

---- Confederate front
line with date

➤ Union Army movements

- ➤ Union Cavalry movements

---- Union front line with date

✕ Battle site

═ Metalled road

— Subsidiary road

a weakened enemy, and at last able to break the shackles of Lincoln's/Halleck's insistence that he keep the Union army between Lee and Washington.

'We are tired of scientific leaders,' Alexander Hays later wrote, 'and regard strategy as it is called – a humbug. Next thing to cowardice. What we want is a leader who will go ahead.' This probably explains why this splendid warrior was still a brigadier general when he was killed at the Wilderness eleven months later, for the Confederates were anxious to repay the treatment they had received and would have been delighted if Meade had 'gone ahead' against them. Lee was above all a deadly counter-puncher and had Meade followed his own instincts, which were not unlike Hays's, the Army of Northern Virginia could still have crowned the campaign with another Fredericksburg. More thoughtful Union commanders recognized the unpalatable fact that they could only defeat Lee's army under very favourable circumstances, so the question is whether such circumstances arose between the repulse of Pickett's Charge and the moment when the last of Lee's army crossed the floodwaters of the Potomac eleven days later.

Retreat/pursuit from Gettysburg

Edwin Coddington and Meade's biographer Freeman Cleaves, both of whom argued that Meade was far more sinned against than sinning, nonetheless agreed that there were two such opportunities: the first was immediately after the battle, when Lee gained a day's march and Meade might have sent a substantial force to hold him up at Fairfield; the second when the Confederate defensive lines around the Potomac bridgehead were left unprobed, permitting Lee to make an orderly withdrawal across the river. The dilemma these pose is that while a lesser man would have thrown away lives to silence the baying of the press and his political masters, a greater general, one possessed of what Liddell Hart called 'the brutality essential for war', might have done so because his predatory instinct would have been aroused by a retreating enemy.

Meade's nature was as paradoxical as Lee's. Confederate Lieutenant General Daniel Hill said he was 'one of our most dreaded foes', and he was known as 'the snapping turtle' by his subordinates, yet he seems to have regarded his aggressiveness as something to guard against and suppress, as he did on these occasions when he summoned informal councils of war, surely knowing that with Reynolds dead and both Hancock and Sickles seriously wounded the consensus of his remaining corps commanders would be in favour of caution. Nor should we underestimate the element of physical and nervous exhaustion that must have overcome him in the adrenalin let-down following the battle, and that he had at that time been in command of the army for only nine days, nearly sleepless, eating on the run, crowded with unfamiliar responsibilities and without even a decent topographical map of Pennsylvania to work with. It is surprising he did not break under the strain.

Perhaps, in a subtle way, he did. Gettysburg was the greatest bloodbath of the war and it takes a very particular type of man to 'pour it on' after such an experience. One Union officer recorded these feelings about the Confederate dead:

> ... some sitting up against trees or rocks stark dead with their eyes wide open staring at you as if they were still alive – others with their heads blown off with shell or round shot others shot through the head with musket balls. Some struck by a shell in the breast or abdomen and blown almost to pieces, others with their hands up as though to fend off the bullets we fired upon them, others laying against a stump or stone with a testament in their hand or a likeness of a friend, as if wounded and had lived for some time. O it was an awful sight!

Also, like many others in his army, Meade had friends and family fighting for the other side. Three of his nephews died in Confederate service and as he fought at Gettysburg Grant's troopers were driving his sister from her home near Vicksburg. After Lee surrendered at Appomattox, Meade rode to pay his respects and encountered his wife's brother-in-law, a Confederate general he had been besieging in Petersburg. Apart from atrocities by irregulars like the psychopath William Quantrill this was one of the least barbaric civil wars ever fought and while we cannot doubt Meade's will to win, he had neither the crusader's persecuting fanaticism of a Stonewall Jackson nor the cold-blooded ruthlessness of a William Tecumseh Sherman. Lincoln eventually found the predators he needed, but although Meade was left in command of the Army of the Potomac for the duration, he was not one of them.

After three days of blasting heat, a thunderstorm broke in the evening of 3 July and torrential rain fell for days. Initially this assisted Lee by concealing the withdrawal begun the night of 4 July, after he realized that Meade was not going to do him the favour of assaulting his now well-entrenched line on Seminary Ridge. But to his rear it swelled the Potomac, such that his intended crossing at Williamsport/Falling Waters was no longer fordable. Meanwhile Major General William French, commander of the 10,000-strong Harper's Ferry garrison that had withdrawn to Frederick at the start of the campaign, sent a cavalry force to destroy Lee's only pontoon bridge. Too much has been made of this – it was a potential catastrophe only if the Union army had been close behind the retreating Confederates, or if French had been ordered to cross the Potomac and contest the Falling Waters crossing from the south. But not far away, at Antietam, the bloodiest single-day battle of the war had been fought the last time Lee seemed to be trapped against the Potomac and there was a marked lack of enthusiasm among the Union commanders for repeating the experience.

If Lee's army had indeed been broken in spirit, as those far from the area of operations believed, then the Union cavalry would have had easy pickings. Instead, during the night of 4–5 July in a mountain pass west of Fairfield, Kilpatrick with about 3,500 men took hours to overcome about 400 troopers of 1st Maryland and 4th North Carolina (Custer once again performing the breakthrough charge) to fall on part of Ewell's wagon train and capture several hundred wounded. But the next day, when 'Kill-cavalry' rode into Hagerstown seeking to cut off Lee's main wagon train, he was given the right about by a scratch force under none other than Alfred Iverson, he of the disaster at McPherson's Wood on the first day at Gettysburg. At the same time

Buford, reunited with the Reserve Brigade and now in command of about 4,000 troopers, approached from the other side of town and was stopped by the irregulars of Brigadier General John Imboden's brigade. Finally, when Kilpatrick and Buford together attempted to cut off the dwindling Confederate rearguard at the Falling Waters crossing on 14 July, although over 700 prisoners were taken and the gallant James Pettigrew was killed, the episode was so overblown by Pleasonton that an outraged Lee issued a refutation.

Three Confederate prisoners captured at Gettysburg

These skirmishes shed a bright light on Confederate morale during the retreat. At Hagerstown Kilpatrick was driven out by the most-punished infantry brigade in Lee's army, while Buford was stopped by a relatively small number of the least dependable horsemen in Confederate service. At Falling Waters the infantry who held open the jaws of the Union cavalry pincer long enough for the rest to escape were from Brockenbrough's brigade, which had shown so little perseverance during the charge on 3 July, and the survivors of Lowrance's brigade, which had been severely mauled. That the detritus of Lee's army was able to prevail over Meade's best-equipped, least-combat-diminished and (in Buford's case) superbly led troops must surely resolve any doubt about what would have happened if the Union army had made a general assault.

Furthermore Lee's army had built a double ring of field fortifications from near Hagerstown to the river and had turned a naturally strong position into what some Union engineers reckoned to have been the most formidable defensive works they ever saw. The informed criticism of Meade was that he did not maintain an aggressive skirmisher presence close to these works, which might have detected when the troops holding them began to withdraw. Perhaps, but we should remember that the Confederates were no mean skirmishers themselves, and that Sickles's strong forward presence did not detect McLaws's division and Alexander's batteries forming for attack on 2 July in a not very dense wood and in broad daylight. The deciding vote in this matter must surely be Lee's disgust that Meade chose not to attack him.

The river crossing is the conventional place to end accounts of the Gettysburg campaign, although operations continued. Twenty days after having command of the Army of the Potomac thrust upon him, Meade responded to increasingly strident criticism from Lincoln/Halleck by offering to resign. It is a measure of his self-restraint and unwillingness to emulate the moral cowardice of Hooker that he did not resign outright. Lincoln's disappointment may also have been tempered by a politely indignant personal letter from Oliver Howard which affirmed that success at Gettysburg was not the foregone conclusion the President seemed to think, and that it was due to the 'energetic operations' of Meade before the battle and his well-timed deployment of reserves during it. Although Howard had been in favour of an attack at Williamsport, he modestly commented:

> ... with the evident difficulties in our way, the uncertainty of a success, and the strong conviction of our best military minds against the risk, I must say that I think the general acted wisely. ... We have, if I may be allowed to say it, a commanding general in whom all the officers with whom I have contact express complete confidence.

Lincoln's impatience was ungenerous and most historians have given it undue importance. It is not my purpose to point out that the idol had feet of clay – like all men, Lincoln was all clay and would have been the first to admit it. My quarrel is with the hagiography that has turned even a petulant letter he wrote and chose not to send into evidence against Meade, as though there had been better instruments to hand. Maybe the colder, more cerebral Slocum would have been a better choice, but he was as guilty as Meade of failing to conceal his opinion that journalists and politicians were the rabble that, with the exception of Lincoln and very few others, they unquestionably were.

Meade's achievement was all the greater because the forces at his disposal were of such extremely variable quality. Recruitment that depended heavily on paid substitutes and bounty men was bound to sweep a large criminal element into uniform, and those citizens of Maryland and Pennsylvania who experienced the passage of both armies judged the Unionists a far greater scourge. Meade later ordered gallows built in each corps encampment, just as George Washington was finally compelled to do during the War of Independence. Short-termism also meant that, for example, immediately after the battle the invaluable Vermonters' nine months' service expired and they went home, to be replaced by the rawest of raw recruits. With all these handicaps Meade faced the finest army the Confederacy ever put in the field, led by the most respected general on either side, and fought it to a standstill. Certainly Lee was not well and his corps commanders underperformed notably; but even so the Union army rallied after a disastrous first day and did not break again despite relentless pressure. It was the Confederates who on two successive days looked over their shoulders in vain for reinforcements, and it was no accident that time after time Union reserves appeared at the right time and place.

'O it was an awful sight'

Union Army
pontoon bridges
across the
Potomac at
Berlin, 21 July
1863

Meade deserved better treatment than he received from his political masters, but the grotesque terms of the 28 January 1864 Congressional Vote of Thanks underline the problems Lincoln no less than Meade had to deal with: '... the gratitude of the American people, and the thanks of their Representatives in Congress, are due, and are hereby tendered, to Major General Joseph Hooker [!] and the officers and soldiers of the Army of the Potomac ... and to Major General George G. Meade and Major General Oliver O. Howard ...' In noble contrast, Lincoln's immortal words at the dedication of the National Cemetery at Gettysburg two months earlier should be considered the military historian's charter and make a fittingly beautiful epitaph for this and many another battle:

> In a larger sense we cannot dedicate, we cannot consecrate, we cannot hallow this ground. The brave men, living and dead, who struggled here, have consecrated it far above our power to add or detract. The world will little note, nor long remember, what we say here, but it can never forget what they did here.

Appendices

APPENDIX A   **MEADE'S PIPE CREEK CIRCULAR**   202

APPENDIX B   **ORDER OF BATTLE AND CASUALTIES –**
ARMY OF THE POTOMAC, USA   204

APPENDIX C   **ORDER OF BATTLE AND CASUALTIES –**
ARMY OF NORTHERH VIRGINIA, CSA   215

APPENDIX D   **DRAMATIS PERSONAE**   224

BIBLIOGRAPHY   229

INDEX   231

HEADQUARTERS ARMY OF THE POTOMAC,
TANEYTOWN, JULY 1, 1863. 12 A.M.

[Italics and parentheses added]

From information received, the commanding general is satisfied that the object of the movement of the army in this direction has been accomplished, viz., the relief of Harrisburg, and the prevention of the enemy's intended invasion of Philadelphia, &c., beyond the Susquehanna. *It is no longer his intention to assume the offensive* until the enemy's movements or position should render such an operation certain of success.

If the enemy assume the offensive, and attack, it is his intention, *after holding them in check sufficiently long*, to withdraw the trains and other impedimenta; to withdraw the army from its present position, and form line of battle with the left resting in the neighborhood of Middleburg, and the right at Manchester, the general direction being that of Pipe Creek. For this purpose, General Reynolds, in command of the left, will withdraw the force at present at Gettysburg, two corps [Reynolds and Howard] by the road to Taneytown and Westminster, and, after crossing Pipe Creek, deploy toward Middleburg. The corps at Emmitsburg [Sickles] will be withdrawn, via Mechanicsville, [changed to 'should be withdrawn via Mechanicstown' in addendum] to Middleburg, or, if a more direct route can be found leaving Taneytown to their left, to withdraw direct to Middleburg. General Slocum will assume command of the two corps at Hanover [Sykes] and Two Taverns [Slocum], and withdraw them, via Union Mills, deploying one to the right and one to the left, after crossing Pipe Creek, connecting on the left with General Reynolds, and communicating his right to General Sedgwick at Manchester, who will connect with him and form the right.

The time for falling back can only be developed by circumstances. *Whenever such circumstances arise as would seem to indicate the necessity for falling back and assuming this general line indicated*, notice of such movement will be at once communicated to these HEADQUARTERS and to all adjoining corps commanders. The Second Corps [Hancock] now at Taneytown will be held in reserve in the vicinity of Uniontown and Frizellburg, to be thrown to the point of strongest attack, should the enemy make it. In the event of these movements being necessary, the trains and impedimenta will all be sent to the rear of Westminster. Corps commanders, with their officers commanding artillery and the divisions, should make themselves thoroughly familiar with the country indicated, all the roads and positions, *so that no possible confusion can ensue*, and that the movement, if made, be done with good order, precision, and care, without loss or any detriment to the morale of the troops. The commanders of corps are requested to communicate at once the nature of their present positions, and their ability to hold them in case of any sudden attack at any point by the enemy.

This order is communicated, *that a general plan, perfectly understood by all*, may be had *for receiving attack, if made in strong force, upon any portion of our present position. Developments may cause the commanding general to assume the offensive from his present positions.* The Artillery Reserve will, in the event of the general movement indicated, move to the rear of Frizellburg, and be placed in position, or sent to corps, as circumstances may require, under the general supervision of the chief of artillery. The chief quartermaster will, in case of the general movement indicated, give directions for the orderly and proper position of the trains in rear of Westminster.

All the trains will keep well to the right of the road in moving, and, in case of any accident requiring a halt, the team must be hauled out of the line, and not delay the movements. The trains ordered to Union Bridge in these events will be sent to Westminster. General HEADQUARTERS will be, in case of this movement, at Frizellburg; General Slocum as near Union Mills as the line will render best for him; General Reynolds at or near the road from Taneytown to Frizellburg. The chief of artillery will examine the line, and select positions for artillery. The cavalry will be held on the right and left flanks after the movement is completed. Previous to its completion, it will, as now directed, cover the front and exterior lines, well out. The commands must be prepared for a movement, and, in the event of the enemy attacking us on the ground indicated herein, to follow up any repulse.

The chief signal officer will examine the line thoroughly, and at once, upon the commencement of this movement, extend telegraphic communication from each of the following points to general HEADQUARTERS near Frizellburg, viz., Manchester, Union Mills, Middleburg, and the Taneytown road.

All true Union people should be advised to harass and annoy the enemy in every way, to send in information, and taught how to do it; giving regiments by number of colors, number of guns, generals' names, &c. All their supplies brought to us will be paid for, and not fall into the enemy's hands. Roads and ways to move to the right or left of the general line should be studied and thoroughly understood. All movements of troops should be concealed, and our dispositions kept from the enemy. Their knowledge of these dispositions would be fatal to our success, and the greatest care must be taken to prevent such an occurrence.

By command of Major-General Meade:
S. WILLIAMS, Assistant Adjutant-General.

APPENDIX B **ORDER OF BATTLE AND CASUALTIES**

ARMY OF THE POTOMAC, USA

MAJ. GEN. GEORGE MEADE COMMANDING

ARMY HEADQUARTERS

Maj. Gen. Butterfield	Chief of Staff
Brig. Gen. Warren	Chief of Engineers
	(the Engineer Corps was at Westminster)
Brig. Gen. Hunt	Chief of Artillery
Brig. Gen. Patrick	Provost Marshal General
	(commanding 549 infantry & 585 cavalry)
Brig. Gen. Williams	Assistant Adjutant General
Brig. Gen. Ingalls	Chief Quartermaster
Capt. Norton	Chief Signals Officer (15 officers and 30 men)
Lt. Edie	Acting Chief Ordnance Officer
Dr. Letterman	Medical Director

HEADQUARTERS GUARD

49 escort (Oneida New York Cavalry) + 250 attached during battle
(1st Massachussetts, previously with VI Corps)
(Staff loss – 4 wounded)

NOTES

• The best estimate for Union battle strength at Gettysburg is 93,534, with 3,149 killed, 14,503 wounded and 5,161 missing, for a total of 22,813 and a casualty rate of 24.4%. But if we subtract Sedgwick's marginalized 13,601 men, the figures are 22,571 casualties out of 79,933 engaged for a casualty rate of 28.2%. If we also factor in the different methodology employed by the Confederates to calculate their killed, wounded and missing (see Appendix C), the casualty returns for the two armies become uncannily similar, a better reflection of a very even battle.

• Contrast the seniority of Meade's HQ staff with Lee's, and the crucial addition of a signals group. In theory the Provost Marshall General also commanded many of the cavalry and infantry units shown as attached to corps and division HQs, but in practice the policing function was decentralized and some of these detachments were used as a tactical reserve.

• Contrast also the standardization of ordnance. The main types were the wrought-iron 3-inch ordnance rifles, the cast-iron 10-pounder (2.9-inch) Parrott rifles (10P) and the bronze 12-pounder (4.62-inch) Napoleon smooth-bores. The only exceptions were the heavy artillery in the Second Volunteer Brigade in the reserve, with 14-pounder James (J) rifles, 12-pounder howitzers (12H) and 20-pounder (3.67-inch) Parrotts (20P). Uniformly equipped batteries hugely simplified resupply, the observation of fall of shot and resulting concentration of fire.

• Cannon weights and ranges with normal loads at 5-degree elevation were as follows: 12H – 778 lbs/1,100 yds; 3-inch ordnance rifle – 816 lbs/1,850 yds; 10P – 890 lbs/2,000 yds; Napoleon – 1,227 lbs/1,620 yds; 20P – 1,750 lbs/2,100 yds. The rifles had far superior performance at higher elevations. Numbers in simple brackets (x) are guns captured, in square brackets [x] captured and recovered.

• The following abbreviations are also employed: C = captured; D = drunk; K = killed; M = missing; P = promoted; W = wounded; * = Congressional Medal of Honor (awarded as late as 1907).

• Sources: John Busey & David Martin, *Regimental Strengths and Losses at Gettysburg* (Highstown: Longstreet House, 1994); Edwin Coddington, *The Gettysburg Campaign: A Study in Command* (New York: Touchstone, 1997); Harry Pfanz, *Gettysburg: The Second Day* and *Gettysburg Culp's Hill and Cemetery Hill* (Chapel Hill: University of North Carolina Press, 1987 & 1993); Stephen Sears, *Chancellorsville* (New York: Houghton Mifflin, 1996).

Division	Brigade	Regiment or Battery		Chancellorsville			Gettysburg				
				K	W	M	Battle Strength	KIA	WIA	MIA	% loss
Brig. Gen. WADSWORTH (11 Staff)	Iron Brigade Brig. Gen. Meredith (W) Col. Robinson (15 Staff/Band)	Col. Williams	19th Indiana	1	4	1	308	27	133	50	68
		Col. Morrow (W)	24th Michigan – see note	4	20	0	496	67	210	86	73
		Col. Fairchild (W)	2nd Wisconsin	0	5	1	302	26	155	52	77
		Lt. Col. Dawes	6th Wisconsin (*)	3	13	0	344	30	116	22	49
		Col. Robinson	7th Wisconsin (*)	3	5	1	364	21	105	52	49
							1,814				
	Brig. Gen.Cutler (17 Staff/Band)	Maj. Grover (K)	76th New York	0	3	0	375	32	132	70	62
		Col. Fowler	84th NY (14th Brooklyn)	1	22	23	318	13	105	99	68
		Col. Biddle (W)	95th New York	0	4	5	241	7	62	46	47
		Lt. Col. Miller (W)	147th New York				380	60	144	92	78
		Col. Hoffman	56th Pennsylvania				252	14	61	55	52
		Col. Grover	7th Indiana – see note	1	4	0	434	2	5	3	2
							2,000				
Brig.Gen. ROBINSON (w) (8 Staff)	Brig. Gen. Paul (W) Cols. Leonard & Root + Lyle and Coulter from Baxter's brigade (3 Staff)	Col. Tilden (c)	16th Maine				298	9	59	164	78
		Col. Leonard (W)	13th Massachussetts	2	7	0	284	7	77	101	65
		Col. Root (W, C)	94th New York	0	1	0	411	12	58	175	60
		Col. Prey (W)	104th New York	0	3	0	286	11	91	92	68
		Col. MacThompson (W)	107th Pennsylvania	0	1	0	255	11	56	98	65
							1,534				
	Brig. Gen. Baxter (4 Staff)	Col. Bates (W)	12th Massachussetts	0	3	5	261	5	52	62	46
		Lt. Col. Moesch	83rd NY (9th Militia)	0	4	1	199	6	18	58	41
		Col. Wheelock (C)	97th New York				236	12	36	78	53
		Col. Coulter (W)	11th Penn – see note				270	1	66	60	47
		Maj. Foust (W)	88th Pennsylvania	0	2	0	274	4	55	51	40
		Col. Lyle	90th Penn (*) – see note	1	7	0	208	8	45	40	45
							1,448				
Maj. Gen. DOUBLEDAY (P) Rowley (D) DOUBLEDAY (13 Staff)	Brig. Gen. Rowley (P, D) Col. Biddle (W) (8 Staff)	Col. Gates	80th New York				287	35	111	24	59
		Col. Biddle (W)	121st Penn. (I Corps HQ)	0	2	1	263	12	106	61	68
		Col. Cummins (K)	142nd Pennsylvania				336	13	128	70	63
		Lt. Col. McFarland (W)	151st Pennsylvania	1	6	9	467	51	211	75	72
							1353				
60 Infantry (149th Pennsylvania)	Col. Stone (W, C) Col. Wister (W) Col. Dana (2 Staff)	Col. Dana	143rd Pennsylvania (*)	0	1	0	465	21	141	91	54
		Lt. Col. Dwight (W)	149th Penn. (Division HQ)	0	1	0	450	53	172	111	75
		Col. Wister (W)	150th Pennsylvania (2*)	0	1	0	400	35	152	77	66
							1,315				
	Col. Stannard (W) Col. Randall (6 Staff)	Col. Randall	13th Vermont (*)	Arrived at Gettysburg evening of 1 July			636	10	103	10	19
		Col. Nichols	14th Vermont				647	19	67	21	16
		Col. Veazey (K)	16th Vermont				661	16	102	1	18
							1,944				
Corps Artillery	Col. Wainwright (7 Staff)	Capt. Hall	2nd Maine Light, B (6 x 3-inch rifles)				117	0	18	0(1)	15
		Capt. Stevens (W)	5th Maine Light, E (6 x Napoleons)	6	22	0	119	3	13	7	19
		Capt. Reynolds (W)	1st New York Light, L (6 x 3-inch rifles)	0	8	0	124	1	15	1(1)	14
		Capt. Cooper	1st Pennsylvania Light, B (4 x 3-inch rifles)				106	3	9	0	11
		Lt. Stewart (W)	4th United States, B (6 x Napoleons)	0	1	2	123	2	31	3	29
12,222 all ranks	8 brigades	37 regiments, 5 batteries, 28 guns		All ranks casualties, Gettysburg				666	3,231	2,162	50

XI CORPS – Maj. Gens. HOWARD (P); SCHURZ; HOWARD
11 Staff – 86 Cavalry (1st Indiana/17th Pennsylvania) – 40 Infantry (8th New York)

Division	Brigade	Regiment or Battery		Chancellorsville K	W	M	Gettysburg Battle Strength	KIA	WIA	MIA	% loss
Brig. Gen. BARLOW (W, C) Ames (4 staff)	Col. von Gilsa (2 staff)	Lt. Col. von Einsiedal	41st New York	2	28	31	218	15	58	2	34
		Maj. Kovacs (C)	54th New York	1	24	18	189	7	47	48	54
		Col. von Bourry	68th New York	3	18	33	230	8	63	67	60
		Col. Freuhauff	153rd Pennsylvania	6	40	39	497	23	142	46	42
							1,134				
	Brig. Gen. Ames (P) Col. Harris (4 Staff)	Lt. Col. Fowler (K)	17th Connecticut	4	38	69	386	20	81	96	51
		Lt. Col. Williams (C)	25th Ohio	15	106	31	220	9	100	75	84
		Col. Harris	75th Ohio	13	61	66	269	16	74	96	69
		Col. Meyer	107th Ohio	6	53	74	458	23	111	77	46
							1,333				
Maj. Gen SCHURZ (P) Schimmelfennig (M) SCHURZ (6 Staff)	Brig. Gen. Schimmelfennig (P) Col. von Amsberg (3 Staff)	Lt. Col. Salomon	82nd Illinois	30	87	38	316	4	19	89	35
		Col. von Amsberg	45th NY (*) – see note	7	25	44	375	11	35	178	60
		Col. Brown	157th New York	13	66	19	409	27	166	114	75
		Col. McGroaty	61st Ohio	33	27	0	247	6	36	12	22
		Col. von Hartung (W)	74th Pennsylvania	8	14	30	333	10	40	60	33
							1,680				
	Col. Krzyzanowski (1 Staff)	Lt. Col. Otto (W)	58th New York	1	10	20	194	2	15	3	10
		Col. Lockman (W)	119th New York	12	66	42	262	11	70	59	53
		Col. Robinson (W)	82nd Ohio	9	47	25	312	17	85	79	58
		Col. Mahler (W)	75th Pennsylvania	1	7	51	208	19	89	3	53
		Lt. Col. Boebel (W)	26th Wisconsin	25	133	40	443	26	129	62	49
							1,419				
Brig. Gen. von STEINWEHR (5 Staff) 33 Infantry (29th New York)	Col. Coster (5 Staff)	Lt. Col. Jackson	134th New York				400	42	151	59	63
		Lt. Col. Allen	154th NY – see note	38	42	160	239	1	21	178	84
		Lt. Col. Cantador	27th Pennsylvania	6	31	19	283	6	29	76	39
		Capt. Kelly	73rd Pennsylvania	10	64	29	290	7	27	0	12
							1,212				
	Col. Smith (1 Staff)	Col. Underwood	33rd Massachussetts	0	4	3	491	7	38	0	9
		Col. Wood	136th New York	0	1	5	482	17	89	3	23
		Col. Gambee	55th Ohio (*)				327	6	31	12	15
		Lt. Col. Long	73rd Ohio (*)	0	1	1	338	21	120	4	43
							1,638				
Corps Artillery	Maj. Osborn (1 Staff)	Capt. Wiedrich	1st New York Light, I	1	10	2	141 (6 x 3-inch rifles)	3	10	0	9
		Lt. Wheeler	13th New York Light	0	11	2	110 (6 x 3-inch rifles)	0	8	3(1)	10
		Capt. Dilger	1st Ohio Light, I	1	10	0	127 (6 x Napoleons)	0	13	0	10
		Capt. Heckman	1st Ohio Light, K	0	3	0	110 (6 x Napoleons)	2	11	2(2)	14
		Lt. Wilkeson (K)	4th United States, G				115 (6 x Napoleons)	2	11	4	15
9,221 all ranks	7 brigades	31 regiments, 5 batteries, 30 guns		All ranks casualties, Gettysburg				369	1,924	1,514	41

Note: 45th and 154th New York share the highest number MIA of all Union regiments at Gettysburg as a result of being among the last to enter Gettysburg, with the Confederates hot on their heels.

Division	Brigade	Regiment or Battery		Chancellorsville			Gettysburg			
				K	W	M	Battle Strength	KIA	WIA	MIA	% loss

Division	Brigade	Regiment or Battery		K	W	M	Battle Strength	KIA	WIA	MIA	% loss
Brig. Gen. GEARY (5 Staff) 28 Infantry (28th Pennsylvania)	Brig. Gen. 'Pop' Greene (3 Staff)	Col. Godard	60th New York	9	44	13	273	11	41	0	19
		Lt. Col. von Hammerstein	78th New York	12	51	68	198	6	21	3	15
		Col. Lane (W)	102nd New York	10	41	39	230	4	17	8	13
		Col. Ireland	137th New York	3	15	36	423	40	87	10	32
		Col. Barnum (W)	149th New York	15	68	103	297	6	46	3	14
							1,421				
	Col. Candy (17 Staff/Band)	Col. Patrick	5th Ohio	6	52	24	302	2	16	0	6
		Col. Creighton	7th Ohio	16	62	21	282	1	17	0	6
		Col. Stevens (W)	29th Ohio	2	42	28	308	7	13	0	12
		Lt. Col. Powell	66th Ohio	3	40	30	303	1	16	0	6
		Capt. Flynn	28th Penn. (Division HQ)	18	61	24	303	3	23	2	9
		Lt. Col. Pardee	147th Pennsylvania	13	57	24	298	5	15	0	7
							1,796				
	Brig. Gen. Kane (ill) Col. Cobham (3 Staff)	Col. Richards	29th Pennsylvania	6	13	2	357	15	43	8	18
		Capt. Gimber	109th Pennsylvania	4	16	2	149	3	6	1	7
		Lt. Col. Walker	111th Pennsylvania	5	14	7	191	15	7	0	11
							697				
Brig. Gen. WILLIAMS (P) Ruger (5 Staff)	Col. McDougall (1 Staff)	Col. Packer	5th Connecticut	1	19	43	221	0	2	5	3
		Lt. Col. Wooster	20th Connecticut	11	60	98	321	5	22	1	9
		Col. Sudsburg	3rd Maryland	12	44	29	290	1	7	0	3
		Lt. Col. Rogers (W)	123rd New York	17	113	18	495	3	10	1	3
		Col. Price	145th New York	4	33	58	245	1	9	0	4
		Col. Selfridge	46th Pennsylvania	3	15	81	262	2	10	1	5
							1,834				
	Brig. Gen. Ruger (P) Col. Colgrove (1 Staff)	Col. Colgrove	27th Indiana	21	125	4	339	23	86	1	32
		Lt. Col. Mudge (K)	2nd Massachussetts	21	110	7	316	23	109	4	43
		Col. Carman	13th New Jersey	18	99	24	347	1	20	0	6
		Col. Crane	107th New York	5	54	24	319	0	2	0	>1
		Col. Hawley	3rd Wisconsin	18	74	9	260	2	8	0	4
							1,581				
	Brig. Gen. Lockwood (3 Staff) *See note*	Col. Maulsby	1st Maryland (Potomac)				674	23	80	1	15
		Col. Ketcham	150th New York				609	7	23	15	7
		Col. Wallace	1st Maryland (East Shore)				532	5	18	2	5
							1,818				
Corps Artillery Lt. Col. Best (P) Lt. Muhlenberg		Lt. Winegar	1st New York Light, M	0	8	0	90 (4 x 10P)	0	0	0	0
		Lt. Atwell	Pennsylvania Light, E	1	8	0	139 (6 x 10P)	0	3	0	2
		Lt. Rugg	4th United States, F	2	9	5	89 (6 x Napoleons)	0	1	0	1
		Lt. Kinzie	5th United States, K				72 (4 x Napoleons)	0	5	0	7
9,788 all ranks	**7 brigades**	**32 regiments, 4 batteries, 20 guns**		All ranks casualties, Gettysburg				204	812	66	11

Note: 1st Maryland, Potomac Home Brigade and 150th New York arrived morning 2 July; 1st Maryland, Eastern Shore, arrived morning 3 July.

Division	Brigade	Regiment or Battery		Chancellorsville			Gettysburg			
				K	W	M	Battle Strength	KIA	WIA	MIA	% loss

Division	Brigade		Regiment or Battery	K	W	M	Battle Strength	KIA	WIA	MIA	% loss
Maj. Gen. BIRNEY (P) Ward (4 Staff)	Semi-independent	Maj. Stoughton	2nd US Sharpshooters	1	9	6	169 482	5	23	15	25
	Brig. Gen. Ward (P) Col. Berdan (6 Staff)	Col. Wheeler (K)	20th Indiana (*)	1	19	4	401	32	114	10	39
		Col. Lakeman	3rd Maine	4	17	42	210	18	59	45	58
		Col. Walker (W)	4th Maine	2	16	10	287	11	59	74	50
		Lt. Col. Higgins (W)	86th New York	8	68	1	286	11	51	4	23
		Col. Ellis (K)	124th New York	29	160	15	238	28	57	5	38
		Maj. Moore	99th Pennsylvania (*)	1	16	9	277 1,699	18	81	11	40
	Brig. Gen. de Trobriand (1 Staff)	Lt. Col. Merrill	17th Maine	10	65	38	350	18	112	3	38
		Col. Pierce (W)	3rd Michigan	7	46	20	237	7	31	7	19
		Lt. Col. Pulford (W)	5th Michigan	7	43	28	216	19	86	4	50
		Col. Egan	40th New York – see note	6	168	145	431	23	120	7	35
		Lt. Col. Jones (W)	110th Pennsylvania	5	18	22	152 1,386	8	45	0	35
	Semi-independent	Col. Berdan	1st US Sharpshooters	11	51	6	313	6	37	6	16
	Brig. Gen. Graham (W, C) Col. Tippin (1 Staff)	Col. Sides (W)	57th Pennsylvania	10	43	18	207	11	46	58	56
		Maj. Dank	63rd Pennsylvania	10	70	38	246	1	29	4	14
		Col. Tippin	68th Pennsylvania	4	34	37	320	13	126	13	47
		Col. Craig	105th Pennsylvania	9	64	3	274	8	115	9	48
		Lt. Col. Cavada (C)	114th Pennsylvania	20	123	38	259	9	86	60	60
		Col. Madill	141st Pennsylvania	23	152	60	209 1,515	25	103	21	71
From Humphreys' division, dispersed ad hoc among Birney's brigades	Col. Burling (2 Staff)	Col. Bailey (W)	2nd New Hampshire				354	20	137	36	54
		Col. Sewell (W)	5th New Jersey	13	102	6	206	13	65	16	46
		Lt. Col. Gilkyson	6th New Jersey	7	52	8	207	1	32	8	20
		Col. Francine (K)	7th New Jersey	7	40	0	275	15	86	13	41
		Col. Ramsey (W)	8th New Jersey	18	101	6	170	7	38	2	28
		Maj. Dunne	115th Pennsylvania	11	78	22	151 1,363	3	18	3	16
Brig. Gen. HUMPHREYS (4 Staff)	Excelsior Brigade Col. Brewster (3 Staff)	Col. Farnum	70th New York	4	11	17	288	20	93	4	41
		Col. Potter	71st New York	1	15	23	243	10	68	13	37
		Col. Austin (W)	72nd New York (*)	12	30	59	305	7	79	28	37
		Maj. Burns	73rd New York	3	31	4	349	51	103	8	46
		Lt. Col. Holt	74th New York	3	22	15	266	12	74	3	33
		Lt. Col. Westbrook (W)	120th New York	4	49	13	383 1,834	32	154	17	53
	Brig. Gen. Carr (2 Staff)	Lt. Col. Baldwin	1st Massachussetts (*)	9	46	40	321	16	83	21	37
		Lt. Col. Tripp	11th Massachussetts	8	65	3	286	23	96	10	45
		Lt. Col. Merriam (W)	16th Massachussetts	8	57	8	245	15	53	13	33
		Col. Langley	12th New Hampshire	41	213	63	224	20	70	2	41
		Col. McAllister (W)	11th N. J. – see note	18	146	5	275	17	124	12	56
		Maj. Bodine	26th Pennsylvania (*)	11	71	9	365 1,716	30	176	7	58
Corps Artillery	Capt. Randolph (W) Capt. Clarke (4 Staff)	Capt. Clarke	2nd New Jersey Light				131 (6 x 10P)	1	16	3	15
		Capt. Winslow	1st New York Light, D	2	12	0	116 (6 x Napoleons)	0	10	8	15
		Capt. Smith	4th New York Light				126 (6 x 10P)	2	10	1(3)	10
		Lt. Bucklyn (W)	1st Rhode Island Light, E	2	13	2	108 (6 x Napoleons)	3	26	1	29
		Lt. Seeley (W)	4th United States, K	7	38	0	113 (6 x Napoleons)	2	19	4	22
10,675 all ranks	7 brigades	42 regiments, 5 batteries, 30 guns		All ranks casualties, Gettysburg				593	3,029	589	39

Note: 40th New York was an amalgamation of several regimental remnants and the casualties for Chancellorsville are only a partial composite. 11th New Jersey had five COs wounded, ending under a lieutenant.

V CORPS – Maj. Gen. SYKES
7 Staff – 78 Cavalry (17th Pennsylvania) – 109 Infantry (12th New York)

Division	Brigade	Regiment or Battery		Chancellorsville			Gettysburg				
				K	W	M	Battle Strength	KIA	WIA	MIA	% loss
Brig. Gen. BARNES (4 Staff)	Col. Vincent (K) Col. Rice (1 Staff)	Col. Chamberlain	20th Maine (2*)				386	29	91	5	32
		Col. Welch	16th Michigan	1	6	0	263	23	34	3	23
		Col. Rice	44th New York	0	4	0	391	26	82	3	28
		Capt. Woodward	83rd Pennsylvania	0	4	0	295	10	45	0	19
							1,335				
	Col. Tilton (1 Staff)	Col. Hayes	18th Massachussetts	1	10	2	139	1	23	3	19
		Lt. Col. Sherwin	22nd Massachussetts	1	0	0	137	3	27	1	23
		Col. Abbott (W)	1st Michigan	2	12	1	145	5	33	4	29
		Lt. Col. Gwynn	118th Pennsylvania	0	8	0	233	3	19	3	11
							654				
	Col. Sweitzer (1 Staff)	Col. Gwiney	9th Mass – see note	0	13	0	412	1	6	0	2
		Col. Prescott	32nd Mass (Arty. Res.)	1	5	5	242	13	62	5	33
		Col. Jeffords (K)	4th Michigan	6	12	2	342	25	64	76	48
		Lt. Col. Hull	62nd Pennsylvania	2	13	0	426	28	107	40	41
							1,422				
Brig. Gen. AYRES (5 Staff)	Brig. Gen. Weed (K) Col. Garrard (4 Staff)	Col. O'Rorke (K)	140th New York	2	12	7	449	26	89	18	30
		Col. Garrard	146th New York	2	17	31	456	4	24	0	6
		Lt. Col. Sinex	91st Pennsylvania	10	41	25	220	3	16	0	9
		Lt. Col. Cain	155th Pennsylvania	3	10	1	362	6	13	0	5
							1,487				
	Col. Burbank (2 Staff)	Maj. Lee (K)	2nd United States	1	27	0	197	6	55	6	34
		Capt. Hancock	7th United States	2	9	5	116	12	45	2	51
		Capt. Clinton	10th United States	0	12	0	93	16	32	3	55
		Maj. Floyd-Jones	11th United States	7	16	5	286	19	92	9	42
		Lt. Col. Greene	17th United States	3	10	1	260	25	118	7	58
							952				
	Col. Day (2 Staff)	Capt. Freedley (W)	3rd United States	0	4	5	300	6	66	1	24
		Capt. Adams	4th United States	1	2	1	173	10	30	0	23
		Capt. Bootes	6th United States	1	21	6	150	4	44	0	29
		Capt. Dunne	12th United States	0	5	18	415	8	71	13	22
		Maj. Giddings	14th United States	3	6	6	513	18	110	4	26
							1,551				
Brig. Gen. CRAWFORD (5 Staff)	Col. McCandless (1 Staff)	Col. Talley	1st Penn. Reserves				379	8	38	0	12
		Lt. Col. Woodward	2nd Penn. Reserves				233	3	33	1	16
		Lt. Col. Ent	6th Penn. Reserves (6*)				324	2	22	0	7
		Col. Jackson	11th Penn. Reserves				327	3	38	0	12
		Col. Taylor (K)	13th Penn. Reserves				298	7	39	2	16
							1,561				
	Col. Fisher (1 Staff)	Lt. Col. Dare	5th Penn. Reserves				285	0	2	0	>1
		Lt. Col. Snodgrass	9th Penn. Reserves				322	0	5	0	2
		Col. Warner	10th Penn. Reserves				401	2	3	0	1
		Col. Hardin	12th Penn. Reserves				273	1	1	0	>1
							1,281				
Corps Artillery	Capt. Martin (3 Staff)	Lt. Walcott	3rd Mass. Light, C				115 (6 x Napoleons)	0	6	0	5
		Capt. Barnes	1st New York Light, C				62 (4 x 3-inch rifles)	0	0	0	0
		Capt. Gibbs	1st Ohio Light, L	2	8	1	113 (6 x Napoleons)	0	2	0	2
		Lt. Hazlett (K)	5th United States, D				68 (6 x 10P)	7	6	0	19
		Lt. Watson (W)	5th United States, I	0	5	0	71 (3 x 3-inch rifles)	1	19	2	31
11,019 all ranks	9 brigades	40 regiments, 5 batteries, 25 guns		All ranks casualties, Gettysburg				365	1,611	211	20

Note: 9th Massachussetts was east of Gettysburg in front of Brinkerhoff's Ridge during the second day battle.

Division	Brigade	Regiment or Battery		Chancellorsville K	W	M	Gettysburg Battle Strength	KIA	WIA	MIA	% loss
Brig. Gen. CALDWELL (7 Staff)	Brig. Gen. Zook (K) Lt. Col. Fraser (4 Staff)	Lt. Col. Freudenberg (W)	52nd New York	4	30	9	134	2	26	10	28
		Lt. Col. Chapman	57th New York	2	28	1	175	4	28	2	19
		Col. Morris (W)	66th New York	1	10	59	147	5	29	10	30
		Col. Roberts (K)	140th Pennsylvania (2*)	7	28	9	515	37	144	60	47
102 Infantry (53rd Pennsylvania) (116th Pennsylvania)							971				
	Col. Cross (K) Col. McKeen (3 Staff)	Lt. Col. Hapgood	5th New Hampshire	0	22	3	179	27	53	0	45
		Lt. Col. Broady	61st New York	1	16	10	104	5	56	0	60
		Col. McKean	81st Pennsylvania	4	38	19	175	5	49	8	35
		Lt. Col. MacFarlane	148th Pennsylvania	31	119	14	392	19	101	5	32
							850				
	Irish Brigade Col. Kelly (2 Staff)	Col. Byrnes	28th Massachussetts	0	11	5	224	8	57	35	45
		Lt. Col. Bentley (W)	63rd New York (2 Coy)	1	3	2	75	5	10	8	31
		Capt. Moroney (W)	69th New York (2 Coy)	3	7	0	75	5	14	6	33
		Capt. Burke	88th New York (2 Coy)	3	23	20	90	7	17	4	31
		Lt. Col. Mulholland	116th Penn (Division HQ)	1	19	4	66	2	11	9	33
							530				
	Col. Brooke (W) (1 Staff)	Lt. Col. Merwin (K)	27th Connecticut (2 Coy)	1	7	283	75	10	23	4	49
		Col. Bailey	2nd Delaware	2	19	40	234	11	61	12	36
		Col. Bingham (W)	64th New York	15	21	8	204	15	64	19	48
		Lt. Col. McMichael	53rd Penn (Division HQ)	0	8	3	135	7	67	6	59
		Col. Brown (W)	145th Pennsylvania	2	8	112	202	11	69	10	45
							850				
Brig. Gen. GIBBON (P) Harrow (6 Staff)	Brig. Gen. Harrow (P) Col. Heath (3 Staff)	Col. Heath	19th Maine				439	29	170	4	46
		Col. Ward (K)	15th Massachussetts	0	2	0	239	23	97	28	62
		Col. Colvill (W)	1st Minn (2*) – see note	0	9	0	330	50	173	1	68
		Lt. Col. Huston (K)	82nd New York (*)				335	45	132	15	54
74 Sharpshooters (1st Massachussetts) 2K, 6W							1,343				
	Philadelphia Brigade Brig. Gen.Webb (W, K) (3 staff)	Col. O'Kane (K)	69th Pennsylvania				284	40	80	17	48
		Col. Penn-Smith	71st Pennsylvania (*)				261	21	58	19	37
		Col. Baxter (W)	72nd Pennsylvania				380	44	146	2	50
		Lt. Col. Curry	106th Pennsylvania				280	9	54	1	23
							1,205				
	Col. Hall (2 Staff)	Col. Devereaux	19th Massachussetts (5*)	0	9	0	163	9	61	7	47
		Col. Revere (K)	20th Massachussetts	2	14	1	243	30	94	3	52
		Lt. Col. Steele (K)	7th Michigan	0	7	0	165	21	44	0	39
		Col. Mallon	42nd New York	1	7	7	197	15	55	4	38
		Lt. Col. Thomas (K)	59th New York (*)				152	6	28	0	22
							920				
Brig. Gen. HAYS (P) (8 Staff)	Col. Willard (K) Col. Sherrill (K) Lt. Col. Bull (2 Staff)	Maj. Hildebrandt (W)	39th New York				269	15	80	0	35
		Col. MacDougall (W)	111th New York				390	58	177	14	64
		Lt. Col. Crandall	125th New York (*)				392	26	104	9	35
		Col. Sherrill (K)	126th New York (3*)				455	40	181	10	51
82 Infantry (10th NY Battalion)							1,506				
	Col. Carroll (7 Staff) 36 Infantry (8th Ohio)	Col. Coons	14th Indiana	8	49	7	191	6	25	0	16
		Lt. Col. Carpenter	4th Ohio	14	55	4	299	9	17	5	10
		Lt. Col. Sawyer	8th Ohio (*) (Brig. HQ)	1	10	1	209	18	83	1	49
		Lt. Col. Lockwood	7th West Virginia	3	17	4	235	5	41	1	20
							934				
	Col. Smyth (W) Lt. Col. Pierce (2 Staff)	Maj. Ellis	14th Connecticut (3*)	1	36	19	172	10	52	4	38
		Lt. Col. Harris	1st Delaware (3*)				251	10	54	13	31
		Maj. Hill	12th New Jersey	24	132	22	444	23	83	9	26
		Lt. Col. Pierce	108th New York (*)	3	39	10	200	16	86	0	51
							1,067				

Note: 1st Minnesota and attached 2nd Co. Minnesota Sharpshooters were the only Union troops from west of the Mississippi present at Gettysburg. Also the smallest contingent from any State on either side, giving Minnesota the actuarial distinction of suffering the highest percentage loss during the battle.

Division	Brigade	Regiment or Battery		Chancellorsville			Gettysburg				
				K	W	M	Battle Strength	KIA	WIA	MIA	% loss
Corps Artillery	Capt. Hazard (4 Staff)	Capt. Rorty (K)	1st New York Light, B	0	12	0	116 (6 x 10P rifles)	10	16	0	22
		Capt. Arnold	1st Rhode Island Light, A				117 (6 x 3-inch rifles)	3	28	1	27
		Lt. Brown (W)	1st Rhode Island Light, B				129 (6 x Napoleons)	7	19	2(3)	22
		Lt. Woodruff (K)	1st United States, I	1	1	0	112 (6 x Napoleons)	1	24	0	22
		Lt. Cushing (K)	4th United Statres, A (*)				126 (6 x 3-inch rifles)	6	32	0	30
11,347 all ranks	**11 brigades**	**48 regiments, 5 batteries, 30 guns**		**All ranks casualties, Gettysburg**				**797**	**3,194**	**378**	**38**

VI CORPS – Maj. Gen. SEDGWICK
13 Staff – 86 Cavalry (1st Pennsylvania/1st New Jersey) + 250 temporarily attached (1st Massachussetts, later to Army HQ)

Division	Brigade	Regiment or Battery		Chancellorsville			Gettysburg			
				K	W	M	Battle Strength	KIA	WIA	MIA	% loss
Maj. Gen. NEWTON (transfer to I Corps) Wheaton (3 Staff)	Brig. Gen. Wheaton (P) Col. Nevin (1 Staff)	Lt. Col. Hamilton	62nd New York	10	55	55	237	1	11	0	5
		Col. Nevin	93rd Pennsylvania	8	53	18	234	0	10	0	4
		Maj. Kohler	98th Pennsylvania	8	20	13	351	0	11	0	>1
		Col. Collier	139th Pennsylvania	12	53	11	443	1	19	0	4
							1,265				
	Brig. Gen. Shaler (3 Staff)	Col. Hamblin	65th New York	1	13	3	277	4	5	0	3
		Col. Cross	67th New York	2	16	11	349	0	0	1	>1
		Col. Titus	122nd New York	0	7	0	396	10	32	2	11
		Lt. Col. Glenn	23rd Pennsylvania (*)	4	17	40	467	1	13	0	3
		Col. Bassett	82nd Pennsylvania	1	32	13	278	0	6	0	2
							1,767				
	Brig. Gen. Eustis (1 Staff)	Lt. Col. Harlow	7th Massachussetts	22	125	3	320	0	6	0	2
		Lt. Col. Parson	10th Massachussetts	10	57	2	361	0	4	5	2
		Col. Edwards	37th Massachussetts	1	10	5	593	2	26	19	8
		Col. Rogers	2nd Rhode Island	8	67	6	348	1	5	1	2
							1,622				
Brig. Gen. WRIGHT (6 Staff) 80 Infantry (4th New Jersey)	Brig. Gen. Torbert (2 Staff)	Lt. Col. Henry	1st New Jersey	7	71	27	253	0	0	0	0
		Lt. Col. Wiebecke	2nd New Jersey	4	36	9	357	0	6	0	2
		Lt. Col. Campbell	3rd New Jersey	11	69	15	282	0	2	0	>1
		Col. Penrose	15th New Jersey	24	126	4	410	0	3	0	>1
							1,302				
	Brig. Gen. Bartlett (4 Staff)	Col. Edwards	5th Maine	12	57	27	293	0	0	0	0
		Col. Upton	121st New York	49	172	55	410	0	2	0	>1
		Lt. Col. Carroll	95th Pennsylvania	23	113	20	309	1	1	0	>1
		Maj. Lessig	96th Pennsylvania	16	54	9	309	0	1	0	>1
							1,321				
	Brig. Gen. Russell (6 Staff)	Col. Burnham	6th Maine	24	110	35	378	0	0	0	0
		Lt. Col. Hulings	49th Pennsylvania	1	3	5	276	0	0	0	0
		Col. Ellmaker	119th Pennsylvania	11	77	38	404	0	2	0	>1
		Col. Allen	5th Wisconsin	36	121	36	420	0	0	0	0
							1,478				
Brig. Gen. HOWE (3 Staff)	Brig. Gen. Neill (16 Staff/Band)	Lt. Col. Connor	7th Maine	12	49	31	216	0	6	0	3
		Capt. Gifford	33rd NY (detachment)	18	129	74	60	0	0	0	0
		Lt. Col. Wilson	43rd New York	15	53	87	370	2	2	1	1
		Col. Bidwell	49th New York	1	16	18	359	0	2	0	>1
		Lt. Col. French	77th New York	7	46	30	368	0	0	0	0
		Lt. Col. Smith	61st Pennsylvania	9	63	16	386	0	1	1	>1
							1,759				
	Brig. Gen. Grant (16 Staff/Band)	Col. Walbridge	2nd Vermont	18	114	0	444	0	0	0	0
		Col. Seaver	3rd Vermont	3	22	0	365	0	0	0	0
		Col. Stoughton	4th Vermont	4	27	22	381	0	1	0	>1
		Lt. Col. Lewis	5th Vermont	3	11	9	295	0	0	0	0
		Col. Barney	6th Vermont	5	54	15	331	0	0	0	0
							1,816				
Corps Artillery	Col. Tompkins (3 Staff)	Capt. McCartney	1st Mass. Light, A	1	1	0	135 (6 x Napoleons)	0	0	0	0
		Capt. Cowan	1st New York Light				103 (6 x 3-inch rifles)	4	8	0	12
		Capt. Harn	3rd New York Light				111 (6 x 10P)	0	0	0	0
		Capt. Waterman	1st Rhode Island Light, C				116 (6 x 3-inch rifles)	0	0	0	0
		Capt. Adams	1st Rhode Island Light, G	5	18	0	126 (6 x 10P)	0	0	0	0
		Lt. Williston	2nd United States, D	1	0	0	126 (6 x Napoleons)	0	0	0	0
		Lt. Butler	2nd United States, G	0	0	14	101 (6 x Napoleons)	0	0	0	0
		Lt. Martin	5th United States, F	0	8	1	116 (6 x 10P)	0	0	0	0
13,601 all ranks	9 brigades	44 regiments, 8 batteries, 48 guns		All ranks casualties, Gettysburg				27	185	30	2

Division	Brigade	Regiment or Battery	Chancellorsville K	W	M	Gettysburg Battle Strength	KIA	WIA	MIA	% loss
Brig. Gen. BUFORD (4 Staff)	Col. Gamble (4 Staff)	Maj. Beveridge — 8th Illinois	0	0	2	470	1	5	1	1
	Col. Chapman (2 sqdns each)	12th Illinois	2	3	30	233	4	10	6	9
		3rd Indiana	1	3	20	313	6	21	5	10
	Lt. Col. Markell	8th New York	0	5	0	580	2	22	16	7
						1,596				
	Attached artillery	Lt. Calef — 2nd United States, A (6 x 3-inch rifles)				75	0	12	0	16
	Col. Devin (5 Staff)	Maj. Beardsley — 6th NY (II Corps HQ)	5	17	53	218	0	1	8	4
		Col. Sackett — 9th NY (XII Corps HQ)				367	2	2	7	3
		Col. Kellogg — 17th Penn (XI Corps HQ)	0	9	5	464	0	0	4	>1
		Capt. Conger — 3rd West Virginia				59	0	0	4	7
						1,108				
Brig. Gen. GREGG 44 Cavalry (1st Ohio)	Col. McIntosh (19 Staff/Band)	Lt. Col. Deems — 1st Maryland	0	0	10	285	0	2	1	1
		Capt. Duvall — Purnell Legion (Md)				66	0	0	0	0
		Maj. Beaumont — 1st NJ (VI Corps HQ)				199	0	9	0	4
		Capt. Craft — 1st Penn. (*) (VI Corp HQ)				355	0	0	2	>1
		Lt. Col. Jones — 3rd Pennsylvania (1*)				335	0	15	6	6
						1,240				
	Attached artillery	Capt. Rank — 3rd Penn. Artillery, H (2 x 3-inch rifles)				52	0	0	0	0
	Col. Gregg (8 Staff)	Lt. Col. Smith — 1st Maine (I & Cav. Corps)	1	1	24	315	1	4	0	92
		Maj. Avery — 10th New York				333	2	4	3	3
		Lt. Col. Doster — 4th Pennsylvania				258	1	0	0	>1
		Lt. Col. Robison — 16th Pennsylvania				349	2	4	0	2
						1,255				
	Attached artillery	Capt. Randol — 1st United States, E/G (4 x 3-inch rifles)				85	0	0	0	0
Part of Kilpatrick's Division, 'borrowed' by Gregg on 3 July	Brig. Gen. Custer (1 Staff)	Col. Town — 1st Michigan				427	10	43	20	17
		Col. Alger — 5th Michigan				646	8	30	18	9
		Col. Gray — 6th Michigan				477	1	26	1	6
		Col. Mann — 7th Michigan				383	13	48	39	26
						1,933				
	Attached artillery	Lt. Pennington — 2nd United States, M (6 x 3-inch rifles)				117	0	1	0	>1
Brig. Gen. KILPATRICK (3 Staff) 41 Cavalry (1st Ohio)	Brig. Gen. Farnsworth (K) Col. Richmond (1 Staff)	Maj. Hammond — 5th New York				420	1	1	4	1
		Lt. Col. Brinton — 18th Pennsylvania				509	2	4	8	3
		Lt. Col. Preston — 1st Vermont (*)				600	13	25	27	11
		Col. Richmond — 1st West Virginia				395	4	4	4	3
						1,924				
	Attached artillery	Lt. Elder — 4th United States, E (4 x 3-inch rifles)				61	1	0	0	2
Reserve Horse Artillery	Capt. Robertson (2 staff) *See note*	Lt. Heaton — 2nd United States, B/L (6 x 3-inch rifles)				99	0	0	0	0
		Capt. Martin — 6th New York (6 x 3-inch rifles)				103	0	1	0	>1
		Capt. Daniels — 9th Michigan (6 x 3-inch rifles)				111	1	4	0	4
10,896 all ranks	**7 brigades**	**33 regiments, 8 batteries, 38 guns**	**All ranks casualties, Gettysburg**				**82**	**326**	**392**	**7**

Note: On paper there were two brigades of Reserve Horse Artillery, five batteries under Robertson and four under Capt. Tidball. Six were distributed among the other brigades and the remaining three joined the army artillery reserve, command of which devolved on Robertson when Tyler suffered a heatstroke. Tidball was an acting staff officer with Meade at the time of Pickett's charge, reason unknown.

CAVALRY CORPS – Maj. Gen. PLEASONTON (continued from previous page)
At Mechanicstown, then at Fairfield – 6th United States heavily engaged there on 3 July

Division	Brigade	Regiment or Battery		Chancellorsville			Gettysburg				
				K	W	M	Battle Strength	KIA	WIA	MIA	% loss
BUFORD's Reserve Brigade	Brig. Gen. Merritt (4 Staff)	Maj. Haseltine	6th Pennsylvania	0	0	2	242	3	7	2	5
		Capt. Lord	1st United States	0	0	18	362	1	9	5	4
		Capt. Rodenbaugh	2nd United States	0	0	11	407	3	7	7	4
		Capt. Mason	5th United States	1	3	33	306	0	4	1	2
		Maj. Starr (W, C)	6th United States	0	0	11	471	6	28	208	
							1,788				
	Attached artillery	Capt. Graham	1st United States, K				114 (6 x 3-inch rifles)	2	1	0	3

ARTILLERY – Brig. Gen. HUNT

Artillery Reserve	Brigade		Battery	Chancellorsville			Gettysburg				
				K	W	M	Battle Strength	KIA	WIA	MIA	% loss
Brig. Gen. TYLER (heatstroke) Robertson of the Reserve Horse took over (46 Staff – including Ordinance Detachment) 45 Infantry (4th New Jersey) + 273 with ammunition train (32nd Massachussetts)	First Regular Capt. Ransom (W) Eakin (W) (2 Staff)	Lt. Eakin (W)	1st United States, H	3	18	0	129 (6 x Napoleons)	1	8	1	8
		Lt. Turnbull	3rd United States, F/K	1	16	1	115 (6 x Napoleons)	9	14	1(4)	21
		Lt. Thomas	4th United States, C	3	12	0	95 (6 x Napoleons)	1	17	0	19
		Lt. Wier	5th United States, C				104 (6 x Napoleons)	2	14	0(3)	15
	First Volunteer Lt. Col. McGilvery (2 Staff)	Capt. Philips	9th Mass. Light, E – see note				104 (6 x 3-inch rifles)	4	17	0	20
		Capt. Bigelow (W)	9th Mass. Light (*)				110 (6 x Napoleons)	8	18	2(4)	27
		Capt. Hart (W)	15th New York Light				70 (4 x Napoleons)	3	13	0	23
		Capt. Thompson (W)	Penn. Ind., Light C & F (*)				105 (6 x 3-inch rifles)	2	23	3(1)	27
	Second Volunteer Capt. Taft (2 Staff)	Capts. Booker, Pratt	1st Connecticut Heavy				See note	0	3	2	5
		Capt. Sterling	2nd Connecticut Light				109 (4 x J, 2 x 12H)	?	?	?	?
		Brigade commander	5th New York				146 (6 x 20P)	1	2	0	3
	Third Volunteer Capt. Huntington (2 Staff)	Capt Edgell	1st N. Hampshire Light, A				86 (4 x 3-inch rifles)	0	3	0	3
		Lt. Norton	1st Ohio Light, H	0	5	3	99 (6 x 3-inch rifles)	2	5	0	7
		Capt. Ricketts	1st Penn. Light, F & G				144 (6 x 3-inch rifles)	6	14	3	16
		Capt. Hill	1st West Virginia Light, C				100 (4 x 10P)	2	2	0	4
	Fourth Volunteer Capt. Fitzhugh (2 Staff)	Lt. Dow	6th Maine Light, F				87 (4 x Napoleons)	0	13	0	15
		Capt. Rigby	1st Maryland Light, A	0	3	0	106 (6 x 3-inch rifles)	0	0	0	0
		Lt. Parsons	1st New Jersey Light, A				98 (6 x 10P)	2	7	0	9
		Capt. Ames	1st New York light, G				84 (6 x Napoleons)	0	7	0	8
		Capt. Fitzhugh	1st NY Light, K – see note				122 (6 x 3-inch rifles)	0	7	0	6
2,376 all ranks	5 brigades		20 batteries, 118 guns	All ranks casualties, Gettysburg				43	187	12	10

Notes: 1st Connecticut Heavy, B & M, was siege artillery at Westminster during the battle.
10th New York battery was divided between 5th Massachussetts Light, E and 1st New York Light, K.

APPENDIX C ORDER OF BATTLE AND CASUALTIES

ARMY OF NORTHERN VIRGINIA, CSA

GEN. ROBERT E. LEE,   COMMANDING

ARMY HEADQUARTERS

Col. Chilton	Chief of Staff and Inspector General
Maj. Venable	ADC and Assistant Inspector General
Brig. Gen. Pendleton	Chief of Artillery
Col. Long	Military Secretary and acting Assistant Chief of Artillery
Maj. Marshall	ADC and Assistant Military Secretary
Lt. Col. Baldwin	Chief of Ordnance
Lt. Col. Cole	Chief of Commissary
Lt. Col. Corley	Chief Quartermaster
Lt. Col. Taylor	ADC and Acting Adjutant General
Maj. Young	Judge Advocate General
Capt. Johnston	Acting Chief Engineer
Dr. Guild	Medical Director

HEADQUARTERS GUARD
91 cavalry (39th Virginia Cavalry Battalion)

NOTES

• The best estimate of the battle strength of the Confederate army at Gettysburg is 70,226, but their record-keeping was notoriously carefree and this is certainly low. Regimental returns must be treated with caution: note what looks like averaging among the Georgia regiments in Pender's division (III Corps) and McLaws' division (I Corps), and the identical battery returns in Stuart's horse artillery.

• Casualties were 4,637 killed, 12,391 wounded and 5,846 missing, for a total of 22,874 and a rate of 32.6%, but these figures are also suspect. By contrast with the more immediately post-battle Union returns, Confederate KIA lists included those who died of their wounds up to the end of 1863 or who were missing and did not appear in any hospital and prisoner list, which optimistically discounted the possibility of successful desertion. WIA included those wounded and captured, so the MIA figure was for confirmed, unwounded POWs, and many regiments refused to admit that any of their men fell into this category.

• See artillery note in Appendix B for a clarification of the pounder vs. barrel bore issue, cannon weights, ranges, etc. Confederate inferiority lay not in its equipment, which was comparable, but in its flawed organization. Note the absence of an army reserve and the logistical nightmare of mixed ordnance at battery level. With the exception of the three-gun Louisiana batteries in I Corps, Confederate batteries were supposed to be four-gun, but there were many exceptions. Abbreviations employed are: 10–24H = 10–24-pounder howitzers; 3–4R = 3–4-inch rifles; 3NR = 3-inch naval rifles; 10–20P = 10–20-pounder Parrott rifles; B and W = Blakely and Whitworth (2-inch) British breech-loading rifles; N = 12-pounder Napoleon smooth-bores. Until the invention of a recoil-absorbing mechanism, breech-loading did not improve rate of fire.

• The following abbreviations are also used: A = absent without leave; C = captured; K = killed; P = promoted; W = wounded.

• Sources are as cited in Appendix B.

Division	Brigade	Regiment or Battery	Chancellorsville K	W	M	Gettysburg Battle Strength	KIA	WIA	MIA	% loss
Maj. Gen. HETH (W) Pettigrew* (8 Staff)	Brig. Gen. Archer (C) Col. Fry (W, C) Lt. Col. Shepard (4 Staff)	Col. Fry (W, C) 13th Alabama				308	11	46	157	69
		Maj. Van de Graaff 5th Alabama Battalion				135	3	30	15	36
		Maj. Buchanan 1st Tenn. Prov. Army				281	16	67	95	63
		Lt. Col. Shepard 7th Tennessee				249	24	38	54	47
		Capt. Philips 14th Tennessee				220	15	37	75	58
* K during retreat						1,193				
	Brig. Gen. Davis (6 Staff)	Col. Stone (W) 2nd Miss – see note				492	56	176	0?	47
		Col. Green 11th Mississippi				592	102	168	42	53
		Col. Miller 42nd Miss – see note				575	75	190	0?	46
		Col. Connally (W) 55th North Carolina				640	55	143	22	34
						2,299				
	Brig. Gen. Pettigrew (P) Col. Marshall (K) (4 Staff)	Col. Leventhorpe (W) 11th NC – see note				617	108	200	58	59
		Col. Burgwyn (K) 26th NC – see note				840	172	443	72	82
		Col. Faribault (W) 47th North Carolina				567	53	159	5	38
		Col. Marshall (K) 52nd North Carolina				553	51	112	14	32
						2,577				
	Col. Brockenbrough (A) Col. Mayo (4 Staff)	Capt. Betts 40th Virginia	14	71	9	253	10	37	18	26
		Col. Mayo 47th Virginia	3	47	3	209	13	35	0?	23
		Col. Christian 55th Virginia	20	90	10	268	9	37	3	18
		Maj. Bowles 22nd Virginia Battalion	6	23	16	237	3	21	0	10
						967				
Maj. Gen. PENDER (K) Lane TRIMBLE (W, C) Lane (W) (11 Staff)	Brig. Gen. Lane (P, W) Col. Avery (4 Staff)	Capt. Turner (W, C) 7th North Carolina	49	148	13	291	32	66	61	55
		Col. Barry 18th North Carolina	34	99	21	346?	16	38	34	25
		Col. Lowe (W) 28th North Carolina	14	91	2	346?	65	135	37	68
		Col. Avery 33rd North Carolina	32	101	68	368	30	54	48	36
		Co. Barbour 37th North Carolina	36	194	8	379	35	83	58	46
						1,730				
	Brig. Gen. Scales (W) Col. Lowrance (W) (4 Staff)	Col. Hyman (W) 13th North Carolina	31	178	7	232	55	98	26	77
		Capt. Stowe 16th North Carolina	17	73	15	321	24	61	38	38
		Col. Conner 22nd North Carolina	30	129	15	267	37	79	50	62
		Col. Lowrance (W) 34th North Carolina	18	110	20	311	19	55	30	33
		Col. Hoke (W) 38th North Carolina	18	84	11	216	40	63	27	60
						1,347				
	Col. Perrin (4 Staff)	Maj. McCreary 1st SC Prov. Army	12	88	4	328	35	60	16	34
		Capt. Hadden 1st SC Rifles	20	91	2	366?	3	8	0?	3
		Col. Miller 12th South Carolina	0	2	0	366?	21	111	0?	36
		Lt. Col. Brockman 13th South Carolina	6	84	1	390	42	88	0?	33
		Lt. Col. Brown (W) 14th South Carolina	8	137	0	428	27	182	0?	49
						1,878				
	Brig. Gen. Thomas (4 Staff)	Col. Brown 14th Georgia	8	67	0	331?	6	27	11	13
		Capt. Duke 35th Georgia	6	28	4	331?	11	37	42	27
		Lt. Grice 45th Georgia	4	36	1	331?	5	32	8	14
		Col. Player 49th Georgia	4	30	4	329?	12	31	42	26
						1,322				
Maj. Gen. ANDERSON (7 Staff)	Brig. Gen. Wilcox (5 Staff)	Lt. Col. Herbert 8th Alabama	9	43	4	477	40	146	80	56
		Capt. King 9th Alabama	23	89	1	306	8	32	76	38
		Col. Forney (W, C) 10th Alabama	18	54	28	311?	15	89	0?	33
		Col. Sanders (W) 11th Alabama	16	75	24	311?	7	68	0?	24
		Col. Pinckard (W) 14th Alabama	13	104	34	316	8	40	0?	15
						1,721				
	Perry's Brigade Col. Lang (3 Staff)	Maj. Moore (W, C) 2nd Florida	5	30	0	242	24	71	49	59
		Capt. Gardner (W) 5th Florida	8	20	0	321	39	77	63	56
		Brigade commander 8th Florida	10	36	0	176	17	80	35	75
						739				

Note: The casualty returns of the two Mississippi regiments involved in Davis's first attack were outrageously falsified, probably to spare President Davis embarrassment. Witnesses on both sides concur that the better part of 2nd Mississippi and some of 42nd Mississippi were surrounded in railway cuts and surrendered *en masse*. 11th and 26th North Carolina, particularly the latter, suffered by far the highest number of killed and wounded in the entire army and all the senior officers in Pettigrew's/Marshall's brigade were casualties.

Division	Brigade	Regiment or Battery		Chancellorsville			Gettysburg				
				K	W	M	Battle Strength	KIA	WIA	MIA	% loss
(continued) Maj. Gen. ANDERSON (7 Staff)	Brig. Gen. 'Rans' Wright (4 Staff)	Col. Walker	3rd Georgia	10	129	0	441	49	139	31	50
		Col. Wasden (K)	22nd Georgia	5	54	0	400	41	70	60	43
		Col. Gibson (W, C)	48th Georgia	7	65	0	395	70	97	57	57
		Maj. Rose (W)	2nd Georgia Battalion	3	23	0	173	24	37	21	47
							1,409				
	Brig. Gen. Posey (4 Staff)	Col. Taylor	12th Mississippi	3	28	23	305	1	11	1	4
		Col. Baker	16th Mississippi	22	57	25	385	3	16	7	7
		Col. Harris	19th Mississippi	6	39	6	372	5	26	3	9
		Col. Jayne	48th Mississippi	10	50	11	256	6	27	6	15
							1,318				
	Brig. Gen. Mahone (4 Staff)	Col. Rogers	6th Virginia	8	33	6	288	0	4	6	3
		Col. Weisener	12th Virginia	5	31	50	348	3	11	8	6
		Col. Ham	16th Virginia	1	17	19	270	2	15	5	8
		Col. Parham	41st Virginia	6	23	19	276	2	10	0	4
		Col. Grover	61st Virginia	4	30	3	356	5	10	0	7
							1,538				
Corps Reserve Artillery Col. Walker (4 Staff)	Maj. McIntosh	Capt. Rice	Danville (Va)				114 (4 x N)	0	1	1	2
		Capt. Hurt	Hardaway (Al)				71 (2 x 3R, 2 x W)	0	4	4	11
		Lt. Wallace	2nd Rockbridge (Va)				67 (2 x 3R, 2 x N)	3	3	0	9
		Capt. Johnson	Johnson's Richmond (Va)				96 (2 x 3R, 2 x N)	5	1	4	10
	Maj. Pegram Capt. Brunson	Capt. Crenshaw	Crenshaw's Richmond	1	5	0	76 (2 x 12H, 2 x N)	1	14	0	20
		Capt. Marye	Fredericksburg (Va)	2	6	0	75 (2 x 10P, 2 x N)	2	0	0	3
		Capt. Brander	Letcher (Va) – *not engaged*	2	5	0	65 (2 x 10P, 2 x N)	3	11	3	26
		Lt. Zimmerman	Pee Dee (SC)	0	0	0	65 (4 x 3R)	1	?	?	NA
		Capt. McGraw	Purcell (Va)	0	0	0	89 (4 x N)	1	5	0	7
Heth's Division Artillery	Lt. Col. Garnett (9 Staff)	Capt. Maurin	Donaldsonville (La)	0	1	0	114 (2 x 3R, 2 x 10P)	0	2	4	5
		Capt. Moore	Huger (Va)				77 (4 x 3R)	?	?	?	NA
		Capt. Lewis	Pittsylvania (Va)	0	6	0	90 (4 x 3R)	?	?	?	NA
		Capt. Grandy	Norfolk (Va) Blues	1	3	0	106 (2 x 3R, 2 x 10P)	0	1	1	2
Pender's Division Artillery	Maj. Poague (4 Staff)	Capt. Wyatt	Ablemarle (Va)				94 (see note)	0	12	1	14
		Capt. Graham	Charlotte (NC)				125 (2 x 12H, 2 x N)	0	0	5	4
		Capt. Ward	Madison (Miss) Light				91 (2 x 12H, 2 x N)	?	?	?	NA
		Capt. Brooke	Warrenton (Va)				58 (2 x 12H, 2 x N)	1	2	2	9
Anderson's Division Artillery	Maj. Lane (9 Staff)	Capt. Ross	Sumter (Ga), A – 6 guns				130 (see note)	1	11	1	10
		Capt. Patterson	Sumter (Ga), B – 6 guns	0	3	0	124 (4 x 12H, 2 x N)	2	6	1	7
		Capt. Wingfield (W)	Sumter (Ga), C – 5 guns				121 (3NR, 2 x 10P)	0	18	2	16
22,026 all ranks	**18 brigades**	**57 regiments, 20 batteries, 85 guns**		**All ranks casualties, Gettysburg**				**1,690**	**4,524**	**1,835+**	**36+**

Note: Wyatt's battery had three 3" rifles, one 12-pounder howitzer and one 10-pounder Parrott. Ross' battery had three 10-pounder Parrotts, one 3" rifle, one 12-pounder howitzer and one Napoleon.

Division	Brigade	Regiment or Battery	Chancellorsville K	W	M	Gettysburg Battle Strength	KIA	WIA	MIA	% loss
Maj. Gen. RODES (14 Staff)	Brig. Gen. Iverson (A) (4 Staff) *See note*	Capt. West (W) — 5th North Carolina	8	61	9	473	64	125	100	61
		Lt. Col. Davis — 12th North Carolina	12	96	11	219	12	60	7	36
		Col. Slough (W) — 20th North Carolina	15	67	18	372	41	94	118	68
		Col. Christie (K) — 23rd North Carolina	32	106	35	316	65	120	97	89
						1,380				
	Col. O'Neal (3 Staff)	Col. Battle — 3rd Alabama	16	127	16	350	17	74	0?	26
		Col. Hall — 5th Alabama	24	133	121	317	26	116	67	66
		Col. Lightfoot (W) — 6th Alabama	26	122	14	382	15	62	88	42
		Col. Pickens — 12th Alabama	13	79	10	317	17	66	0?	26
		Lt. Col. Goodgame — 26th Alabama	12	77	27	319	8	57	65	41
						1,685				
	Brig. Gen. Doles (4 Staff)	Lt. Col. Winn (K) — 4th Georgia	29	115	11	341	12	26	15	15
		Col. Willis — 12th Georgia	12	58	2	327	12	28	13	16
		Col. Mercer — 21st Georgia	15	64	10	287	4	11	23	13
		Col. Lumpkin (W) — 44th Georgia	20	96	5	364	18	41	16	21
						1,319				
	Brig. Gen. Daniel (4 Staff)	Col. Brabble — 32nd North Carolina				454	39	111	31	40
		Col. Kenan (W) — 43rd North Carolina				572	40	116	31	33
		Lt. Col. Boyd (W, C) — 45th North Carolina				460	63	156	?	48+
		Col. Owens — 53rd North Carolina				322	43	74	?	36+
		Lt. Col. Andrews (K) — 2nd NC Battalion				253	46	78	75	83
						2,061				
	Brig. Gen. Ramseur (4 Staff)	Maj. Hurtt (W) — 2nd North Carolina	55	155	49	243	9	37	21	28
		Col. Grimes — 4th North Carolina	47	155	58	196	10	29	30	35
		Col. Bennett (W) — 14th North Carolina	23	120	0	306	9	42	13	21
		Col. Parker (W) — 30th North Carolina	26	99	1	278	11	41	23	27
						1,023				
Maj. Gen. EARLY (12 Staff) Approx. 475 on attachment from Cavalry Division during march north. (17th Virginia & 35th Va. Battalion)	Brig. Gen. Hays (3 Staff)	Maj. Hart — 5th Louisiana	11	37	28	196	7	30	30	34
		Lt. Col. Hanlon — 6th Louisiana	14	68	99	218	8	32	21	28
		Col. Penn — 7th Louisiana	7	75	36	235	13	40	5	25
		Col. Lewis (K) — 8th Louisiana	17	64	89	296	14	50	11	21
		Col. Stafford — 9th Louisiana	21	53	42	347	19	35	19	21
						1,292				
	Col. Avery (K) Col. Godwin (2 Staff)	Maj. Tate — 6th North Carolina	8	42	17	509	47	118	43	41
		Col. Kirkland — 21st North Carolina	16	72	43	436	27	76	36	32
		Col. Godwin — 57th North Carolina	12	64	57	297	18	19	28	22
						1,242				
	Brig. Gen. Gordon (6 Staff)	Col. Smith — 13th Georgia	4	54	28	312	37	75	25	44
		Col. Atkinson — 26th Georgia	3	21	0	315	2	13	17	10
		Col. Evans — 31st Georgia	3	22	1	252	13	44	8	26
		Col. McLeod — 38th Georgia	2	18	0	341	18	62	53	39
		Capt. Jones — 60th Georgia	5	30	4	299	12	28	19	20
		Col. Lamar — 61st Georgia	0	32	3	298	30	75	6	38
						1,817				
	Brig. Gen. Smith (4 Staff)	Col. Hoffman — 31st Virginia	6	35	17	267	19	16	24	22
		Lt. Col. Gibson — 49th Virginia	1	16	0	281	18	73	9	36
		Lt. Col. Skinner — 52nd Virginia	4	9	0	254	9	26	19	21
						802				

Note: Iverson's brigade was shattered on 1 July and lost so many field officers that Ramseur assumed command of it as well as his own brigade when Iverson suffered a moral collapse.

Division	Brigade	Regiment or Battery		Chancellorsville			Gettysburg				
				K	W	M	Battle Strength	KIA	WIA	MIA	% loss
Maj. Gen. JOHNSON (9 Staff)	Stonewall Brigade	Col. Nadenbousch	2nd Virginia	8	58	0	333	3	12	10	7
		Maj. Terry	4th Virginia	18	148	3	257	18	63	56	53
	Brig. Gen. Walker	Col. Frank	5th Virginia	9	111	5	345	14	33	11	17
	(4 Staff)	Lt. Col. Shriver	27th Virginia	9	63	1	148	11	29	8	32
		Capt. Golladay	33rd Virginia	10	50	0	236	19	36	15	30
							1,319				
	Nicholl's Brigade	Capt. Willett	1st Louisiana	7	29	10	172	11	28	0?	23
		Lt. Col. Burke	2nd Louisiana	15	90	21	236	15	47	0?	26
	Col. Williams	Maj. Powell	10th Louisiana	15	51	20	226	22	69	19	49
	(3 Staff)	Lt. Col. Zable	14th Louisiana	4	60	17	281	15	50	0?	16
		Maj. Brady	15th Louisiana	5	37	62	186	3	35	0?	20
							1,101				
	Brig. Gen. Jones (W)	Capt. Moseley	21st Virginia	4	40	0	236	8	32	10	21
		Lt. Col. Higgenbotham (W)	25th Virginia				280	9	61	0?	25
	Lt. Col. Dungan	Lt. Col. Withers (W)	42nd Virginia	15	120	0	265	16	47	26	33
	(7 Staff)	Maj. Cobb (W)	44th Virginia	15	62	0	227	8	48	0?	25
		Lt. Col. Dungan	48th Virginia	19	84	9	265	20	38	29	33
		Lt. Col Slayer	50th Virginia	8	110	0	240	16	66	17	41
							1,513				
	Brig. Gen. 'Maryland' Steuart (5 Staff)	Lt. Col. Herbert (W)	1st Maryland Batt.				400	56	118	15	47
		Lt. Col. Brown	1st North Carolina	32	140	27	377	14	40	97	40
		Maj. Parsley	3rd North Carolina	39	176	17	548	48	140	30	40
		Col. Warren	10th Virginia	25	107	25	276	8	17	52	28
		Lt. Col. Walton	23rd Virginia	10	70	2	251	3	15	18	14
		Maj. Wood	37th Virginia	22	101	9	264	20	55	23	37
							2,116				
Corps Artillery Reserve Col. Brown (4 Staff)	~~Capt. Dance~~ (9 Staff)	Capt. Watson	2nd Richmond (Va)				64 (4 x 10P)	2	1	0	5
		Capt. Smith	3rd Richmond (Va)				62 (4 x 3R)	1	1	2	6
		Lt. Cunningham	Powhatan (Va)	2	16	2	78 (4 x 3R)	0	3	12	19
		Capt. Graham	Rockbridge (Va)				85 (4 x 20P)	0	14	7	25
		Lt. Griffin	Salem (Va)				69 (2 x 3R, 2 x N)	0	2	5	10
	~~Lt. Col. Nelson~~ (9 Staff)	Capt. Kirkpatrick	Amherst (Va)				105 (2 x 3R, 2 x N)	0	0	13	12
		Capt. Massie	Fluvanna (Va)				90 (2 x 3R, 2 x N)	0	1	10	12
		Capt. Milledge	Georgia battery				69 (2 x 3R, 2 x 10P)	?	?	?	NA
Rodes' Division Artillery	~~Lt. Col. Carter~~ (4 Staff)	Capt. Reese	Jeff Davis (Al)				79 (4 x 3R)	0	0	8	10
		Capt. Carter	King William (Va)	9	37	0	103 (2 x 10P, 2 x N)	7	4	12	22
		Capt. Page (W)	Morris Louisa (Va)				114 (4 x N)	7	25	7	34
		Capt. Fry	Orange (Va)				80 (2 x 3R, 2 x 10P)	0	0	7	8

SECOND CORPS *(continued from previous page)*

Division	Brigade	Regiment or Battery		Chancellorsville			Gettysburg				
				K	W	M	Battle Strength	KIA	WIA	MIA	% loss
Early's Division Artillery	Lt. Col. Jones (9 Staff)	Capt. Carrington	Charlottesville (Va)				71 (4 x N)	0	0	2	3
		Capt. Tanner	Courtney (Va)	0	21	0	90 (4 x 3R)	0	0	2	2
		Capt. Green	Louisiana Guard				60 (2 x 3R, 2 x 10P)	2	5	0	12
		Capt. Garber	Staunton (Va)				60 (4 x N)	0	1	0	2
Johnson's Division Artillery	Maj. Latimer (K) Capt. Raine (9 Staff)	Capt. Dement	1st Maryland	3	6	0	90 (4 x N)	1	4	0	6
		Capt. Carpenter	Alleghany (Va)	1	3	0	91 (2 x 3R, 2 x N)	10	14	0	26
		Capt. Brown (W)	Chesapeake (Md)	3	6	0	76 (4 x 10H)	8	9	0	22
		Capt. Raine	Lee (Va)	1	3	0	90 (3R, 10P, 20P)	2	2	0	4
20,503 all ranks	18 brigades	61 regiments, 20 batteries, 80 guns		All ranks casualties, Gettysburg				1,295	3,693	1,689	33

Division	Brigade	Commander	Regiment or Battery	Chancellorsville K	W	M	Gettysburg Battle Strength	KIA	WIA	MIA	% loss
Maj. Gen. HOOD (W) Law (11 Staff)	Brig. Gen. Law (P) Col. Sheffield (4 Staff)	Lt. Col. Scruggs	4th Alabama				346	21	45	21	25
		Col. Oates	15th Alabama				499	31	50	90	34
		Col. Perry	44th Alabama				363	24	66	4	26
		Col. Jackson (W)	47th Alabama				347	14	26	4	13
		Col. Sheffield	48th Alabama				374	9	66	7	27
							1,929				
	Texas Brigade Brig. Gen. Robertson (W) (5 Staff)	Lt. Col. Work	1st Texas				426	29	46	22	23
		Col. Key (W)	4th Texas				415	28	53	31	27
		Col. Powell (W, C)	5th Texas				409	54	112	45	52
		Col. Manning (W)	3rd Arkansas				479	41	101	40	38
							1,729				
	Brig. Gen. Benning (4 Staff)	Lt. Col. Harris (K)	2nd Georgia				348	25	66	11	29
		Col. DuBose	15th Georgia				368	14	58	99	46
		Col. Hodges	17th Georgia				350	31	66	11	31
		Col. Jones (K)	20th Georgia				349	25	84	28	39
							1,415				
	Brig. Gen. 'Tige' Anderson (W) Lt. Col. Luffman (temp) Col. White (10 Staff)	Col. White	7th Georgia				377	5	10	6	6
		Col. Towers	8th Georgia				312	36	103	29	54
		Lt. Col. Mounger (K)	9th Georgia				340	34	123	32	56
		Col. Little (W)	11th Georgia				310	40	156	5	65
		Col. Brown (W)	59th Georgia				525	37	75	30	27
							1,864				
Maj. Gen. McLAWS (11 Staff)	Brig. Gen. Kershaw (6 Staff)	Col. Kennedy	2nd South Carolina				412	53	100	17	41
		Maj. Maffett	3rd South Carolina				406	22	59	6	21
		Col. Aiken	7th South Carolina	12	90	2	408	29	79	7	28
		Col. Henagan	8th South Carolina				300	31	74	0	35
		Col. de Sausurre (K)	15th South Carolina				448	31	74	0	32
		Lt. Col. Rice	3rd SC Battalion				203	14	31	3	24
							2,177				
	Brig. Gen. Semmes (K) Col. Bryan (4 Staff)	Col. Weems	10th Georgia				303?	17	73	11	33
		Col. Manning	50th Georgia	85	492	26	302?	17	65	14	32
		Col. Ball	51st Georgia				303?	15	40	40	31
		Col. Simms	53rd Georgia				422	30	61	8	23
							1,330				
	Brig. Gen. Barksdale (K) Col. Humphreys (4 Staff)	Col. Carter	13th Mississippi				481	39	171	33	50
		Col. Holder	17th Mississippi	43	208	341	469	64	108	98	58
		Col. Griffin	18th Mississippi				242	20	81	36	57
		Col. Humphreys	21st Mississippi				424	18	110	11	33
							1,616				
	Brig. Gen. Wofford (4 Staff)	Col. Bryan	16th Georgia				303?	20	41	43	34
		Lt. Col. Ruff	18th Georgia				302?	3	16	17	12
		Col. McMillan	24th Georgia	74	479	9	303?	10	29	46	28
		Lt. Col. Glenn	Cobb's (Ga) Legion				213	6	16	?	10+
		Lt. Col. Barclay	Phillips' (Ga) Legion				273	6	41	19	24
		Brigade commander	3rd Batt. Ga Sharpshooters				209	3	3	7+	6+
							1,603				
Maj. Gen. PICKETT (11 Staff)	Brig. Gen. Kemper (W, C) Lt. Col. Mayo (W) (11 Staff)	Col. Williams (K)	1st Virginia				209	27	73	13	54
		Lt. Col. Mayo (W)	3rd Virginia				332	30	41	57	39
		Col. Patton (K)	7th Virginia				335	31	82	36	44
		Lt. Col. Otey (W)	11th Virginia				359	34	86	26	41
		Lt. Col. Terry (W)	24th Virginia				495	47	83	33	41
							1,730				

(continued overleaf)

Division	Brigade	Regiment or Battery		Chancellorsville K	W	M	Gettysburg Battle Strength	KIA	WIA	MIA	% loss
(continued) Maj. Gen. PICKETT (11 Staff)	Brig. Gen. Garnett (K) Maj. Peyton (4 Staff)	Lt. Col. Hunton (W)	8th Virginia– *see note*				193	39	79	60	92
		Lt Col. Carrington (W)	18th Virginia				312	54	134	57	78
		Lt. Col. Gantt (W)	19th Virginia				328	42	41	68	46
		Col. Allen (K)	28th Virginia				333	44	65	73	55
		Col. Stuart (K)	56th Virginia				289	51	72	66	65
							1,455				
	Brig. Gen. Armistead (K) Col. Aylett (W) (4 Staff)	Col. Owens (K)	9th Virginia				257	24	70	83	69
		Col. Hodges (K)	14th Virginia				422	45	?	?	NA
		Col. Edmonds (K)	38th Virginia				356	55	135	40	65
		Lt. Col. Aylett (W)	53rd Virginia				435	30	?	?	NA
		Col. Magruder (K)	57th Virginia				476	32	?	?	NA
							1,946				
Corps Reserve Artillery Col. Walton (4 Staff)	Col. Alexander (9 Staff)	Capt. Woolfolk (W)	Ashland (Va) – 6 guns	6	35	24	103 (2 x 20P, 4N)	3	24	1	28
		Capt. Jordan	Bedford (Va)				78 (4 x 3R)	1	7	1	11
		Lt. Gilbert	Brooks (SC)				71 (4 x 12H)	7	29	0	51
		Capt. Moody	Madison (La) Light				1,35 (4 x 24H)	4	29	0	24
		Capt. Parker	Richmond (Va)				90 (3 x 3R, 10P)	3	14	1	20
		Capt. Taylor	Bath (Va)				95 (4 x N)	4	8	1	14
	Maj. Eshleman (9 Staff)	Capt. Squires	Washington (La) 1st Co	4	8	27	77 (3 x N)	1	0	3	5
		Capt. Richardson	Washington (La) 2nd Co				80 (2N, 1 x 3R)	2	3	1	7
		Capt. Miller	Washington (La) 3rd Co				93 (3 x N)	5	2	3	11
		Capt. Norcom (W)	Washington (La) 4th Co				80 (2N, 1 x 12H)	0	6	4	12
Hood's Division Artillery	Maj. Henry (9 Staff)	Capt. Latham	Branch (NC) – 5 guns				112 (4N, 1 x 12H)	1	2	0	3
		Capt. Reilly	Rowan (NC) – 6 guns				148 (see note)	2	4	0	4
		Capt. Garden	Palmetto (SC) – 5 guns				63 (2N, 3 x 10P)	2	5	0	11
McLaws' Division Artillery	Col. Cabell (4 Staff)	Capt. Manley	1st North Carolina, A	1	10	0	131 (2 x 3R, 2 x N)	3	10	0	10
		Capt. Fraser (W)	Pulaski (Ga)	1	2	2	63 (3R, 10P)	7	12	0	30
		Capt. McCarthy	1st Richmond	2	2	0	90 (2 x 3R, 2 x N)	3	10	0	14
		Capt. Carlton (W)	Troup (Ga) – 2 guns	1	10	0	90 (12H, 10P)	2	5	0	8
Pickett's Division Artillery	Maj. Dearing (9 Staff)	Capt. Stribling	Fauquier (Va) – 6 guns				134 (4N, 2 x 10P)	1	4	0	4
		Capt. Caskie	Richmond Hampton				90 (2N, 3R, 10P)	0	3	1	4
		Capt. Macon	Richmond Fayette				90 (2 x N, 2 x 10P)	3	1	1	6
		Capt. Blount	Lynchburg				96 (4 x N)	5	3	2	10
20,935 all ranks	16 brigades	53 regiments, 22 batteries, 99 guns		All ranks casualties, Gettysburg			1,607	4,045+	2,087+	37+	

Note: 8th Virginia suffered the highest percentage loss in the entire army. Of the field officers in Pickett's division only staff Col. Cabell survived unhurt. Rowan's battery had two each 10-pounder Parrotts, 3" rifles and Napoleons

CAVALRY DIVISION

Division	Brigade		Regiment or Battery	Chancellorsville			Gettysburg				
				K	W	M	Battle Strength	KIA	WIA	MIA	% loss
Led Ewell's corps up the Cumberland Valley, rejoined Stuart at Gettysburg	Brig. Gen. Jenkins (W) Col. Ferguson (4 Staff)	Col. Thoburn	14th Virginia				265	4	2	0	2
		Col. Ferguson	16th Virginia				265	1	0	0	>1
		Col. French	17th Va (with EARLY)				241	0	2	6	3
		Lt. Col. Witcher	34th Va Battalion				172	?	?	?	NA
		Lt. Col. White	35th Va Batt. (with EARLY)				232	?	?	?	NA
		Col. Ferguson	36th Va Battalion				125	1	0	0	>1
		Capt. Jackson	Jackson's battery				107? (4 x 3R) 1,300	0	1	0	>1
Main cavalry force, rode east around the Union army Maj. Gen. STUART (20 Staff)	Brig. Gen. Hampton (W) Col. Baker (5 Staff)	Lt. Col. Warring	Jefferson Davis Legion				246	4	10	1	6
		Col. Barker	1st North Carolina				407	2	17	25	11
		Brigade commander	1st South Carolina				339	1	9	4	4
		Col. Butler	2nd South Carolina				186	2	5	0	4
		Col. Young	Cobb's (Ga) Legion				330	9	5	7	6
		Lt. Col. Phillips	Phillips (Ga) Legion				238 1,746	3	7	0	4
	Brig. Gen. Fitzhugh Lee	Maj. Gilmor	1st Maryland (with EWELL)				310	0	2	15	5
		Col. Drake	1st Virginia				310	6	7	10	7
		Col. Munford	2nd Virginia				385	1	4	11	4
		Col. Owen	3rd Virginia	0	15	0	210	0	5	1	3
		Col. Wickham	4th Virginia	1	1	4	544	0	1	32	6
		Col. Rosser	5th Virginia				150 1,909	?	?	?	NA
	Col. Chambliss (4 Staff)	Col. Spruill	2nd North Carolina				145	1	2	6	6
		Col. Beale	9th Virginia				490	2	9	7	4
		Col. Davis	10th Virginia	0	4	31	236	1	9	2	5
		Col. Phillips	13th Virginia				298 1,169	1	11	5	6
	Horse Artillery Maj. Beckham (9 Staff)	Capt. Breathed	Breathed's (Va)	1	0	0	106? (4 x 3R)	0	1	0	>1
		Capt. McGregor	McGregor's (Va)	3	6	8	106? (2N, 2 x 3R)	0	0	2	2
		Capt. Griffin	Griffin's (Md)				106? (4 x 10P)	?	?	?	NA
		Capt. Hart	Hart's (SC) – 8 guns				107? (3 x B)	1	0	0	>1
6,934 all ranks	**5 brigades**		**22 regiments, 5 batteries, 24 guns**	**All ranks casualties, Gettysburg**				**40+**	**111+**	**134+**	**4+**

CAVALRY BRIGADES NOT AT GETTYSBURG

Division	Brigade		Regiment or Battery				Battle Strength				
With main army up the Cumberland Valley, posted as flank guard at Fairfield	Brig. Gen. Robertson (i/c) (4 Staff)	Col. Ferebee	4th North Carolina				504				
		Col. Garrett	5th North Carolina				458				
		Capt. Moorman	Moorman's (Va) battery				112 (4 x 3R?) 962				
	Brig. Gen. 'Grumble' Jones (4 Staff)	Maj. Flournoy	6th Virginia				625				
		Lt. Col. Marshall	7th Virginia				428				
		Col. Lomax	11th Virginia				424				
		Capt. Chew	Chew's (Va) battery				99 (4 x 3R?) 1,477				
Joined army in the Cumberland Valley, baggage guard at Cashtown	Brig. Gen. Imboden (4 Staff)	Col. Smith	62nd Virginia Infantry				1095				
		Brigade commander	18th Virginia				914				
		Capt. McNeill	Partisan Rangers (Va)				90				
		Capt. McClanahan	Staunton Horse Artillery				142 (4 x 3R?) 2,099				
4,916 all ranks	**3 brigades**		**8 regiments, 3 batteries, 12? guns**				**No casualties at Gettysburg**				

APPENDIX D **DRAMATIS PERSONAE**

Includes states of origin, previous military experience and identity of units commanded.

UNION
(*see also* Appendix A)

Ames, Brig. Gen. Adelbert (1835–1933).
Maine, West Point 1861. 2nd Bde/1st
Div, Howard's Corps.

Ayres, Brig. Gen. Romeyn (1825–88).
New York, West Point 1847. 2nd Div,
Sykes's Corps.

Barlow, Brig. Gen. Francis (1835–96).
New York, volunteer. 1st Div, Howard's
Corps.

Barnes, Brig. Gen. James (1801–69).
Pennsylvania, West Point 1829.
1st Div, Howard's Corps.

Baxter, Brig. Gen. Henry (1821–73).
Michigan, volunteer. 2nd Bde,
Robinson's Div, Reynold's Corps.

Berdan, Col. Hiram (c.1823–93).
New York, volunteer. Sharpshooter
Bde, Birney's Div, Sickles's Corps.

Birney, Maj. Gen. David (1825–64).
Pennsylvania, volunteer. 1st Div,
Sickles's Corps.

Brewster, Col. William (1828–69).
Connecticut, militia. 2nd Bde,
Humphreys's Div, Sickles's Corps.

Brooke, Col. John (1838–1926).
Pennsylvania, volunteer. 4th Bde,
Caldwell's Div, Hancock's Corps.

Buford, Brig. Gen. John (1826–63).
Kentucky, West Point 1848. 1st Div,
Cavalry Corps.

Burbank, Col. Sidney (1802–82).
Massachussetts, West Point 1829.
2nd Bde, Ayres's Div, Sykes's Corps.

Burling, Col. George (?–1885).
New Jersey, volunteer. 3rd Bde,
Humphreys's Div, Sickles's Corps.

Caldwell, Brig. Gen. John (1833–1912).
Maine, volunteer. 1st Div, Hancock's
Corps.

Candy, Col. Charles (1832–?). Kentucky,
US Army trooper. 1st Bde, Geary's Div,
Slocum's Corps.

Carr, Brig. Gen. Joseph (1828–95). New
York, volunteer. 1st Bde, Humphreys's
Div, Sickles's Corps.

Carroll, Col. Samuel (1832–93).
Washington D.C., West Point 1856,
1st Bde, Hays's Div, Hancock's Corps.

Cobham, Col. George (?–1864). England,
volunteer. 2nd Bde, Geary's Div,
Slocum's Corps.

Coster, Col. Charles (?–1888). New York,
militia. 1st Bde, von Steinwehr's Div,
Howard's Corps.

Crawford, Brig. Gen. Samuel (1829–92).
Pennsylvania, army surgeon.
3rd Division, Sykes's Corps.

Cross, Col. Edward (1832–63). New
Hampshire, Mexican Army, 1st Bde,
Caldwell's Div, Hancock's Corps.

Custer, Brig. Gen. George (1839–76).
Ohio, West Point 1861 (last). 2nd Bde,
Kilpatrick's Div, Cavalry Corps.

Cutler, Brig. Gen. Lysander (1807–66).
Mass., volunteer. 2nd Bde,
Wadsworth's Div, Reynolds's Corps.

Day, Col. Hannibal (1804–91). Army
family, West Point 1823. 1st Bde,
Ayres's Div, Sykes's Corps.

Devin, Col. Thomas (1822–78). New
York, militia. 2nd Bde, Buford's Div,
Cavalry Corps.

Doubleday, Maj. Gen. Abner (1819–93).
New York, West Point 1842. 3rd Div,
Reynolds's Corps.

Farnsworth, Brig. Gen. Elon (1837–63).
Illinois, volunteer. 1st Bde, Kilpatrick's
Div, Cavalry Corps.

Fisher, Col. Joseph (1813–1900).
Pennsylvania, volunteer. 3rd Bde,
Crawford's Div, Sykes's Corps.

Gamble, Col. William (1818–66). Ireland, trooper in UK & US armies. 1st Bde, Buford's Div, Cavalry Corps.

Geary, Brig. Gen. John (1819–73). Pennsylvania, Mexican War. 2nd Division, Slocum's Corps.

Gibbon, Brig. Gen. John (1827–96). Pennsylvania, West Point 1847. 2nd Div, Hancock's Corps.

Graham, Brig. Gen. Charles (1824–89). New York, Mexican War Navy. 1st Bde, Birney's Div, Sickles's Corps.

Greene, Brig. Gen. George (1801–99). Rhode Island, West Point 1823. 3rd Bde, Geary's Div, Slocum's Corps.

Gregg, Brig. Gen. David (1833–1916). Pennsylvania, West Point 1855. 2nd Div, Cavalry Corps.

Gregg, Col. John (1827–92). Pennsylvania, Mexican War. 3rd Bde, Gregg's Div, Cavalry Corps.

Hall, Col. Norman (1837–67). Michigan, West Point 1858. 3rd Bde, Gibbon's Div, Hancock's Corps.

Hancock, Maj. Gen. Winfield (1824–86). Pennsylvania, West Point 1844. II Corps commander.

Harrow, Brig. Gen. William (1822–72). Indiana, volunteer. 1st Bde, Gibbon's Div, Hancock's Corps.

Hays, Brig. Gen. Alexander (1819–64). Pennsylvania, West Point 1844. 3rd Div, Hancock's Corps.

Hooker, Maj. Gen. Joseph (1814–79). Massachussetts, West Point 1837. Meade's predecessor.

Howard, Maj. Gen. Oliver (1830–1909). Maine, West Point 1854. XI Corps commander.

Humphreys, Brig. Gen. Andrew (1810–83). Pennsylvania, West Point 1831. 2nd Div, Sickles's Corps.

Hunt, Brig. Gen. Henry (1819–89). Michigan, West Point 1839. Chief of Artillery.

Kane, Brig. Gen. Thomas (1822–83). Pennsylvania, Volunteer. 2nd Bde, Geary's Div, Slocum's Corps.

Kelly, Col. Patrick (?–1864). Ireland, militia. 2nd Bde, Caldwell's Div, Hancock's Corps.

Kilpatrick, Brig. Gen. Judson (1836–81). New Jersey, West Point 1861. 3rd Division, Cavalry Corps.

Krzyzanowski, Col. Wladimir (1824–87). Poland, volunteer. 2nd Bde, Schurz's Div, Howard's Corps.

Lockwood, Brig. Gen. Henry (1814–99). Delaware, West Point 1836. 2nd Bde, Williams's Div, Slocum's Corps.

McCandless, Col. William (?–?). Pennsylvania, volunteer. 1st Bde, Crawford's Div, Sykes's Corps.

McDougall, Col. Archibald (1817–64). New York, volunteer. 1st Bde, Williams's Div, Slocum's Corps.

McIntosh, Col. John (1829–71). Florida, volunteer (previously US Navy). 1st Bde, Gregg's Div, Cavalry Corps.

Meade, Maj. Gen. George (1815–72). Pennsylvania, West Point 1835. Army commander.

Meredith, Brig. Gen. Solomon (1810–75). Indiana, Politician. 1st Bde, Wadsworth's Div, Reynolds's Corps.

Merritt, Brig. Gen. Wesley (1834–1910). Illinois, West Point 1860. Reserve Bde, Buford's Div, Cavalry Corps.

Neill, Brig. Gen. Thomas (1826–85). Pennsylvania, West Point 1847. 2nd Bde, Howe's Div, Sedgwick's Corps.

Nevin, Col. David (?–?). New York, volunteer. 3rd Bde, Wheaton's Div, Sedgwick's Corps.

Newton, Maj. Gen. John (1822–95). Virginia, West Point 1842. Took over Reynolds's Corps.

Paul, Brig. Gen. Gabriel (1813–86). Missouri, West Point 1834. 1st Bde, Robinson's Div, Reynolds's Corps.

Pleasanton, Maj. Gen. Alfred (1824–97). Washington D.C., West Point 1844. Cavalry Corps commander.

Reynolds, Maj. Gen. John (1820–63). Pennsylvania, West Point 1841. I Corps commander.

Robinson, Brig. Gen. John (1817–97). New York, expelled West Point 1838. 2nd Div, Reynolds's Corps.

Rowley, Brig. Gen. Thomas (1808–92). Pennsylvania, politician. 1st Bde, Doubleday's Div, Reynolds's Corps.

Ruger, Brig. Gen. Thomas (1833–1907). New York, West Point 1854. 3rd Bde, Williams's Div, Slocum's Corps.

Schimmelfennig, Brig. Gen. Alexander (1824–65). Prussia, volunteer. 1st Bde, Schurz's Div, Howard's Corps.

Schurz, Maj. Gen. Carl (1829–1906). Prussia, politician. 3rd Div, Howard's Corps.

Sedgwick, Maj. Gen. John (1813–64). Connecticut, West Point 1837. VI Corps commander.

Shaler, Brig. Gen. Alexander (1827–1911). New York, militia. 1st Bde, Wheaton's Div, Sedgwick's Corps.

Sickles, Maj. Gen. Daniel (1819–1914). New York, politician. III Corps commander.

Slocum, Maj. Gen. Henry (1827–94). New York, West Point 1852, militia. XII Corps commander.

Smith, Col. Orland (1825–?). Ohio, Volunteer. 2nd Bde, von Steinwehr's Div, Howard's Corps.

Smyth, Col. Thomas (1832–65). Ireland, volunteer. 2nd Bde, Hays's Div, Hancock's Corps.

Stannard, Brig. Gen. George (1820–86). Vermont, militia. 3rd Bde, Doubleday's Div, Reynolds's Corps.

Stone, Col. Roy (?–1901). Pennsylvania, volunteer. 2nd Bde, Doubleday's Div, Reynolds's Corps.

Sweitzer, Col. Jacob (?–1888). Pennsylvania, volunteer. 2nd Bde, Barnes's Div, Sykes's Corps.

Sykes, Maj. Gen. George (1822–80). Delaware, West Point 1842. V Corps commander.

Tilton, Col. William (?–1889). Massachussetts, volunteer. 1st Bde, Barnes's Div, Sykes's Corps.

Trobriand, Col. Philippe de (1816–97). France, volunteer. 3rd Bde, Birney's Div, Sickles's Corps.

Vincent, Col. Strong (1837–63). Pennsylvania, volunteer. 3rd Bde, Barnes's Div, Sykes's Corps.

von Gilsa, Col. Leopold (?–?). Prussian officer, volunteer. 1st Bde, Barlow's Div, Howard's Corps.

von Steinwehr, Brig. Gen. Baron Adolph (1822–77). Prussian officer, volunteer. 2nd Div, Howard's Corps.

Wadsworth, Brig. Gen. James (1807–64). New York, politician. 1st Division, Reynolds's Corps.

Ward, Brig. Gen. John (1823–1903). New York, Mexican War. 2nd Bde, Birney's Div, Sickles's Corps.

Webb, Brig. Gen. Alexander (1835–1911). Pennsylvania, West Point 1855. 2nd Bde, Gibbon's Div, Hancock's Corps.

Weed, Brig. Gen. Stephen (1831–63). New York, West Point 1854. 3rd Bde, Ayres's Div, Sykes's Corps.

Willard, Col. George (1828–63). New York, non-West Point regular. 3rd Bde, Hays's Div, Hancock's Corps.

Williams, Brig. Gen. Alpheus (1810–78). Connecticut, Mexican War. 1st Div, Slocum's Corps.

Zook, Brig. Gen. Samuel (1821–63). Pennsylvania, militia. 3rd Bde, Caldwell's Div, Hancock's Corps.

CONFEDERATE
(*see also* Appendix B)

Anderson, Maj. Gen. Richard (1821–79). South Carolina, West Point 1842. Div, Hill's Corps.

Anderson, Brig. Gen. 'Tige' (1824–1901). Georgia, Mexican War. Bde, Hood's Div, Longstreet's Corps.

Archer, Brig. Gen. James (1817–64). Maryland, non-West Point regular. Bde, Heth's Div, Hill's Corps.

Armistead, Brig. Gen. Lewis (1817–63). Virginia, expelled West Point 1837 (for breaking a plate on Jubal Early's head). Bde, Pickett's Div, Longstreet's Corps.

Avery, Col. Isaac (1828–63). North Carolina, volunteer. Bde, Early's Div, Ewell's Corps.

Barksdale, Brig. Gen. William (1821–63). Mississippi, politician. Bde, McLaws's Div, Longstreet's Corps.

Benning, Brig. Gen. Henry (1814–75). Georgia, politician. Bde, Hood's Div, Longstreet's Corps.

Brockenbrough, Col. John (1830–92). Virginia Military Institute, volunteer. Bde, Heth's Div, Hill's Corps.

Daniel, Brig. Gen. Junius (1828–64). North Carolina, West Point 1851. Bde, Rodes's Div, Ewell's Corps.

Davis, Brig. Gen. Joseph (1825–96). Mississippi, politician. Bde, Heth's Div, Hill's Corps.

Doles, Brig. Gen. George (1830–64). Georgia, Mexican War. Bde, Rodes's Div, Ewell's Corps.

Early, Maj. Gen. Jubal (1816–94). Virginia, West Point 1837. Div, Ewell's Corps.

Ewell, Lt. Gen. Richard (1817–72). Virginia, West Point 1840. II Corps commander.

Garnett, Brig. Gen. Richard (1817–63). Virginia, West Point 1841. Bde, Pickett's Div, Longstreet's Corps.

Gordon, Brig. Gen. John (1832–1904). Georgia, volunteer. Bde, Early's Div, Ewell's Corps.

Hampton, Brig. Gen. Wade (1818–1902). South Carolina, millionaire. Bde, Cavalry Div.

Hays, Brig. Gen. Harry (1820–76). Louisiana, Mexican War. Bde, Early's Div, Ewell's Corps.

Heth, Maj. Gen. Henry (1825–99). Virginia, West Point 1847 (last). Div, Hill's Corps.

Hill, Lt. Gen. Ambrose (1825–65). Virginia, West Point 1847. III Corps commander.

Hood, Maj. Gen. John (1831–79). Kentucky/Texas, West Point 1853. Div, Longstreet's Corps.

Imboden, Brig. Gen. John (1823–95). Virginia, politician. Irregular cavalry commander.

Iverson, Jr., Brig. Gen. Alfred (1829–1911). Georgia, Mexican War. Bde, Rodes's Div, Ewell's Corps.

Jenkins, Brig. Gen. Albert (1830–64). West Virginia, politician. Bde, cavalry Div.

Johnson, Maj. Gen. Edward (1816–73). Kentucky, West Point 1838. Div, Ewell's Corps.

Jones, Brig. Gen. 'Grumble' (1824–64). Virginia, West Point 1848. Bde, cavalry Div.

Jones, Brig. Gen. John (1820–64). Virginia, West Point 1841. Bde, Johnson's Div, Ewell's Corps.

Kemper, Brig. Gen. James (1823–95). Virginia, politician. Bde, Pickett's Div, Longstreet's Corps.

Kershaw, Brig. Gen. Joseph (1822–94). South Carolina, Mexican War. Bde, McLaws's Div, Longstreet's Corps.

Lane, Brig. Gen. James (1833–1907). Virginia Military Institute 1854. Bde, Pender's Div, Ewell's Corps.

Lang, Col. David (1838–1917). Florida, Georgia Military Institute. Bde, Anderson's Div, Hill's Corps.

Law, Brig. Gen. Evander (1836–1920).
South Carolina Military Institute. Bde,
Hood's Div, Longstreet's Corps.

Lee, Brig. Gen. Fitzhugh (1835–1905).
Virginia, West Point 1856. Bde,
cavalry Div.

Lee, Gen Robert (1807–70). Virginia,
West Point 1829. Army commander.

Longstreet, Lt. Gen. James (1821–1904).
Georgia, West Point 1842. I Corps
commander.

Mahone, Brig. Gen. William (1826–95).
Virginia Military Institute. Bde,
Anderson's Div, Hill's Corps.

McLaws, Maj. Gen. Lafayette (1821–97).
Georgia, West Point 1842. Division,
Longstreet's Corps.

O'Neal, Col. Edward (1818–90).
Alabama, politician. Bde, Rodes's Div,
Ewell's Corps.

Pender, Maj. Gen. William (1834–63).
North Carolina, West Point 1854.
Div, Hill's Corps.

Pendleton, Brig. Gen. William
(1809–83). Virginia, West Point 1830.
Chief of artillery.

Pettigrew, Brig. Gen. Johnston
(1828–63). North Carolina, militia.
Bde, Heth's Div, Hill's Corps.

Pickett, Maj. Gen. George (1825–75).
Virginia, West Point 1846 (last).
Div, Longstreet's Corps.

Posey, Brig. Gen. Carnot (1818–63).
Mississippi, Mexican War. Bde,
Anderson's Div, Hill's Corps.

Ramseur, Brig. Gen. Stephen (1837–64).
North Carolina, West Point 1861.
Bde, Rodes's Div, Ewell's Corps.

Robertson, Brig. Gen. Jerome (1815–91).
Texas, politician. Texas Bde, Hood's
Div, Longstreet's Corps.

Rodes, Maj. Gen. Robert (1829–64).
Virginia Military Institute 1848.
Div, Ewell's Corps.

Scales, Brig. Gen. Alfred (1827–92).
North Carolina, politician. Bde,
Pender's Div, Hill's Corps.

Semmes, Brig. Gen. Paul (1815–63).
Georgia, militia. Bde, McLaws's Div,
Longstreet's Corps.

Smith, Brig. Gen. William (1797–1887).
Virginia, politician. Bde, Early's Div,
Ewell's Corps.

Steuart, Brig. Gen. George (1828–1903).
Maryland, West Point 1848. Bde,
Johnson's Div, Ewell's Corps.

Stuart, Maj. Gen. 'Jeb' (1833–64).
Virginia, West Point 1854.
Commander cavalry div.

Trimble, Maj. Gen. Isaac (1802–88).
Maryland, West Point 1822.
Took over Pender's Div, Hill's Corps.

Walker, Brig. Gen. James (1832–1901).
Expelled Virginia Military Institute
1852 for challenging Stonewall Jackson
to a duel. Ironically, commanded
Stonewall Bde, Johnson's Div, Ewell's
Corps at Gettysburg.

Wilcox, Brig. Gen. Cadmus (1824–90).
Tennessee, West Point 1846. Bde,
Anderson's Div, Hill's Corps.

Williams, Col. Jesse (1831–64).
Louisiana, volunteer. Bde, Johnson's
Div, Ewell's Corps.

Wofford, Brig. Gen. William (1824–84).
Georgia, politician. Bde, McLaws's Div,
Longstreet's Corps.

Wright, Brig. Gen. 'Rans' (1826–72).
Georgia, politician. Bde, Anderson's
Div, Hill's Corps.

BIBLIOGRAPHY

• As emphasized in the text, this interpretation is based on three keystone works: Coddington, E., *The Gettysburg Campaign: A Study in Command* (New York: Touchstone, 1997); Pfanz, H., *Gettysburg: The Second Day* and *Gettysburg: Culp's Hill and Cemetery Hill* (Chapel Hill: University of North Carolina Press, 1987 & 1993).

• The following CD-ROMs from Guild Press of Carmel, Indiana (www.guildpress.com) contain the indispensable primary sources for the war overall: *The War of the Rebellion: A Compilation of the Official Records of the Union and Confederate Armies; Confederate Military History*; and *The Southern Historical Society Papers*.

• Ladd, D. & A. (eds.), *The Bachelder Papers*, 3 vols. (Dayton: Morningside House, 1994–95), contains the comprehensive oral history of the battle collected from 1863 to 1894 by John Bachelder. Morningside House also publishes *The Gettysburg Magazine*, organ of the on-line Gettysburg Discussion Group, and many other excellent works.

• Personal visits are essential but vital terrain features can emerge from a comparison between the CD-ROM *The Atlas of the Official Records of the Civil War*, also from Guild Press, and the *Digital Topographic Maps of Civil War Battlefields* by the Digital History Corporation of Oakton, VA (www.DigHistory.com).

• Busey, J. & Martin, D., *Regimental Strengths and Losses at Gettysburg* (Highstown: Longstreet House, 1994) is the definitive source for casualty figures.

• Nobody can write about battle without acknowledging a debt to: Holmes, R., *Firing Line* (London: Jonathan Cape, 1985); Keegan, J., *The Face of Battle* (London: Chaucer Press, 1976); Hanson, V., *The Western Way of War* (New York: Alfred A. Knopf, 1989); and Dixon, N., *On the Psychology of Military Incompetence* (London: Jonathan Cape, 1976).

• Grossman, Lt. Col. D., *On Killing: The Psychological Cost of Learning to Kill in War and Society* (New York: Back Bay Books, 1996) and Linderman, G., *Embattled Courage: The Experience of Combat in the American Civil War* (New York: The Free Press, 1987) are also useful discussions of men in battle.

Other essential works are:

Beringer, R., Hattaway, H., Jones, A. & Still, W. Jr. (eds.), *Why the South Lost the Civil War* (Athens: University of Georgia Press, 1986).

Boritt, G., *The Gettysburg Nobody Knows* (Oxford: Oxford University Press, 1997).

Cleaves, F., *Meade of Gettysburg* (Norman: University of Oklahoma Press, 1960).

Donald, D., *Lincoln* (London: Jonathan Cape, 1995).

Gallagher, G. (ed.), *The First Day at Gettysburg* and *The Second Day at Gettysburg* (Kent: Kent State University Press, 1992 & 1993); *The Third Day at Gettysburg and Beyond* and *Fighting for the Confederacy: The Personal Recollections of General Edward Porter Alexander* (Chapel Hill: University of North Carolina Press, 1994 & 1989).

Hattaway, H. & Jones, A. (eds.), *How the North Won: A Military History of the Civil War* (Urbana: University of Illinois Press, 1983).

Longacre, E., *The Cavalry at Gettysburg* (London: Associated University Presses, 1986).

McPherson, J., *Ordeal by Fire: The Civil War and Reconstruction* (New York: Alfred A. Knopf, 1982); *Battle Cry of Freedom: The Civil War Era* (New York: Oxford University Press, 1988); and with Cooper, W. Jr. (eds.), *Writing the Civil War: The Quest to Understand* (Columbia: University of South Carolina Press, 1998).

Reardon, C., *Pickett's Charge in History and Memory* (Chapel Hill: University of North Carolina Press, 1997).

Rollins, R. (ed.), *Pickett's Charge! Eyewitness Accounts* (Redondo Beach: Rank and File Publications, 1994).

Sears, S., *Chancellorsville* (New York: Houghton Mifflin, 1996).

Shaara, M., *The Killer Angels: A Novel* (New York: David McKay, 1974).

Shultz, D., *'Double Canister at Ten Yards': The Federal Artillery and the Repulse of Pickett's Charge* (Redondo Beach: Rank and File Publications, 1995).

Sifakis, S., *Who Was Who in the Civil War* (New York: Facts on File, 1988).

Tagg, L., *The Generals of Gettysburg* (Campbell: Savas Publishing Co., 1998).

Thomas, E., *Bold Dragoon: The Life of J.E.B. Stuart* (New York: Harper and Row, 1986) and *Robert E. Lee: A Biography* (London: W.W. Norton, 1995).

Wert, J., *General James Longstreet: The Confederacy's Most Controversial Soldier* (New York: Simon & Schuster, 1993).

INDEX

Alexander, Col. Porter 78, 101, 119, 123, 126, 175, 181, 186, 195
Ames, Brig. Gen. Adelbert 57, 58, 139, 144–5, 146
Anderson, Brig. Gen. 'Tige' 87, 99–100, 105–6, 110, 115, 116
Anderson, Maj. Gen. Richard 77, 83, 127–30, 133, 140, 146, 186
Archer, Brig. Gen. James 45, 47, 52
Armistead, Brig. Gen. Lewis 181–5
Avery, Col. Isaac 57, 59, 61, 139, 144–6
Ayres, Brig. Gen. Romeyn 109, 113, 115

Barksdale, Brig. Gen. William 26, 79, 104, 109, 112, 114, 117, 119, 123–6
Barlow, Brig. Gen. Francis 57–62, 91, 139
Barnes, Brig. Gen. James 99, 100–1, 105, 109
Baxter, Brig. Gen. Henry 45, 52
Benning, Brig. Gen. Henry 87, 100
Berdan, Col. Hiram 117
Birney, Maj. Gen. David 62, 85, 90, 95, 112, 184
    Peach Orchard 117–19
    Stony Hill 99, 101, 105, 106
Brockenbrough, Col. John 45, 53, 170, 180, 195
Brooke, Col. John 109, 110–11
Buford, Brig. Gen. John 38, 41, 77, 81–3, 164, 188, 195
    first day 43, 45, 50, 51
    Howard's battle 65–6
Burbank, Col. Sidney 113
Burling, Col. George 99, 124

Caldwell, Brig. Gen. John 106, 107–9, 110, 111–12, 113, 132
Candy, Col. Charles 149, 153, 158–9
Carr, Brig. Gen. Joseph 131, 132, 133
Carroll, Col. Samuel 139, 146, 180
Chamberlain, Col. Joshua 13, 29, 87, 95–6, 115, 177
Cobham, Col. George 153
Coster, Col. Charles 57, 61
Crawford, Brig. Gen. Samuel 109, 115
Cross, Col. Edward 109–10, 112
Custer, Brig. Gen. George 162–4, 193
Cutler, Brig. Gen. Lysander 45, 47, 52, 69, 73

Daniel, Brig. Gen. Junius 45, 53, 157, 158–60
Davis, Brig. Gen. Joseph 45, 47–50, 180, 185
Day, Col. Hannibal 113
Devin, Col. Thomas 45, 57, 58, 59, 64
Doles, Brig. Gen. George 45, 54, 57, 59, 61

Doubleday, Maj. Gen. Abner 45, 50–4, 57–8, 70, 81, 131

Early, Maj. Gen. Jubal 45, 50, 59, 65–6, 77, 79, 140–6, 150–2, 157
Ewell, Lt. Gen. Richard 37, 40–2, 50, 58, 77, 81, 83, 162, 165
    artillery 174
    Cemetery Hill 64–6, 132, 136, 140–2, 144
    Cemetery Ridge 127, 130
    Culp's Hill 150, 154, 157, 160

Farnsworth, Brig. Gen. Elon 188
Fisher, Col. Joseph 115

Gamble, Col. William 45, 47, 52, 57, 64
Garnett, Brig. Gen. Richard 181, 184–6
Geary, Brig. Gen. John 69, 72–3, 81, 149, 151, 153–4, 155, 159, 161
Gibbon, Brig. Gen. John 62, 131, 133, 146, 170, 172, 187
Gordon, Brig. Gen. John 57, 59, 66, 69, 71, 80, 145–6
Graham, Brig. Gen. Charles 117–19, 123, 124, 132
Greene, Brig. Gen. George 73, 139, 149, 151–3, 155, 159
Gregg, Brig. Gen. David 150, 157, 162–4
Gregg, Col. John 38

Hall, Col. Norman 132, 133, 136
Hampton, Brig. Gen. Wade 80, 162, 164
Hancock, Maj. Gen. Winfield 41, 62, 64, 69–70, 72, 74–5, 81–3, 126, 176
    Cemetery Ridge 129, 131–3
    Pickett's Charge 184, 187
    Wheatfield 107
Harrow, Brig. Gen. William 131–2, 133
Hays, Brig. Gen. Alexander 170, 180–1, 184–5, 187, 191
Hays, Brig. Gen. Harry 57, 59, 61, 139, 144, 145–6
Heth, Maj. Gen. 'Harry' 45, 50, 53, 80
Hill, Lt. Gen. Ambrose 37, 43, 50, 64–5, 77, 80, 139, 174
    Cemetery Hill 132, 140
    Cemetery Ridge 129, 130, 136
Hood, Maj. Gen. John 77, 82, 83–4, 87, 90–1, 115–16
Hooker, Maj. Gen. Joseph 12, 18, 33–40, 43, 72, 82, 196, 200

Howard, Maj. Gen. Oliver 40–1, 50–2, 53, 54–66, 82, 151, 196, 200
    Cemetery Hill 139, 145–6
    Slocum's front 69–70, 72, 74
Humphreys, Brig. Gen. Andrew 82, 99, 119, 122–4, 129–32
Hunt, Brig. Gen. Henry 40, 77, 90, 155–7, 172–6

Imboden, Brig. Gen. John 195
Iverson, Jr., Brig. Gen. Alfred 45, 52–3, 58, 193–5

Jenkins, Brig. Gen. Albert 162
Johnson, Maj. Gen. Edward 71, 143–5, 150, 153, 157–8, 159
Jones, Brig. Gen. 'Grumble' 161–2, 188
Jones, Brig. Gen. John 150, 151, 159

Kane, Brig. Gen. Thomas 40, 73, 149, 153, 159
Kelly, Col. Patrick 40, 107, 109, 111
Kemper, Brig. Gen. James 184, 185, 186
Kershaw, Brig. Gen. Joseph 80, 99–101, 104–6, 109–10, 112, 115, 119
Kilpatrick, Brig. Gen. Judson 38, 41, 162, 164, 188, 193–5
Krzyzanowski, Col. Wladimir 57, 59, 61

Lane, Brig. Gen. James 180, 184
Lang, Col. David 129, 131, 133, 167, 186–7
Law, Brig. Gen. Evander 87, 167
Lee, Brig. Gen. Fitzhugh 164
Lee, Gen. Robert 9, 11–12, 18, 22–3, 30, 75, 127–9, 161–2, 167–71
    artillery 40, 174
    Cemetery Hill 64, 77, 140–1
    miscalculations 64–5, 77–8
    move to Gettysburg 33, 41, 42
    non-professionals 80
    Pickett's Charge 165, 174, 186
    Plum Run Valley 87
    post-Gettysburg 191–3, 195, 197
    Second Manassas 20
    simultaneous assaults 83
    Stony Hill 101
    view of Meade 37
    Wheatfield 112
Lincoln, Abraham 9, 12, 18–20, 35–6, 38, 78, 189–91, 193, 196, 200
Lockwood, Brig. Gen. Henry 40, 119, 126, 147–9, 157, 160
Longstreet, Lt. Gen. James 65, 77–8, 81, 83–4, 165–7, 171, 174, 185–6
    Cemetery Hill 141, 144
    Cemetery Ridge 127–30, 136

Peach Orchard 122
Plum Run Valley 87
Stony Hill 100–4
Wheatfield 112, 114–16

McCandless, Col. 'Buck' 115
McDougall, Col. Archibald 157, 161
McGilvery, Lt. Col. Freeman 101, 114, 123, 132, 173–4, 176, 184–5
McIntosh, Col. John 164
McLaws, Maj. Gen. Lafayette 77, 80, 83–4, 100, 112, 115, 122, 167, 195
Mahone, Brig. Gen. William 130
Meade, Maj. Gen. George 9, 15–19, 21–2, 37–8, 40–2, 75, 131, 176
    appointment 12–13, 35–7
    Cemetery Ridge 127, 129, 133, 136, 171–2
    Culp's Hill 149, 154
    Hancock 70
    miscalculations 77–8, 81–4, 187, 188
    Newton promotion 54
    Peach Orchard 126
    Plum Run Valley 90
    post-Gettysburg 189, 191–3, 195–200
    Right Wing 157
    Slocum's front 69, 71–2, 74
Meredith, Brig. Gen. Solomon 45, 47, 52, 69
Merritt, Brig. Gen. Wesley 188

Neill, Brig. Gen. Thomas 157, 161
Nevin, Col. David 109, 114
Newton, Maj. Gen. John 54

O'Neal, Col. Edward 45, 52, 58, 157, 158
Osborn, Maj. Thomas 137, 173–4, 176, 184

Paul, Brig. Gen. Gabriel 52, 54
Pender, Maj. Gen. William 45, 53, 140, 167
Pendleton, Brig. Gen. William 40, 171, 181, 185
Pettigrew, Brig. Gen. Johnston 45, 53, 167, 170, 174, 180, 184–6, 195
Pickett, Maj. Gen. George 15, 80, 83, 127, 167, 170, 173–4, 180, 184–7
Pleasanton, Maj. Gen. Alfred 38, 43, 77, 81–2, 164, 188, 195
Posey, Brig. Gen. Carnot 129, 130, 132–3, 186

Ramseur, Brig. Gen. Stephen 45, 54, 139, 140, 144
Reynolds, Maj. Gen. John 35, 36, 41–2, 45, 50, 54, 58, 78, 82
Robertson, Brig. Gen. Jerome 87–90
Robinson, Brig. Gen. John 81, 136
Rodes, Maj. Gen. Robert 45, 50, 52–4, 59, 140, 145, 157, 167

Rowley, Brig. Gen. Thomas 45, 53
Ruger, Brig. Gen. Thomas 73, 147, 149, 155

Scales, Brig. Gen. Alfred 53
Schimmelfennig, Brig. Gen. Alexander 57, 58,
  59, 61, 63
Schurz, Maj. Gen. Carl 57, 58–9, 139, 149, 151
Sedgwick, Maj. Gen. John 41, 71, 91, 114, 127,
  147, 157, 161, 173, 187
Semmes, Brig. Gen. Paul 101, 109, 110, 112,
  115, 116
Shaler, Brig. Gen. Alexander 157, 161
Sickles, Maj. Gen. Daniel 19, 41, 63, 75, 77,
  81–4, 143, 189, 195
  Cemetery Ridge 131
  Culp's Hill 149
  Peach Orchard 99, 112, 119, 122–3, 126
  Plum Run Valley 87, 91
  Stony Hill 101, 105
  Wheatfield 107–9, 112
Slocum, Maj. Gen. Henry 40–1, 63–5, 67–74,
  126, 136, 187, 196
  Culp's Hill 147, 149, 150, 154
  Right Wing 155, 158, 161
Smith, Brig. Gen. William 'Extra Billy' 65, 69,
  71, 77, 79, 157, 158–60
Smith, Col. Orland 57, 63–4, 140
Smyth, Col. Thomas 180
Stannard, Brig. Gen. George 40, 51, 129, 136,
  186–7
Steuart, Brig. Gen. George 149–51, 153, 157,
  159–60
Stevens, Capt. Greenleaf 69, 72, 139, 145
Stone, Col. Roy 45, 52, 53
Stuart, Maj. Gen. 'Jeb' 38–9, 41, 65–6, 154, 157,
  161–2, 164
Sweitzer, Col. Jacob 99, 100, 105, 111, 112
Sykes, Maj. Gen. George 41, 69, 71–2, 74, 77,
  83–4, 90–1, 173
  Culp's Hill 147, 150
  Stony Hill 100–1
  Wheatfield 107–9, 113–14

Tilton, Col. William 99, 100, 105, 114
Trimble, Maj. Gen. Isaac 167, 170, 174, 180,
  184–6
Trobriand, Col. Philippe de 87, 94–5, 97–100,
  105–6, 110, 116, 117

Vincent, Col. Strong 87, 90, 95–6, 100, 116, 153
von Gilsa, Col. Leopold 57, 59, 139, 145
von Steinwehr, Brig. Gen. Baron Adolph 58, 140

Wadsworth, Brig. Gen. James 47, 50, 72–3, 81,
  139, 149, 152

Wainwright, Col. Charles 51, 53–4, 139, 143,
  173–4
Walker, Brig. Gen. James 69, 150, 157, 159
Ward, Brig. Gen. John 85, 91, 95, 99, 105, 117,
  184
Warren, Brig. Gen. Gouverneur 69, 72, 77, 84,
  90–1, 96
Webb, Brig. Gen. Alexander 132, 136, 146, 152,
  181, 184, 187
Weed, Brig. Gen. Stephen 87, 91, 96, 110, 113
Wilcox, Brig. Gen. Cadmus 129–31, 133, 167,
  171, 186
Willard, Col. George 119, 126
Williams, Brig. Gen. Alpheus 'Old Pap' 69–71,
  147, 149–51, 154, 155–7
Williams, Col. Jesse 150, 151
Wofford, Brig. Gen. William 109, 111–12, 114,
  119, 122
Wright, Brig. Gen. 'Rans' 80, 129–30, 133, 136,
  167, 186

Zook, Brig. Gen. Samuel 109, 111

PICTURE CREDITS